Integrative Psychotherapy in Theory and Practice

by the same author

Being White in the Helping Professions
Developing Effective Intercultural Awareness
Judy Ryde
ISBN 978 1 84310 936 5
eISBN 978 1 84642 730 5

White Privilege Unmasked
How to Be Part of the Solution
Judy Ryde
ISBN 978 1 78592 408 8
eISBN 978 1 78450 767 1

of related interest

Social Exclusion, Compound Trauma and Recovery
Applying Psychology, Psychotherapy and PIE to
Homelessness and Complex Needs
Edited by Peter Cockersell
ISBN 978 1 78592 284 8
eISBN 978 1 78450 588 2

**A Practical Guide to Therapeutic Work with
Asylum Seekers and Refugees**
Angelina Jalonen and Paul Cilia La Corte
Foreword by Jerry Clore
ISBN 978 1 78592 073 8
eISBN 978 1 78450 334 5

Counselling and Psychotherapy with Older People in Care
A Support Guide
Felicity Chapman
ISBN 978 1 78592 396 8
eISBN 978 1 78450 751 0

Honest Dialogue
Presence, Common Sense, and Boundaries when
You Want to Help Someone
Bent Falk
ISBN 978 1 78592 353 1
eISBN 978 1 78450 689 6

INTEGRATIVE PSYCHOTHERAPY IN THEORY AND PRACTICE

A Relational, Systemic and
Ecological Approach

Peter Hawkins
and Judy Ryde

Jessica Kingsley *Publishers*
London and Philadelphia

First published in 2020
by Jessica Kingsley Publishers
73 Collier Street
London N1 9BE, UK
and
400 Market Street, Suite 400
Philadelphia, PA 19106, USA

www.jkp.com

Library of Congress Cataloging in Publication Data
A CIP catalog record for this book is available from the Library of Congress

British Library Cataloguing in Publication Data
A CIP catalogue record for this book is available from the British Library

ISBN 978 1 78592 422 4
eISBN 978 1 78450 786 2

2

Printed and bound in Great Britain by CPI Group (UK) Ltd, Croydon CR0 4YY

Contents

Part 4: The Fruits and Flowers: Integration in Practice

Acknowledgements

This book has been developing over the course of both our lifetimes, but in particular over the 40-plus years we have lived together. We met and came together through our shared interest and teaching in the creative therapies, and our life together has been rich with conversations, joint explorations and inquiry into the nature of being human, how human beings develop, the nature of mental health and illness, how psychotherapy can help and how you train and supervise psychotherapists. This book is the result of these many conversations and explorations, which also continued and intensified as we wrote this book together.

Many friends thought we were crazy to risk our relationship by trying to write a book together, as co-writing can be fraught with tension and conflict, but it has been a pleasure and a joyful collaborative enterprise.

Many people have been influential in writing this book, and we owe them a great gratitude. Over the years, we have been blessed with great psychotherapy teachers and trainers, supervisors and spiritual teachers, and continue to be supervised by people who enable our learning to deepen and mature.

We would also like to thank our colleagues along the way: the many people who have taught and worked at the Bath Centre for Psychotherapy and Counselling since 1984, as well as the visiting fellows such as Donna Orange, Robert Stolorow, Richard Hycner and Patrick Casement; also our colleagues at the Centre for Supervision Training and Development with whom we have been teaching supervision for over 40 years; and our colleagues at Trauma Foundation South West. We also have learned from psychotherapists leading other training, particularly through our active years in the UK Council for Psychotherapy Humanistic and Integrative section and later college.

Then there are our friends who have been so generous in reading and commenting on early drafts of this book, particularly Michaela von Britzke, Peter Binns, Nick Smith, Kelvin Hall and Tree Staunton, Director of the Bath

Centre for Psychotherapy and Counselling. Michaela read and corrected two early drafts and much improved the readability. Their wisdom and support are such gifts to both of us and this book.

Fiona Benton and Julie Jeffery have been patient and generous in helping us sort out computers when they tried our patience, the permissions for quotes, the references and manuscript and so much more. This book could not have been written without them.

A particular thank you needs to go to our clients in psychotherapy, coaching, spiritual guiding and supervision. It is not an exaggeration to say that each one has been a teacher to us, opening up new vistas and challenges, expanding our range of experience, helping us to find new levels of compassion and patience and discover new parts of ourselves. Life is a great teacher.

Preface and Welcome

Welcome to this book.

Welcome – whether you are an experienced psychotherapist, a psychotherapist in training, a psychotherapy client or just beginning to think about having psychotherapy. This book is for all of you. It is also written to be of value to psychologists, counsellors, spiritual guides and coaches, all of whom have roles which greatly overlap with the role of psychotherapists. We also hope it will be useful to people in various other helping professions, such as psychiatrists, general practitioners (family doctors), social workers, nurses, occupational therapists, physiotherapists and so on. We all need to be aware that all distress, disturbance and 'dis-ease' are in some form or other psychosomatic, involving body and brain; all illness has relational and social aspects and is not just an individual phenomenon. The book is also for parents and those who are en route to becoming parents. We hope the book will be useful for teachers at all levels, as teaching, like parenting, is one of the most valuable roles needed by humanity at this time in our development.

We will now address each of these groups and say how we believe there will be particular value in reading this book.

Psychotherapists and those training to be psychotherapists

Both of us spent much of our twenties working in the field of mental health while undertaking training in various psychotherapies. In our thirties, we established the Bath Centre for Psychotherapy and Counselling as, at that time, there was very little training available outside London and very few places providing an integrative approach. We have written many handouts and informal papers for our students over the years, but only now do we feel ready to write a more comprehensive book on our approach to integrative psychotherapy. We have both had many years of practice, supervision, our own further psychotherapy and spiritual trainings, explorations of the field in dialogue and learning with other psychotherapists and schools, to arrive at our own mature integration. We now feel ready to attempt to bring it all together into a coherent whole. That is not to say that we consider this to be a final word, but as work in progress, made available for others to build on.

We always encourage our students to find their own integration, and still believe this is an important process (see Chapter 14 on training integrative psychotherapists). However, we now believe that trained psychotherapists need to be able to read and witness other psychotherapists' integration, written from the experience of those who have been longer in the field, not so they can slavishly follow others' ways of making an integration, but to use it as a springboard for their own integrative work.

We encourage all readers, as we do our own students, to read the book dialogically. By that we mean start every chapter by considering why you want to learn from this chapter. What are the questions and answers you bring to it? Imagine you are embarking on a series of conversations with us, the authors, and feel free to object to, challenge and question what we have written. This ensures that you avoid the trap of introjecting the book and the ideas within it – or become reactive to what is written and reject it. Instead, give yourself space to chew on the ideas, play with them and discover what may be useful and what you can integrate into your training, your approach and your practice.

Counsellors, psychologists, spiritual guides and coaches

We believe all four of these roles have a great deal of overlap with psychotherapy. We have in our career taught people in all four of these differently named professions/roles and have found more overlap than difference. We have also been involved in many long and intense discussions about defining these differences. Some conversations were fruitful, but many went round and round in circles. Of course, we occasionally came up against people more interested in protecting their own sphere of activity and vested interests than engaging collaboratively with our project, but many people entered into fruitful dialogue with us and we hope we honour their voices in these explorations.

However, we do not think all these roles are the same or serve the same purpose. We believe that psychotherapy and counselling can be seen as a continuum, with a good deal of overlap in the middle. The two ends are easier to distinguish. Psychotherapy tends to be based on a longer-term contract with the aim to address, integrate and heal past distress, traumas and patterns of disturbance, including work with the 'here and now' relationship between psychotherapist and client, and areas of transference and countertransference. Counselling at the other end of the spectrum will tend to be shorter term, stay more in an adult–adult relational pattern, address current issues, and avoid encouraging transference with the client. In the middle is a large area of overlap where short-term, cognitive and behavioural psychotherapies intersect with longer-term relational counselling, and whether these areas are called counselling or psychotherapy is more dependent on historical and social construction.

Coaching, like some therapies less based on unconscious processes, is focused on a more adult-to-adult relationship, and aims to explore specific issues. Differently from counselling (Hawkins, 2018b), coaching often takes place within an organisational or work context and is paid for by the organisation. This means that the coach needs specific training in working to serve multiple clients. Peter has addressed this format in his latest coaching book written with Eve Turner, *Systemic Coaching: Delivering Value Beyond the Individual* (Hawkins & Turner, 2019). Their book parallels this book in showing the importance of relational, systemic and eco-systemic perspectives in the work. Coaches can become overly individually focused and get caught up in their own doctrinaire frameworks and limiting beliefs – issues which Peter outlined in his article 'Cracking the shell: Unleashing our coaching assumptions (Hawkins, 2015).

We believe that counsellors, psychologists, spiritual guides and coaches can benefit greatly by absorbing the relational, systemic and ecological perspectives we lay out in this book. Spiritual guides tend to focus more on the unfolding potential of the individual than unfinished work from their past (but sometimes this cannot be ignored whatever your role!). They will be particularly interested in Chapter 3, where we explore how the individual can develop, not just through the ego-focused, socio-focused and self-authoring stages of human development, but also into the post-conventional and transpersonal stages of spiritual development. We also take up these issues in Chapter 9, where we show the connections between eco-systemic and spiritual approaches, and how the deeper you go within, the broader your external focus becomes.

Other helping professionals

Some helping professionals, such as general practitioners, receive a training that is scientifically based and focused on the body. Increasingly, research is showing that all distress and disturbance and dis-ease is in some way psychosomatic and involves the body and the brain (Van der Kolk, 2015). To add to the complexity, illness also has relational and social aspects and is not just an individual phenomenon, which shows that the medical professional needs training in therapeutic skills to enhance their professional effectiveness. Social workers' training is based largely on a societal perspective, thus asking them to attend to manage and remedy the social context of their clients' distressing situation. They might feel more confident in responding to the psychological and interpersonal distress their clients may raise if they had some appropriate training in this (which used to be a taken-for-granted part of the social work role).

All helping professionals are dealing with complex relationships with their clients and need training in emotional and whole intelligence (see Chapter 13), empathy and compassion, managing their own responses and retriggered distress, as well as tools for managing the relational field, as we have long argued (Hawkins & Shohet, 2012; Hawkins & Smith, 2006). We are convinced that all helping professionals need regular and competent supervision from trained supervisors in order to work most satisfactorily within their fields of competence (see also Chapter 12).

Parents

The book is also for parents, and those who are en route to becoming parents. Being a parent is one of the most important and difficult roles in the world and, despite there being much more awareness and knowledge about parenthood and its pitfalls generally, it is probably getting harder, rather than easier, because our world is getting more complex and almost over-rich in choices. We have been privileged to have had three children and watched them grow up, develop and find their own way in the world, but we recognise that parenting never ends, just transforms into new stages. We have also been blessed with five grandchildren, and to watch the interactions between them, and between them and their parents. Our children (and grandchildren) are so often our teachers: reconnecting us with parts of ourselves that we have left behind; giving us a second and third opportunity to work through phases of our own childhood that remain unfinished within us; pushing up against our limits and helping us notice when we become reactive rather than receptive.

We would encourage all parents to read the sections on how important it is for parents to have worked through and integrated the narrative of their own childhood, since this can make a great difference to their parenting. The sections on birth, infancy and childhood in Chapter 3 will be helpful both for the parenting process and for working through our individual histories. It is almost unnecessary to emphasise the importance of early attachment – but then it cannot be emphasised enough.

Teachers

The book is also for teachers at all levels, for teaching – like parenting – is one of the most valuable roles humanity needs at this time in our development. Our children and grandchildren are going to grow up in a world that has bigger, more complex and interconnected challenges than anything our most privileged generation has had to face (see Chapter 2) and it is essential that we support their learning and development to adequately meet these challenges. So often our society teaches children to acquire facts, solve linear problems, pass exams, and behave in socially acceptable ways. These may all be important skills in life, but they are by no means sufficient for a psycho-logically healthy and meaningful life in the 21st century.

We believe it is important for all teachers to have a good grounding in understanding human development (see Chapter 3), how the brain and mind develop (Chapter 4), attachment processes and disturbances (Chapter 4), mental health and individual flourishing (Chapter 4). It is all too easy to teach children and young people to acquire the knowledge and skills that were necessary for yesterday's world when we were growing up, rather than what they will need for tomorrow's world. It is essential that all teachers have a training in future foresight of the nature of the world and the curriculum of challenges that the children in today's classroom will face when they are adults (some of these challenges are addressed in Chapter 2).

Part 1

The Ground that is Shaking

Introduction

We are living in an age in which the ground is shifting and the
foundations are shaking. I cannot answer for other times and places.
Perhaps it has always been so. We know it is true today.

Laing, 1990:108

Welcome to Part 1 of this book.

It is the first of four parts, each growing out of the previous parts, but each in turn feeding back into what has come before.

1. *The Ground that is Shaking.* In this opening section, we will explore the ground that provides the foundations on which integrative psychotherapy stands.

2. *The Roots: Revisioning the History of Psychotherapy.* Here we will offer two chapters outlining the history of psychotherapy, the first from the 19th century to the end of the Second World War, and the second focusing on the last half of the 20th century.

3. *The Three Epistemological Stems or Strands.* These chapters explore in depth three core plants that have emerged from the ground and the roots. Each represents a major turn in our ways of perceiving the world and the nature of psychotherapy (our epistemology) and our ways of being as psychotherapists (our ontology). These are seeing the world as relational and intersubjective; seeing all living beings as living and evolving in dynamic relationship to all the many levels of system they are nested within; and finally recognising that the human and the more-than-human world of ecology are inextricably bound together.

4. *The Fruits and Flowers: Integration in Practice.* The fourth and final part explores the nature of the practice that grows from weaving together the three strands of Part 3. In Chapter 10, we show how to set the frame, the setting and form the working alliance necessary to do the psychotherapeutic work, and, in Chapter 11, how the work unfolds. Then we look at how such an approach necessitates regular integrative supervision (Chapter 12), relational, systemic and ecological ethics (Chapter 13) and the training necessary to do this profound and demanding work (Chapter 14).

You are free to choose whether you read the book from the ground up, that is, the order it is presented, or whether your learning needs and style require a different entry point. We have designed the book so that it can be read in separate sections and in any order.

At the end of the book, we provide a stand-alone chapter in which we reflect on the many themes and offer a provisional integration of all the various elements. It is provisional because we do not want to create artificial closure, but rather a springboard for readers, other writers and scholars to further the inquiry and take forward the urgent questions and explorations we have opened up.

Part 1: The Ground that is Shaking

So, returning to this first part, we will explore the ground from which integrative psychotherapy grows. We will address a number of the important questions that every integrative psychotherapist needs to address at the beginning of their training and revisit at all stages of their career.

- Who are we as human beings?

- What is a self?

- How are we formed?

- How do we change and develop?

- How are we both separate and also embedded in our families, communities and cultures?

- How do we flourish and what makes us psychologically healthy or mentally ill?

- What are the challenges of our time, how do these show up and how can they be addressed in the psychotherapy relationship?

None of these questions has an easy, fixed or permanent answer. They are questions that ignite continuous and evolving human inquiry. Thus, they are questions that are at the heart of the very work of psychotherapy.

In Chapter 1, we will explore what is meant by 'integrative' and look at different types of psychotherapy integration that have been developed. We will then describe our own integration, which will be explored throughout the rest of the book.

Then, in Chapter 2, we will address the question of why is there is a need for a new integration in psychotherapy. We will explore the specific challenges of our time and the even bigger challenges that are coming over the horizon. We will tackle the paradox of why it is, at a time when those living in privileged white western countries are safer, richer, healthier, live longer and have more access to education and travel, that mental illness, teenage suicide and general anxiety are all increasing?

In Chapter 3, we explore the questions of identity and the nature of the self. We will draw on pre-modern, modern and post-modern approaches to understanding the self and then offer an integration of both psycho-social approaches to understanding the many stages of each person's development, as well as the internal evolution of our consciousness.

In Chapter 4, we will look at psychological health and human flourishing and also psychological illness, distress, disturbance and dis-ease. Then we will explore the role of psychotherapy in enabling the former and ameliorating the latter.

Some readers may be surprised to find a psychotherapy book starting with such wide-ranging explorations drawing on such differing fields as philosophy, anthropology, sociology, psychology, science, neuroscience, evolution, religion and spirituality and last, but most importantly, ecology. We believe that without addressing the fundamentals of human existence, development and health, our psychotherapy integration will have shallow roots and unrecognised and unquestioned assumptions that we have absorbed from our culture and upbringing. Throughout this book, we will be arguing that we live in extraordinary times which are providing challenges that require human beings to think, relate and engage in radically new ways.

Later in the book, we will write about the challenges of living in a globally interconnected human community, rather than in localised niches, and the ecological crisis that needs urgent and radical change if climatic disaster is to be avoided. Many argue that the next 10–15 years are critical to lessen the life-threatening damage our species has done, is, and will be doing to all life on this planet. Others, like ourselves, have been arguing that we can only step up to this challenge with a major evolution in our ways of thinking, perceiving and being in the world.

Psychotherapy can either sleepwalk in this global crisis, and live on the fringes, helping individuals cope with increasing rates of anxiety and mental illness (see Chapter 4), or it can bring its great collective experience and learning to address the revolution in our thinking, being and doing, which is an essential foundation of the ecological war we are all part of (see Chapter 9).

For every profession, the choice has become either to begin to radically disrupt yourself and revise what you are doing or wait for the external world to disrupt you. This is true for doctors, lawyers, accountants and clergy, so why should psychotherapists be different? We could stay on the sidelines and try to deal individually with the personal anxiety, depression and mental illness that will no doubt increase with the side effects of these global and climatic changes. Another alternative is to take a step back, look critically at our profession, our history and what we are doing in the world. This is what we have attempted in writing this book. It leads us to a position where we believe it is not enough just to integrate the best of what is already in the rich field of psychotherapy, but rather embrace the radical shaking of the very foundations and revision psychotherapy so that it is fit for the 21st century.

CHAPTER 1

An Integrative Psychotherapy for the 21st Century

In this chapter, we lay out the multi-faceted ways we use the term 'integrative' to define and shape the particular approach to psychotherapy that this book explores and which we have been teaching and practising for 35 years. Over this time, the approach has evolved and developed through our practice and our teaching, through countless dialogues with many people, ranging from leading psychotherapists to students at the beginning of their training as well as writers from many other schools of psychotherapy, and through our explorations of the new paradigms in science, neuroscience, philosophy, ethics and psychology.

The need for integration in psychotherapy is apparent at many levels. There is a proliferation of different forms of psychotherapy, each with its own language, models and practices. And each making claims for its own approach, and many for their unique superiority. Yet there is much research to show that many are equally effective (Wampold, 2001; Lambert, 1992). Psychotherapy – like many fields of study in the internet age – provides an overwhelming amount of theories, concepts and techniques for the beginning trainee to engage with. With this proliferation of approaches also comes a 'Tower of Babel' phenomenon of different schools each developing their own technical and theoretical language, so dialogue between approaches becomes harder and harder. We need to evolve some common languages whereby psychotherapists and theorists from different schools can speak to each other and make it possible for the field of psychotherapy to have a language that can engage with other disciplines. As we will show later in this book, we live in times of rapid paradigm change, where the new paradigms no longer just emerge from one field of study, be it Descartes in philosophy or Newton in physics, but where much of the new thinking increasingly emerges from interdisciplinary connections and breakthroughs. In this process, psychotherapy has to play its part more collectively and that requires greater internal collaboration and integration, as well as increased external co-creative dialogue. How this is done will be explored later in this chapter and throughout the book

As we explained in more detail in the preface, we have written this book for a variety of audiences. These include psychotherapists in training as well as experienced psychotherapists but also those in parallel professions such as counselling, coaching, organisational development, psychology, social work, medicine, nursing and teaching. We believe that ideas and methods drawn from the rich panoply of psychotherapy have much to offer all of you in your important and demanding work. This book follows our work in using integrative psychotherapy approaches to aid better supervision for all the helping professions (Hawkins & Shohet, 2012: Hawkins & McMahan, in press), which has been used widely across many countries and a great variety of professions and more. This also for those who are in, or thinking of having, psychotherapy and want to discover more about the breadth, depth and history of the psychotherapy world.

History of integration in psychotherapy

We will show in Chapter 5 how the early history of psychotherapy grew out of great collaboration and dialectical differences, but was characterised by strong personalities with both loyal adherents and rebels who then split away to start their own schools, which in turn had strong adherents and rebels. This led to both dogmatic sectarianism and fragmentation. We would argue that the most creative episodes in the history of psychotherapy have happened in periods of rich collaboration between people of different professional and academic backgrounds, drawing from different theoretical schools and forms of practice. Besides the great dialogues of Freud and his early circle (see Chapter 5), we might point to the Macy Conferences just after the Second World War, where anthropologists, sociologists, psychologists and cyberneticists brought about new systemic understanding (see Chapter 8), and the early conferences that brought together the existential, phenomenological and early humanistic psychologists, researchers and psychotherapists.

Our own early training was also seeped in creative collaboration. We were both involved very early in collaborative groups that focused on bringing together the various creative therapies – art, drama, music, movement – integrating these with approaches from both psychoanalytic and humanistic group work, as well as therapeutic community approaches (see Chapter 8). Through the Association of Therapeutic Communities (now known as The Consortium for Therapeutic Communities) we worked closely with psychiatrists, psychologists and psychotherapists of many different orientations, at both conferences and jointly run experiential events. Peter was deeply influenced by being part of the New Paradigm Research Group in London in the late 1970s and early 1980s, comprising great thinkers like John Heron, John Rowan, and Peter Reason. When we first started the Bath Centre for Psychotherapy and Counselling in the mid-1980s, we very soon joined what was the Rugby Conference, where UK psychotherapists from all persuasions came together to explore how to organise the nascent professionalisation of psychotherapy. Despite many inter-organisational prejudices, projections and fears, collaboration and cross-learning began to take root, and people who would not have previously talked or listened to each other began to work together. This was driven by having a common enemy and collective endeavour. There was the threat that the government was going to regulate psychotherapy unless the profession started to better regulate itself, and no school wanted to be either left out or part of a profession that let just anyone in. The Rugby Conference formed itself into the UK Council for Psychotherapy (UKCP), which soon created different sections, including the psychoanalytic, the psychodynamic, the children's and family sections, the behaviourists and hypnotherapists and the humanistic and integrative strands. Peter was the first chair of the humanistic and integrative psychotherapy section, which, in itself, was an integration of specialised schools in psychodrama, gestalt, transactional analysis, psychosynthesis, transpersonal approaches, body-orientated therapies, and those with stronger integrations such as our own school, the Bath Centre for Psychotherapy and Counselling, and The Minster Centre and parts of The Metanoia Institute.

However, it was not long before divisions raised their head once more and the psychoanalytic section broke away and formed its own organisation (The British Confederation of Psychotherapists). The British Association of Counselling (BAC) decided it also wanted to include psychotherapists and became the British Association of Counselling and Psychotherapy (BACP). At this time, we were also deeply involved in developing integrative approaches to supervision (Hawkins & Shohet, 2012) (see Chapter 12).

During these periods of collaborative creativity in psychotherapy there were many serious attempts to integrate different approaches to psychotherapy and overcome the divisions and antagonistic tendencies towards separation that often existed between different schools, each of which was battling to take the academic and moral high ground. The early attempts at integration were mostly focused on combining two or more approaches. The earliest were probably the work of psychotherapists like French (1933), Kubie (1934) and Sears (1944), combining approaches from psychoanalysis with behavioural approaches based on conditioning. After the Second World War, this was continued by Dollard and Miller (1950) and Alexander (1963), integrating psychoanalysis and learning theory. This was taken further by Wachtel (1977), Wachtel and Watchel (1986) and Wachtel and McKinney (1992) in what was termed an 'integrative psychodynamic approach', which integrated psychodynamic concepts, showing how the past influences present choices, behaviours and actions, with the cyclical nature of causality and interactions. Most of the approaches before the late 1980s and early 1990s were about combining behavioural and psychodynamic approaches, although Thoresen in 1973 was one of the first to try and connect behavioural and humanistic approaches (O'Leary, 2006:4). With the enormous upsurge in writings, approaches and teaching of integrative psychotherapy in the late 1980s and early 1990s and with more and more psychotherapists calling themselves integrative, Norcross and Goldfried (1992) reported that between a third and a half of psychotherapy practitioners in the United States claimed that their approach was integrative or eclectic, indicating a need to distinguish different forms of integration (Norcross & Grencavage, 1989; Lazarus, 1973; McCleod, 1993).

The most common distinctions are between: a) technical eclecticism and integration; b) theoretical integration; and c) common factors.

Technical eclecticism and integration. This term was first used by Lazarus in 1967 and later developed by him (Lazarus, 1992), for psychotherapists and psychologists who use techniques and interventions from different approaches, without necessarily incorporating or agreeing with their theoretical foundation. Finlay calls this approach a 'pragmatic, instrumental integration' (Finlay, 2016:5).

Theoretical integration. In contrast to technical eclecticism, this form of integration brings together the theory and approach of two or more schools of psychotherapy, from which is created a new gestalt or whole (McCleod, 1993).

Common factors. This approach to integration looks for the common factors in a number of different approaches to psychotherapy. It can be dated back to Rosenzweig (1936) and others' work that showed that many very different therapies were equally effective, and so they became interested in finding out what were the effective elements they shared. These include what Gold (1996) calls the 'supportive factors', including the relationship (see Chapter 7), the personality of the psychotherapist, empathy, positive regard and so forth, and what Gold calls 'the technical factors', which are found in the therapist's interventions.

In this book and in the many years of our practice, our integration has been built first from (b) integrating humanistic and psychodynamic theoretical approaches and then from a growing interest in (c). Our interest in common factors came from our realisation that many schools of psychotherapy are now fundamentally 'relational' in their approach, including the modern post-Winnicottian 'object-relations' school, the American intersubjective systemic therapists; existential and phenomenological schools of psychotherapy; relational gestalt; and other approaches using dialogical and conversational approaches (Erskine, 2015).

In more recent years, we recognised that there were two other paradigm shifts that needed to be incorporated into psychotherapy approaches. First, the systemic understanding that human beings are not just born into and develop through interpersonal relationships but are also in dynamic co-creative interchange with the many group, social, cultural and physical environments they inhabit. Second, we became increasingly concerned that psychotherapy was very human-centric, at a time when human-centricity was destroying many species of animals, insects and vegetation with which we share this planet, polluting the atmosphere and oceans on which all of our lives depend. It became clear that all human sciences and fields of study need to go beyond their current paradigms and put ecological understanding at the heart of their theories and practice.

We will show how these three approaches have emerged in a synchronistic way from parallel schools of psychotherapy, as well as in other fields of physical sciences, human sciences, including psychology, anthropology and sociology and the humanities. However, we might better call them strands, for they do not stand alone but flow through and inform each other, and form a new integrative synthesis.

From this understanding we now see that there are three main strands, which we call the relational, systemic and ecological, that have become the foundation of our psychotherapy integration and provide us with frames through which we can revisit the history of psychotherapy (see Chapters 5 and 6), and different psychotherapy theories (see Chapters 7–9) and construct a new integrative practice (see Chapters 10–14).

There are many hurdles to overcome to be truly integrative. Hawkins and Nestoros (1997:53–57) (not the Hawkins of this book) outline seven major hurdles:

1. Partisan zealotry and territorial interest.

2. Divergent visions of life and health, psychopathology and change.

3. Inadequate empirical and clinical research on psychotherapeutic change and insufficient evaluation of psychotherapy outcomes.

4. Lack of a common language for psychotherapies.

5. Insufficient training in eclectic and integrative psychotherapy.

6. Differences in the effectiveness of psychotherapies.

7. The proliferation of different schools of eclectic and integrative psychotherapies.

In this book, we will attempt to make a small but important contribution to overcoming many of these hurdles. In doing so we are cognisant of London's warning (London, 1988: quoted in O'Leary 2006:5) that psychotherapy integration was 'overly ambitious and essentially impossible…because of scientific incompatibilities and philosophical differences among the various schools of psychotherapy'. We do not believe this to be true, but proceed with the approach of Antonio Gramsci (1975), to combine 'optimism of the will, with pessimism of the intellect'! For, as we will lay out in the next chapter, we believe that an encompassing psychotherapy integration is not just useful but essential in making its contribution to facing the great challenges of our time.

What is integrative in integrative psychotherapy?

Many psychotherapy approaches call themselves integrative and many mean different things when they use this word. As we saw above, some mean they integrate two or more psychotherapy approaches, others that they draw on techniques and interventions from many sources. Beyond the three types of integration we mentioned, we also come across other psychotherapists who call themselves integrative because they see integration as a key goal for the individual client (Finlay, 2016:120). As explained above, our own theoretical integration for praxis is built on three critical strands: the relational, systemic and ecological. We also use the term 'integrative' in a specific and multi-faceted way, which we will now describe. Many other psychotherapies would share some of these facets but only psychotherapies that share our approach would share all of them.

1 The individual's journey to integration is the core of the psychotherapeutic endeavour

When Fritz Perls, the founder of gestalt psychotherapy, was asked what three things he thought were most essential to gestalt psychotherapy he said: 'Integrate, integrate, integrate' (Perls, 1969). In Chapter 3, we outline how we see the role of psychotherapy as assisting the individual in developing their sense of self and aligning various aspects of their identity, both internal and external, individual and collective, historic and current, to achieve a coherent, healthy functioning, a positive, resilient and adaptable sense of self. We explore the way this move to integration is a continuously evolving process. Reg Revans (1982), the founder of action learning, pointed out that any organism needs to learn at the same or greater rate than its changing environment. In today's world of exponential change and transformation on so many levels, the individual and the human species are having to adapt and learn faster and in more complex ways than ever before. As we learn and adapt to new challenges and contexts, the work of integrating these new learnings and aspects becomes a perpetual, life-long task. This does not mean we need to always have a psychotherapist, but that we learn to work psychotherapeutically ourselves as part of our everyday life.

2 A holistic integration

Integrative psychotherapy does not just work with the cognition, nor solely with the emotions, nor just focused on the body or on the spirit of the individual, for we do not see these as existing separately from each other. We do not see the mind as existing just in the brain, or the emotions just in the body. We do not see what the transpersonal psychotherapists call the higher self as being something located within us. All these elements are not locatable things, but complex systems that flow across the boundaries that many see as containing them. Therefore, the integrative psychotherapist must work in a way that attends to all four elements of this quaternity of cognition, emotions, body and spirit, in an integrated way.

3 Historically integrative

Psychotherapy has evolved within certain historical and cultural contexts, which have shaped and informed it. Its theories and approaches were always created in response to the human needs of the time and emerged from the cultural and epistemological thinking that permeated the zeitgeist of the historical context. Freud's early work grew out of late 19th-century Vienna, capital of the then Austro-Hungarian Empire, which at the time was a rich centre, both economically and in cultural innovation. His thinking was rooted in the medical science of his time, which was informed by mechanical ways of understanding the body and mind, and many of his patients were people suffering from what was termed hysterical symptoms. Mental illness was understood as residing in the individual – individually generated. As psychotherapy spread in the 20th century throughout Europe and North America, and out from psychiatry into non-medical practice, it evolved in the different contexts and cultures in which it took root.

Yuval Noah Harari, a historian we both admire, writes how 'Each and every one is born into a given historical reality, ruled by particular norms and values, and managed by a unique economic and political system' (Harari, 2015:59). He goes on to say:

> Movements seeking to change the world often begin by rewriting history, thereby enabling people to reimagine the future...the first step is to retell their history. The new history will explain that our present situation is neither natural nor eternal. Things were different once. Only a string of chance events created the unjust world we know today. If we act wisely, we can change that world and create a much better one. (Harari, 2015:59–60)

This is true, not just of social and political movements, but of psychotherapy theory, and in Chapters 5 and 6, we too undertake this task of retelling and reconfiguring the history and development of psychotherapy theory and practice, not only so we can be informed by and learn from it, but so we can be liberated to create a new psychotherapy, more fitting for the mid-21st century. The current and future world is a million miles from Freud's Vienna or even a very long way from the post Second World War America where humanistic psychotherapy had its roots.

Harari goes on to say that what is true of grand social revolutions is equally true at the micro level of everyday life. Each psychotherapy client also needs to retell their history and find new ways of understanding and reconfiguring that narrative. Like the change-architects of revolution who

28

planned on a grand scale, they too 'aim not to perpetuate the past, but rather to be liberated from it' (Harari, 2015:60).

4 Theoretically integrative

Psychotherapy theory is like a prism – whichever lens you look through you see something new and different. Each psychotherapy school or approach illuminates some aspect of the whole, but each inevitably occludes other aspects and has its blind spots. In order not to be caught in the rigidity of a closed approach, it is necessary to look at any issue from multiple perspectives and through different theoretical lenses. Thus, integrative psychotherapy always attempts to develop new creative understandings through the dialogue and dialectic created by the thesis and antithesis of differing theories coming into relationship, and, through the emerging dialectical dialogue, creates a third position that transcends the previous duality.

5 Methodologically integrative

Integrative psychotherapy encourages methodological creativity and ex-perimentation in ways of engaging, working with and enabling clients, not for its own sake, but because every client is different and calls for a unique response. How the psychotherapist works should be dictated by each client's needs and what psychotherapy methods enable effective work in each particular situation. Ways of being with clients can become habitual for the psychotherapist and, possibly over-constrained by the ways they were taught, or the ways they experienced with their own therapist. Integrative psychotherapists take a stance of humility and practice, a universalist approach that recognises that we can learn from all cultures and differing schools, no matter how they vary from our own. However, to be effective this needs to be neither an opportunistic nor an eclectic pick-and-mix approach, but selective and informed by principles that give coherence to the work, steering clear of tribal prejudices of 'us' and 'them' that can so easily play out in any professional field.

Debates between different schools of psychotherapy have often been competitive, heated and derogatory, or even dismissive of each other's positions. Yet repeated research and large-scale studies and meta-analyses on effectiveness of different psychotherapies have shown that there is no significant difference between the efficacy of professional practitioners from different approaches, although it is possible to find differences between those who are professionally trained and untrained (Wampold, 2001). Rosenzweig (1936) as long ago as 1936 first created what has become known as the 'Rosenzweig conjecture' or 'Dodo conjecture'. The latter term comes from his reference to Lewis Carroll's *Alice in Wonderland*, where the Dodo organises a race. When the Dodo is asked who won, he replies: 'Everybody has won and they all must have prizes.' Rosenzweig went on to conjecture that if all psychotherapies are equally effective, there must be common ingredients, rather than specific interventions that make them effective. More recent research has suggested that the most important common ingredient is the relationship between the therapist and the client (Wampold, 2001) and how this relationship is perceived by the client (Lambert, 1992). We will explore the conditions that are necessary for an effective psychotherapy relationship in Chapter 7 on the relational turn in psychotherapy and in Chapter 11 on integrative psychotherapy practice.

6 Culturally integrative

Judy (Ryde, 2009, 2019), has written extensively about how psychotherapy has grown up in a very white Eurocentric world. As psychotherapy has spread to other continents, and as our world has become much more migratory and culturally mixed, psychotherapy has needed to be informed by, and adapt to, working with very different cultures with different ideas of mental health and mental illness. One of the key aspects of this is that the white culture is very individualistic, whereas many non-white indigenous cultures are/were more collectively oriented. To work effectively with different cultures, we need to become more aware of such cultural differences, so that we can examine and question our own cultural assumptions (Ryde 2009, 2019) and develop new cultural sensitivities and transcultural inquiry processes within the psychotherapy dialogue (see Chapter 12).

7 Epistemologically integrative

Epistemology is not 'what' we know, but 'how' we know – the frameworks and processes through which we come to know anything. In some ways, these frames are similar to the 'organising principles' which the intersubjective systems theorists describe as the frames that inform our thinking and being (Stolorow & Atwood, 1992). We have seen an epistemological integration of three fundamental epistemological turns in the last 50 years, which is at the heart of integrative psychotherapy. Each of the three pillars on which we build our integration was born out of an epistemological turn or paradigm shift. Part 3 of this book fully explores each of the pillars and the important epistemological turns that underpin them and have taken psychotherapy into new ways of thinking and practising. Here we offer a brief overview of these three epistemological turns:

- *The relational turn.* This recognises that the psychotherapist does not respond objectively, constituting a subject–object relationship, but engages in an intersubjective relationship, where the psychotherapy is co-created and the relationship itself is the main vehicle of the therapy.

- *The systemic turn.* This recognises that an individual is both a whole system but inextricably embedded and nested in other wider systems, including: their original and current family; groups and communities they belong to; cultures they are part of, which inevitably are part of them. These wider systems are not just a backdrop or context, for they flow through the individual and co-create the individual's text or narrative.

- *The ecological or eco-systemic turn.* This recognises that for several millennia there has been a growing split between the human and more-than-human world of our ecological context; that psychotherapy has grown out of this fundamental split, and that, having now entered the Anthropocene Age, where human activity permeates every aspect of life on Earth, our planet will only be sustained if human beings urgently attend to overcoming this dangerous split.

1 Systemically integrative

In integrative psychotherapy, we do not believe that you can study an individual separately from their context. It is not just an individual that turns up in the consulting room, but also, in their wake, their families, communities, groups and cultures appear in and through them. We do not believe that the systems are distinct and bounded; we hold that the group lives in and through the individual, and the individual lives in and through the group. This applies right through all the nested systems of the universe.

In 2014, Peter wrote:

It is never enough to focus on just one level of system. To understand the human individual, we need to understand the sub-systems that comprise the individual; these could be the physical organs that are necessary for their physical well-being, or the many roles and sub-personalities that are integral to their way of being in the world. We also need to look at the systems the individual is part of – their family of origin, their current family, the team and organisation they work within, the national, local and ethnic culture they are part of. As Wendell Berry – the great American farmer philosopher – beautifully shows, we all live within: 'a system of nested systems: the individual human within the family within the community within agriculture within nature' (Berry, 2015:46). (Hawkins, 2014:6)

In 2017, Peter also wrote about the dangers of 'entity thinking' (Hawkins, 2017a), which reifies systems as fixed and objective things, rather than understanding them as temporary and permeable constructs for understanding. In this book, we go further to suggest that all evolution is co-evolution and happens in the relationship between any organism and its eco-system. The species does not just adapt to its ecological niche and compete to be the fittest (i.e. the best fit for the niche), but the species also changes and adapts its niche. Both are constantly changing and being changed by the other. This is the dance of co-evolution. The same happens at other levels of nested systems – the individual is not just responding and adapting to their family, for the family is changed by the individual. The dance of co-creation is happening at the interface between all systemic levels.

2 Integrating being and doing; cognition and action; experience and behaviour

Classical Freudian theory saw the individual as driven by internal drives of which they were mostly unconscious. Early behaviourism looked from the other end of the telescope and saw the individual as driven by external stimuli that triggered patterned responses in them. Only in the mid-20th century did psychotherapy give more attention to the individual creating their own meaning from the givens of their past and their context and being author of their own actions. Many humanistic writers criticised the early psychotherapists for objectifying human beings and viewing them mechanistically (Laing & Anthony, 2010; Maslow, 1972; May, 1969; Rogers, 1965).

Integrative psychotherapy answers the call of Rollo May (1969:40) when he says:

We need a form of psychology that does not dwell on behavior to the exclusion of experience or experience without regard to behaviors, but centers on the relation between experience and behavior.

We argue that you cannot fully understand another human being by separating their behaviour from their cognition and their experience from the meaning-making they have done in relation to this experience, framed by their beliefs and values. Earlier theories were built on linear causality, that saw behaviour as caused by inner complexes, drives or beliefs, or saw beliefs as caused by external events. Developments in neuroscience show how the neural connections and patterns of the brain are influenced by the patterns of our relationships and behaviours, while our behaviour and actions are affected by these patterns of brain activity. In a later chapter, we also address the complex issues of the mind and consciousness and how these operate through the brain but are not contained or bounded by it.

3 An integrating view of what it is to be human

Laing, the Scottish psychiatrist and radical psychotherapist, wrote: 'Any theory not founded on the nature of being human is a lie' (Laing & Anthony, 1967:45). To be human is to be a creature, with many ways of being that are shared with other mammals (see Chapter 3), as well as having god-like powers (Harari, 2015). This means that as a species we have 'conquered' the planet, killed off millions of other species, and created the Anthropocene (St Fleur, 2016). Our view embraces both the *actualities* of our current state and our *potentialities* to change ourselves and our environment (Maslow, 1972); it recognises the human ability to be wilfully blind, deceitful, murderous, destructive and caught in the grip of base emotions and our capability to be loving, generous, self-sacrificing, creative and spontaneous.

Later in the book, we will show how this integrative theory – its key factors described above – translates into practice, both in the psychotherapy relationship (Chapters 7 and 11) and in supervision (Chapter 12).

To provide a foretaste of this we have outlined our manifesto for integrative psychotherapy:

1. The work of psychotherapy is not carried out by the psychotherapist, but is a collaborative practice undertaken jointly by the client and therapist.

2. The therapist is part of the system they are studying and needs to be able to see and listen and actively reflect on: the client, themselves, the emergent relationship and the wider systemic levels they are nested within, including how these are interconnected.

3. Body, mind and spirit are all key parts of the process to be attended to, but do not exist separately from each other and are not bounded by the skin or consciousness of the individual.

4. All evolution is co-evolution.

5. Thoughts are not just created by the individual, but in collaboration with their family, culture and ethnicity which speak through them. Krishnamurti said: 'We think we are thinking our own thoughts, but we are not, we are thinking our culture's thoughts' (Krishnamurti, 1989:32).

6. We can only begin to know another by how we experience them through relationship, and this relationship is co-created between two or more parties and the wider societal and eco-systemic contexts.

7. All human beings operate within organising principles, and these arise within the relational and societal contexts. They can become limiting beliefs.

8. All understanding and assumptions can only be tentative and temporary.

9. Meaning-making is an emergent and dialogic process. New understanding is co-created between the therapist and client.

10. Identity is neither innate nor self-created, but dialogically co-created between the individual and their relational and systemic context.

11. Identity is always emergently evolving, but the self-narrative can become fixed and out of date.

12. Unlearning the old self-narrative and creating a new self-narrative is an important therapeutic process.

13. There is no such thing as an ethical and an unethical psychotherapist, for all of us are capable of being ethical and unethical.

14. Human beings become more ethical when they have the time and space to reflect on their situation and preflect on their future actions. They become even more ethical when they first discuss their options with another.

15. Every psychotherapist needs to be 'held' by themselves, by supervision, and by being part of a community of practice.

16. The psychotherapist is accountable to their clients, themselves, their supervisor, their community of practice, the profession and the wider community.

17. Good psychotherapists are curious about their clients and their lives. While a therapist cannot be knowledgeable in all areas of life, they will always be curious to learn about the areas that are spoken of by clients.

18. Good therapists hold their opinions lightly so that new learning from the client is possible.

19. A good psychotherapist never stops learning.

Conclusion

In the last chapter of this book we will explore the dangers of being integrative as a psychotherapist, as well as the dangers of not being integrative. We will look at ways of overcoming dangers through effective training (see Chapter 14); how we continually develop our personal integration through good supervision (see also Chapter 12); belonging to a community of practice; and having good governance structures. But to embark on the ambitious task of psychotherapy integration, as a writer, reader, researcher, practitioner or client, we need a clear purpose, to sustain the intellectual curiosity and rigorous exploration that this road requires. So, in the next chapter, we will explore why we believe greater psychotherapy integration is critically important for psychotherapy to make its necessary contribution to the great challenges of our time.

CHAPTER 2

The Current and Future Challenge for Our World and for Psychotherapy

So fair and foul a day I have not seen.

Shakespeare's *Macbeth*, Act One Scene Two

You cannot get through a single day without having an impact on the world around you. What you do makes a difference, and you have to decide what kind of difference you want to make.

Goodall, 2018

We live in one of the most privileged generations to have ever lived. Despite what you may imagine from watching the news or reading newspapers, statistically we human beings are less likely to be murdered, die in warfare, suffer from malnutrition, die at birth or in childhood, than ever before. Compared with even recent generations, we live much longer; have access to a much wider range of food; have much better access to health treatment and medication; are better educated; and can travel more. We are just one click away from vast amounts of knowledge and information and have much more free time and choice.

This chapter does something not found in many psychotherapy books. We explore in some detail this global context in which psychotherapy sits. As psychotherapists, we are used to considering the context of the client from the comparatively narrow perspective of their family and workplace, but we are not so used to considering the influence of the global context. This may always have had an influence on us and our clients, but now, more than ever, this wider view needs to be taken account of in our globally connected world.

We hope in this way that we can better understand the fundamental and vitally important challenges of our time. We will show how psychotherapy both is a creature of these times and has a potential to usefully address the especially difficult issues found in the age in which we live.

The benefits of the human progress recently achieved are particularly apparent for those of us who live in the privileged western white world (Ryde, 2019) and we need to continue to be aware that there are parts of the world where warfare, conflict and starvation are still a daily reality. However, all of the above statements are globally true. To give just one example, the child and infant mortality rate globally showed that under-five mortality rate has decreased by 56%, from an estimated rate of 93 deaths per 1000 live births in 1990 to 41 deaths per 1000 live births in 2016. About 20,000 fewer children died every day in 2016 than in 1990 (World Health Organization/Global Health Observatory, 2017a). This a remarkable global achievement.

Yet, at the same time in 2008:

> The American Psychological Association report that one in five young people are suffering from mental health problems, while the Health Organization predicts that by 2020 disorders such as depression and schizophrenia leading to suicide, drug abuse and self-harm in children will increase by 50%, placing them among the five main causes of disability and death. (Greenfield, 2009:158)

A 2016 index of 301 diseases found mental health problems to be one of the main causes of the overall disease burden worldwide (they were shown to account for 21.2% of years lived with disability worldwide). According to the 2013 Global Burden of Disease study, the predominant mental health problem worldwide is depression, followed by anxiety, schizophrenia and bipolar disorder. Globally, an estimated 300 million people are affected by depression (World Health Organization/Global Health Observatory, 2017b). In 2013, depression was the second leading cause of years lived with disability worldwide and in 26 countries, depression was the primary driver of disability. Depressive disorders also contribute to the likelihood of suicide as well as heart disease and hence to mortality and disability; they have both a direct and an indirect impact on the length and quality of life.

A large amount of mental illness remains unaddressed. The World Health Organization estimates that between 35% and 50% of people with severe mental health problems in developed countries, and 76–85% in developing countries, receive no treatment. A third of people (36.2%) who self-identified as having a mental health problem in the 2014 Adult Psychiatric Morbidity

Survey (National Health Service, 2014) have never been diagnosed by a professional.

Since 2000, there has been a slight steady increase in the proportion of people with symptoms of common mental health problems and nearly half (43.4%) of adults think that they have had a diagnosable mental health condition at some point in their life (35.2% of men and 51.2% of women). A fifth of men (19.5%) and a third of women (33.7%) have had diagnoses confirmed by professionals. In 2014, 19.7% of people in the UK aged 16 and older showed symptoms of anxiety or depression – a 1.5% increase from 2013 (National Health Service, 2014).

So why, when the human species is getting richer, physically healthier and more resourced, is mental illness becoming more prevalent and happiness not increasing? We suggest that there are four main factors that go some way to explaining this:

- Psychological overload.

- The conscious or unconscious registering of ecological devastation.

- The fragmentation of the psychological containers in and through which we psychologically process our experience and form our sense of meaning and individuality.

- Human-centrism and living in what we have termed the 'Age of More', an addicted society that is searching for happiness in ways that can never be satiated.

We will now take these four factors and explore them in more detail.

Psychological overload

We now connect with more people than ever before, play a greater variety of roles, and are exposed to more sources of data and information than ever. At the same time, we have less space alone or time to process the vast deluge of data and sensory input and experience we daily absorb.

Today more information is instantaneously available to us, at the click of the cell-phone or computer, than our grandparents would have accessed in their lifetime. We no longer need to wonder or argue about who wrote a book, or appeared in a film, for Google can tell us! But our information arrives in bite-sized fragments – by Twitter, YouTube, Facebook, television headlines and email. We take in much more information every day than previous generations but have less 'pause space' to connect and digest it. We do not have the time to engage in the process of turning data into information, information into knowledge and knowledge into wisdom, before the next flood of data arrives.

The internet age has brought many benefits to human beings, but with it has come informational overload by the media and other sources with such a large volume of information that it could overload even a powerful computer, according to US scientific research. A study, conducted by researchers at the University of California San Diego, under Roger Bohn (Bohn & Short, 2012), believes that people are inundated every day with the equivalent amount of 34 gigabytes of information, a sufficient quantity to overload the average laptop within a week.

Through mobile phones, the internet, electronic mail, television, radio, newspapers, books, social media and so on, western individuals receive every day about 105,000 words or 23 words per second in the hours when they are not sleeping or eating. There is no way we are able to process everything that is estimated to reach our eyes and ears every day – or the videos, pictures and videos games that together create the estimated 34 gigabytes of information per day we receive. Much of the data, images and voices are disconnected, uncurated and discordant; it is as if we are constantly eating fragments of contrasting raw food and then wondering why we have indigestion.

Modern technology has not just increased the psychological pressure we feel as a result of this information overload, but in addition, screen experience is very addictive in nature. The average British person checks their mobile phone once an hour or 10,000 times a year and many people check it much more often than that – in the middle of meals and meetings or even in bed (Barr, 2017).

Susan Greenfield, a brain scientist and Oxford Professor of Synaptic Pharmacology and Director of the Institute for the Future of the Mind, writes about how the effect of screen time – the amount of time we spend in front of screens, particularly when living through virtual reality in second life or on video games – is changing the very nature of the human brain, as well as human identity and social interaction. She quotes a survey from 2008, that showed that even then, 8–18-year-olds in the UK spent an average of 6.5 hours using electronic media and often more than one device at a time, stretching the daily timeframe to 8.5 hours. She suggests that 'the technology, now assumed to be as indispensable and integral to our daily existence is actually becoming ever more pervasive, invasive and startling' (Greenfield, 2009:1). She sees this as a threat to humanity as big as climate change (not a view we share).

The world of video games, visual entertainment and daily news engages our emotions and feelings in intense ways, so that we imaginatively enter other, and often extreme, worlds. In minutes we can be taken from warfare in Syria, with children being bombed and gassed, to floods in India, to sport in Australia, and then into the virtual world of dragons and mythical enemies, then into Facebook intimacy with multiple friends, while listening to a kaleidoscopic playlist of music, and half-aware that the children are fighting downstairs and we are late for picking up our partner from the station!

Not only do we take in more, but we move through a greater variety of roles in each day, from parents negotiating our children's education with a teacher, to caregiver for our own parents; from our partner's lover to co-parent, to joint manager of the family house and finances; from work roles where we now may belong to multiple teams, or have a portfolio career involving many different ways of being; and from being a passionate sports fan to volunteering on the local soup run to the homeless. Yet psychotherapy encourages us to be authentic and autonomous and discover our integration in this one-man or one-woman ever-changing repertory show.

Additionally, many have written about how life is becoming increasingly VUCA, which stands for volatile, uncertain, complex and ambiguous (Stiehm & Townsend, 2002). Psychological overload is not just about the amount of information we take in, the range of experience and virtual experience we absorb, and the multifarious roles we are required to play, but also that we know more, but can predict less in our lives. The contexts we inhabit are changing faster and with more interconnected complexity than ever. To give just two examples, the time it takes for any innovation to become obsolete is becoming shorter and shorter, as is the average life expectancy of organisations. The average lifespan of a company in the Standard & Poor's index has fallen from 67 years a century ago to just 15 years today, and it is predicted that 40% of today's largest companies (listed on the Fortune 500 index) won't exist a decade from now (Ismail, 2014:203). At the same time, we are seeing a meteoric rise in successful start-ups. YouTube began as an angel-funded enterprise from a makeshift office in a garage in 2005 and was acquired by Google for $1.65 billion just 18 months later. By 2009, it was receiving 129 million views a day. In March 2013, the number of unique users visiting YouTube every month reached 1 billion (Diamandis & Kotler, 2014:35, 84).

Most of what today's students learn in college is out of date within fewer years than it took them to learn it, and they no longer choose a career but recognise that in their working life they will undertake many different work roles, having to retrain and reinvent themselves many times. Some have predicted that over half of the jobs now being carried out in America and Europe will not exist within 20 years, due to digitalisation, robotics and artificial intelligence.

Human beings have been incredibly successful at adapting to multiple environmental niches, from the tropical jungle to the Arctic tundra, and from the desert to urban living, but now, for better or worse, we have created one interconnected, fast-changing, global niche, and as a species we have no idea how to thrive within this context.

The pain of ecological devastation

For many years, human beings have been wilfully blind to the ecological destruction that has resulted from their so-called success. The massive pollution of the atmosphere from the carbon-driven economies originated in the Industrial Revolution – and the effects last for hundreds of years. Climate changes that have emerged from the effect of the so-called greenhouse gases are already driving more extreme weather patterns in many parts of the world and causing sea level rises from melting polar ice-caps. There is devastation of many ecological niches of the world through exploitation of nature's resources, including deforestation of many of the world's jungles and forests, termed by some the 'earth lungs'; the hunting of many animals that has caused unprecedented loss of species diversity; the mining of carbon sources (coal, gas, oil) and of minerals to fuel and adorn and enable human lifestyles; and the conversion of diverse wild natural areas into human-controlled mono-cultures.

This is now becoming impossible to ignore, despite the best attempts of the politicians, communities and companies, who have large vested interests in sustaining the carbon industry and currying populist favour. Evidence reaches around the world from scientific reports, films and television programmes, and direct experience of living in cities where you can sense the pollution you are breathing, or where your communities are wrecked by forest fires, hurricanes or rising sea levels. Even those living in more protected areas are becoming affected by the migration of those who have been directly or economically impacted by climate change, and this will inevitably increase.

The devastation of our shared planetary home has enormous and increasing impact on the mental and emotional lives of each and every one of us, for some consciously and for all unconsciously. This gives rise to direct or indirect feelings of: grief and loss; guilt for one's part in the destruction; fear for oneself, one's community, and/or for future generations; or anger at others who the individual sees as more responsible for the devastation than themselves. These can emerge through the dreams of the client or their reactions to current events, or even through nameless and unlocatable emotions. Whatever way, the wider ecology and what is happening to it will arrive in the therapeutic relationship, bidden or unbidden, recognised or unrecognised.

Nature has traditionally been a major place and source of physical and mental healing. Yet with the unprecedented migration of human beings to urban environments and the parallel destruction and humanisation of many natural ecologies, this resource is less and less available to larger percentages of the human population. Many have lost their living connection to other mammals and to plants, or ease of access to places of unspoilt beauty away from human noise and interference. Many of us have lost our healthy living connection to our source, and life has become plastic-packaged, humanised, noisy and crowded. Many people have written about the consequences of a flattened world (Wilber, 2000); the disenchantment of the world (Abram, 1996; Reason, 2017); and the subsequent human alienation and loss (Marcuse, 2002; Habermas, 2015; Mumford, 2015; Whitehead, 2010).

In Chapter 9, we will specifically address how the ecological enters the therapeutic relationship and work, as well as how the 'more-than-human' world can be a part of the healing process. Here we need to start by recognising that mental health in the individual is inextricably linked to, and affected by, health at other systemic levels. To offer a modern rendering of the Chinese philosopher Lao Tsu's wise words:

If there is not health in the ecology of the planet, there will not be harmony between species.

If there is not harmony between humans and the more-than-human world, there will not be peace between nations.

If there is not peace between nations, there will not be health within communities.

If there is not health within communities, there will not be health within families and other groups that reside in those communities.

If there is not health in groups and families, there will not be peace or health in the individual.

If there is not health in the individual, this will impact on all the larger systemic levels, as well as on all the sub-systems within the individual.

All these systemic levels affect all of us and arrive in the psychotherapy consulting room. And although we may focus mostly on one of them, the others cannot be ignored as not only do they provide the context in which the individual lives, thinks, feels and breathes, but also these larger systemic levels reside within the individual, as we will show in later chapters.

Fragmentation

In this book, we will explore how it is natural for human beings to be engaged, not just in living but in life-making, which turns life that is lived and experienced into lived meaning, through creating narratives that connect: past, present and future; inner experience and outer experience; and personal meaning with group, community and cultural meaning. These give a sense of continuity and integration to episodic experience.

We will show that, although individuals can be considered makers of their own life and authors of their own narratives, these narratives and meanings are always co-created dialogically, that is, in relation to others, both individual others and the collective groups of which we and they are part, as well as permeated by the cultures they are both born in and live within – their stories framed by the languages, customs, mores and belief systems of those cultures. Thus, human beings create their individuality out of relational and collective ingredients in the same way that a unique individual plant creates its individuality not just out of the genetic inheritance of its genus, but out of the soil, sunlight, weather, rain, insects and companion plants that make up its own unique micro-niche.

The materials from which we build our identity and meaning have become much more fractured and fragmented in recent years:

- *Families* are more transitory, with parents changing partners, and many children having life split between separated parents, engaging with different half- and step-brothers and sisters.

- *Community* – our holding container in previous generations was not just our immediate nuclear family, for this was often contained within a wider extended family of grandparents, aunts, uncles and cousins who lived locally. The local village or urban estate would be a known community with and through whom you created an identity.

Lesley, who comes from Bath and works with us, describes her sisters coming home with boyfriends from Bristol just 14 miles away. The local Bath boys attacked them, telling them to go back to where they belonged and not try and take 'our girls'. This would have been in the 1970s. Our communities are now often spread round the world and consist of people we connect with digitally via Facebook, Snapchat, Instagram and so on.

- *Place* – in the past children would more often grow up in a rooted location. Even 50 years ago two-thirds of the world's population was rural, intimately connected with growing their food and looking after their animals within an ecological locale to which they felt deeply connected. Peter has written elsewhere about how nearly all of us have lost the sense of creating our meaning in relation to a given ecological context (Hawkins, 2018a, 2018b). Poets like Seamus Heaney, R. S. Thomas and Wordsworth still provide us with a sense of forming our identity in relation to place.

- *A collective rhythm* – traditionally, cultures would have collective rhythms that gave shape and meaning to the day, week, season and year. As children, both of us went to church on Sundays, both experiencing a clearer distinction between the working week and the weekends. The school day began with an assembly of prayers and hymns. We experienced the fasting of Lent, Whit walks, Harvest festivals, May Day dancing around the maypole and Christmas that was not just a consumerist indulgence. We have lived through the blurring of these boundaries and thus the weakening of the containers between work and play. With digital technology, work can happen anywhere, anytime and emails and messages chase us round the world.

- *Shared beliefs* – the celebrations of the year's rhythm were rooted in collective beliefs, shared by the extended family, school and local community. In the West, these were based in a Christian culture, but many of the festivities like May Day, Easter bunnies and Easter eggs and Christmas had roots that went back in our culture to older pre-Christian festivals. Our family, community, town or village and festivities were an interconnected web which expressed and communicated shared beliefs. In the last 100 years, not only have we become more migratory and less rooted, but much more secular and individualistic in our beliefs. This is particularly true in the western world.

- *Digitalisation of human interactions* – a 75-year-old friend of ours told us that, in the past, he would, while collecting his pension, have a conversation with the local post office; counter-clerk; buy his train ticket in conversation with the ticket officials and discuss his finances with the bank manager. All of these conversational interactions have now been replaced with digital online transactions with faceless processes on his computer. This can also disadvantage those who receive Universal Credit and are required to apply online but have no access to a computer.

Nevertheless, many of these social changes are both liberating and empowering as well as socially fragmenting. In the same way that the printing press massively increased people's direct access to books and the Bible unmediated by priests, so the internet has democratised information. Individuals are less constrained and oppressed by the dominant beliefs and prejudices of their families, communities or peer groups and are able to move away from the place and the communities to which they belong, if they so wish. However, there is increasing global evidence that many individuals and social communities and groups are struggling to create a positive sense of identity in the midst of the exponential changes of our time. Some of the symptoms of greater human unease can be seen in the rapid increase in mental illness, particularly among the young, and in the growing feeling of alienation in many communities, with an increasing mistrust in both their political leaders and in 'experts'. Some argue that the political move back to nationalism and more right-wing agendas is fuelled by people's reaction to this fragmentation and loss of social identity.

We are in the midst of what has been termed the 'fourth industrial revolution': Klaus Schwab, founder and executive chairman of the World Economic Forum, wrote in 2016:

> We stand on the brink of a technological revolution that will fundamentally alter the way we live, work, and relate to one another. In its scale, scope, and complexity, the transformation will be unlike anything humankind has experienced before. We do not yet know just how it will unfold, but one thing is clear: the response to it must be integrated and comprehensive, involving all stakeholders of the global polity, from the public and private sectors to academia and civil society.

He went on to say: 'The fourth great Industrial Revolution…is characterised by a fusion of technologies that is blurring the lines between the physical, digital, and biological spheres' (Schwab, 2016).

Revolutions in the digital world, artificial intelligence, virtual reality and 'presencing' through mixed reality, robotics and bio-technology will come together to change not only the workplace, but human connectedness, social organisation and individuals' sense of self, in as yet unimaginable ways and at accelerating speeds. Harari (2015) has argued that liberal humanism in its many forms, such as modern democracy, customer-centrism and secular values, has been based on the individual being the sole arbiter of what is right, the assumption that the individual knows themselves and what they believe. He then argues that this assumption will be undermined by modern technology, that can collect and process 'big data' about us, via the internet. Internal data through medical and cognitive implants, and technological systems will soon potentially know more about us than we do ourselves!

The coming of human-centrism and the 'Age of More'

Central to human mental health and well-being is a sense of purpose which gives meaning to one's life (see Chapter 4). For the early hunter-gathers, purpose was collective or tribal and centred on survival, how the tribe could collectively organise itself to secure the necessary food, drink and warmth to sustain life. Only with the coming of the agrarian revolution, accompanied by larger human cities, with greater diversity of human roles, and the growth of more complex language and culture, was there the development of the search for conceptual and intellectual meaning. Karen Armstrong (2006) has shown how the Axial Age, the period 800–200 BCE, proved pivotal to human cultural development. It brought about the beginnings of conceptual religions and philosophies, based on cultural stories and narratives that were shared by much wider human groups. With this movement came a new purpose, centred on knowledge, understanding and intellectual meaning, turning information into knowledge and knowledge into wisdom. In the 5th century BCE, we have the 'great wisdom teachers' emerging in very different cultures: Confucius and Lao Tzu in China; Gautama Buddha in India; and Socrates and Plato in Greece. Each of them is concerned with asking the question, 'What is a good life?'

The influence of all four of them, and the schools that followed them, has permeated human thinking and narratives, right through to our modern world. First, their questions and explorations influenced the development and growth of many of the world's main religions; not only were some named after particular thinkers such as Confucianism and Buddhism, but Greek philosophy also had a major impact on all three of the world's monotheistic religions (Judaism, Christianity and Islam).

Thus, the Axial Age gave birth to the age of large-scale religion, where humans were schooled in the religion of their community and culture, and people no longer fought just for food and territory, but religious wars became prominent, where cultures would try both to protect and to impose their dominant meaning narrative on others.

Two major historical trends began to undermine collectively received meaning: the beginnings and development of modern science in the Islamic, Christian and Chinese cultures, from the 10th century onwards; and the invention of printing in the late 15th century, that was as impactful on its time as the computer and internet have been in the last 50 years.

Modern science at first grew slowly within the dominant religious frameworks and belief systems. Inevitably, it led to discoveries that would begin to challenge religious orthodoxy, such as Copernicus and Galileo, challenging the Christian church's belief that the sun and planets revolved around the Earth; or much later the discovery that human beings had evolved from other life forms. In parallel, the growth of printing and literacy meant that individual human beings could have direct access to the knowledge of others, rather than having to rely on that mediated by the local priest, imam or guru.

Gradually, these trends built towards the 'Age of Enlightenment' and the birth of 'liberal humanism', which Harari (2015) argues is the dominant religion of our time in the West. Whereas the Copernican revolution put the sun at the centre of our solar system and relegated the Earth to an orbiting planet, the Protestant Reformation put the individual mind and conscience at the centre of the universe and relegated the priest to an orbiting organism that would sometimes come for tea. Secular liberal humanism has put individual feelings and happiness at the centre of the universe and the environment as something to fulfil our individual needs. Harari (2014) describes the 20th century as being dominated by the wars between three different 'humanisms': *liberal humanism*, which centred on the importance of the individual, social democracy and capitalist markets; *social humanism*, which privileges the collective over the individual, and state control over market forces; and *evolutionary humanism*, which sees some cultures as more evolved than others and an inevitable battle for the more evolved to dominate over the less evolved ruled by 'more enlightened' dictators. These three took global shape in Capitalism, Communism and Fascism, and Harari suggests that even in the 1970s it looked very unlikely that liberal humanism would dominate, as the majority of countries at that time were dominated by a communist or dictatorial politics. However, in the last 50 years he suggests that liberal humanism has become globally dominant, albeit in different manifestations, because 'the supermarket is more attractive than the Gulag' (Harari, 2014:265). But liberal humanism brings with it its own shadow. For capital markets rely on growth, and growth relies on constantly increasing consumerism.

Alan Durning (1992:69) wrote:

> Our enormously productive economy…demands that we make consumption our way of life, that we convert the buying and use of goods into rituals, that we seek our spiritual satisfaction, our ego satisfaction, in consumption… We need things consumed, burned up, worn out, replaced, and discarded at an ever-increasing rate.

Durning goes on to say:

> Only population growth rivals consumption as a cause of ecological decline and at least population growth is now viewed as a problem by many governments and citizens of the world. Consumption, in contrast, is almost universally seen as a good – indeed, increasingly it is the primary goal of national economic policy. (p.70)

Armies of advertisers, marketing experts and 'spin doctors' have to convince human beings that to be happy, to be healthy, to be successful they need to acquire 'more': more food, drink, clothes, cars, travel, holidays, books, films, electronic gadgets, computers, belongings of every kind. Increasingly, in the rich cultures 'more' has begun to move away from acquisition of material things, to acquisition of experiences, which you can tell your friends about via social media; a move from 'you are what you own' to 'you are what you have experienced'.

The 'Age of More' is also the age of the sore neck, for everyone is looking upwards to those that have more than they have. Consumerism requires conspicuous inequality, and rich, attractive celebrities, to increase the mass aspiration for more. Some people may be in the wealthiest 1% of the world's population, but if the people they see on our televisions and YouTube, the celebrities in our sports events and popular entertainment, the top executives in our organisations, are much wealthy than they are, they feel poor and under-privileged. Alan Durning who we quoted above went on to quote Lewis Lapham, the editor of *Harper's* magazine as saying:

> A depressing number of Americans believe that if only they had twice as much, they would inherit the estate of happiness promised them in the Declaration of Independence. The man who receives $15,000 a year is sure that he could relieve his sorrow if he had $30,000 a year; the man with $1 million a year knows that all would be well if he had $2 million a year ... Nobody ever has enough. (Durning, 1992:70)

Harari (2015:218) writes about how: 'modernity...inspired people to want more and dismantled the age old disciplines that curbed greed'. Furthermore, globalisation and the internet has meant that 'the rest know what the best are having' (Hawkins, 2017a:2), and, in the 'Age of More', this has led to massive increase in migration.

Psychotherapy, like Protestant thinking and ethics before it, can be seen as a child of liberal humanism, for liberal humanism preaches that meaning is only to be found by individuals looking inside themselves. For Protestants, meaning was found by consulting your own conscience, developing your personal relationship with God, who could be found, not in the teachings of the priest or Holy Book, not in the sky, but inside you, in your heart, for God was 'the ground of your being'. As liberal humanism became more and more secularised, psychotherapy still encouraged the individual to look inside themselves, to consult their own reason and their own feelings. Autonomy, individuation and self-actualisation became the goal not just of psychotherapy (see Chapter 4), but for living. Material growth became paralleled by 'personal growth' as many of us 'tried to find the fastest escalator up "Maslow's pyramid"' (Hawkins, 2017b:255).

A number of governments have increasingly begun to focus on how we can replace the measurement of national GDP (Gross Domestic Product), which merely measures the level of economic activity, with national GDH (Gross Domestic Happiness), a revival of the 18th-century utilitarianism of Bentham and Mill (Mill, 2001), defining the purpose of society to be to create the greatest happiness of the greatest number.

As experiences have become more valued than material possessions, for those who live in the materially more affluent societies, many have become consumers of experiences, many are centring their sense of purpose on a 'healthy body', 'great relationships', 'more mindfulness', 'an expanded and enlightened consciousness'. These, too, have their armies of marketing advertisers and seductive sales forces.

Anne Wilson Schaef (2013, first published 1987) wrote an important book, *When Society Becomes an Addict*, applying what we know about the nature of individual addiction to wider western society. The nature of addiction entails that, whatever you become addicted to, you need increasing amounts of it to meet your habituated need. 'More' no longer brings you the pleasure it once did. 'More' no longer brings you happiness, but instead brings you the longing for 'even more'.

The 'Age of More', with its aspiration, acquisition and addiction, supports gross inequality and the exponential growth of consuming the Earth's resources, beyond sustainable levels. With over three times more people in the world than when we were both born, all being globally connected, all being encouraged to want more, our human species urgently needs to find a new sense of personal and collective meaning. Harari (2015) wrote that liberal humanism, having addressed the historical challenges of famine, plague and war, will move on to three new human-centric aspirations: becoming immortal and overcoming human death; greater happiness; and becoming God-like through technological augmentation. We believe that liberal humanism has reached its highest point and humans have already played at being God far too long for the good of the planet's eco-system. Until we have discovered how to live well on this planet, we have no moral right to even think about colonising other planets. What is needed is a major paradigm shift in human consciousness, from human-centricity to humility; and from assuming the environment is there to serve human want, to becoming aware of the environment as being part of us. Without this shift we have no healthy or sustainable life.

Conclusion

We have explored our tentative answers to the question, 'How come humans on average are richer, better fed, less in danger of dying from warfare or murder, living longer and with more access to knowledge than ever before – and yet, we are no happier and, indeed, suffer a significant increase in mental illness?' We have looked at psychological overload, fragmentation of the psychological containers we have traditionally used to create meaning and integrating narratives; and have considered liberal humanism and the 'Age of More', which has brought immeasurable benefits, but also great psychological and social costs.

Psychotherapy is both a symptom and an offspring of these global trends but is also a potential remedy. It can collude in reinforcing narcissistic self-centredness, and beliefs that we are the centre of the universe and that our feelings are the ultimate arbiter of truth. It can be part of the human-centric zeitgeist that sees human happiness as the ultimate goal, and the rest of the living universe as there to serve not only our needs, but also our culturally induced wants. It can encourage the client to see themselves as separate from the world around them and even collude with their sense of being a victim of 'Them' – that which they see as evil others and the bad environment. Or it can go to the other extreme and encourage the individual to see themselves as solely responsible for whatever happens to them and around them. It can get entrapped in dualistic polarisations that can become unhealthy splitting: victim or autonomous independent individual; myself and other; good and bad; them and us; internal me and external not me; human and environment.

What the human species and the more-than-human world needs is a psychotherapy that is an antidote to our individual and collective human sickness, an integrative psychotherapy that draws on the best and deepest that psychotherapy can offer, irrespective of which school or approach it comes from. A psychotherapy that is: non-dualistic, relational, seeing the individual as co-creating themselves and their world in dynamic relation to the many systems they are part of, a psychotherapy which attends to healing the split between the human and 'more-than-human world'.

Our time is both frightening and exciting, but above all crucial. For in the next 25 years we are in the midst of what Macy and Johstone (2012) describe as the 'Great Turning', which Elkington and Zeitz (2014) describe as the time when human systems will either break down or break through, and Peter Diamandis, with his abundant optimism, sees as a period that 'can remake the world' (Diamandis & Kotler, 2014:27). We live in a time when the human species needs to evolve faster than ever before, and in the Anthropocene Age (St Fleur, 2016) we need to take responsibility for the effect we are having on the evolution and extinction of many other species and ecologies in the eco-system. It is a time when, not just psychotherapists, but all of us need to listen to what is happening both in us and all around us, re-examine our deeply held assumptions and beliefs and constantly reinvent and innovate any field we work in.

Carl Jung was extremely prescient when he said as early as 1958 in a television interview with John Freeman:

> The only real danger that exists is man himself. He is the great danger, and we are pitifully unaware of it. We know nothing of man, far too little. His psyche should be studied, for we are the origin of all coming evil. (Jung, 1977:436)

CHAPTER 3

Identity: In Search of a Self

Nasrudin went into a bank that he did not usually use and asked to withdraw a large sum of money from his account. The bank clerk was naturally suspicious and asked him politely: 'Have you any means of identifying yourself?' Nasrudin reached down into the pockets of his long cloak and found an ornate mirror. He held the mirror up and looked studiously into it and exclaimed to the clerk: 'Yes, that's me all right.'

Hawkins, 2005:36–37

On a later visit after further financial regulation, the bank clerk asked Nasrudin for two forms of identity. He drew out two mirrors one from each pocket and with puzzlement looked from one to the other and explained: 'I think one of those has to be me?'

Hawkins, 2005:36–37

Introduction

We will often start a new psychotherapy relationship by inviting the client to tell us about themselves. The answers come in very diverse narratives. Some new clients describe themselves by their current roles in their family and at work; others tell the chronology of their life; others describe their symptoms of distress and disturbance; and some as a victim of a series of 'bad' people and events. How we each construct the narrative of our lives reflects our personality. We may go on to ask them what matters most to them and what has brought them to psychotherapy. From these questions, often a more relational and emergent sense of their being begins to be revealed. Then we notice how we experience being with them in the room, how they register inside us, and we may invite them to notice what it feels like being here, now, with us. Within just a few minutes, the journey in search of a self has begun, not just the self they can tell us about, or we can interpret, or they can show us in their psychometric assessment or psychiatric diagnosis, but rather a new emergent self that arises in our meeting.

Writing this chapter of the book has been the most difficult of them all and more pages have ended up on the cutting room floor than from all the other chapters put together! Trying to understand the nature of the self and integrate the many different approaches to understanding identity and its development throughout history has been like wrestling a very slippery octopus. As soon as you grasp hold of one of its many limbs, another comes sliding in and intrudes. As we reflected on this image, we recognised how similar this was to the feeling of being in psychotherapy, and the joint search by therapist and client to find a healthier integration of the self of the client and to find a coherence in the many aspects of an individual.

The very notion of a 'self' is extremely slippery, and it has a long history of being contentious. In this chapter, we will explore some of the different concepts about the self and how our unique identity develops. We will offer an integration of ways of understanding individual development that draws on research in many fields, including psychotherapy, social psychology, cognitive science, neuroscience, philosophy and spirituality. In doing so, we will attempt to weave a new tapestry that transcends the polarised opposites that have captured the debates about the nature of self in the modern era.

A short history of pre-modern searches for a 'self'

As far as we can tell, early *Homo sapiens* had no language or concepts of the separate self. The anthropologist Levy-Bruhl (1966, first published 1927) concluded that it was unlikely that early human beings had a concept of having their own 'personality.' Kelson (quoted in Belk, 1984) also noted that most hunter-gatherer cultures had no first-person singular forms in their languages.

It was only with the advent of the agricultural age, when food became plentiful enough to support the growth of cities, a greater division of labour and the growth of more conceptual languages, that individuality became something that was focused on. Most early concepts came from philosophers or religious writers and focused on the notion of soul or spirit. Interestingly, the words 'soul' and 'spirit' have very similar roots to each other: the word for 'soul' in Greek is *psyche*, in Latin, *anima* and in Sanskrit, *atman*, all of which mean breath. The same is true for the word 'spirit', which in Greek is *pneuma*, in Latin, *spiritus* and in Hebrew, *ruah*, all of which also partly mean breath.

Plato in *Phaedo* wrote about the soul as being immaterial but the source of consciousness, of choice and activity. Aristotle followed his teacher and carried out a much more extensive exploration of the soul. For Aristotle, the soul was not only what animated us and drove our actions, but also the agent of perception and the source of knowing and sense-making. Platonic and Aristotelian ideas would permeate western understanding of the soul and the self for many centuries, providing primary frameworks for Jewish (Maimonides), Christian (St Augustine and Thomas Aquinas) and Islamic (Avicenna and Ibn Arabi) philosophers.

It was St Augustine (354–430 BCE) who took Aristotelian ideas and, within a Christian framework, developed ideas of a personal self or soul who could reflect on itself, but who could only come to perfection through God's love. Many gnostics, neo-Platonists, Sufis, Buddhists and Asian spiritual teachers developed sophisticated models of the stages of human and spiritual development with their differentiated 'stations' and 'states', but these remained esoterically available only to the privileged few. (For further understanding of these from different traditions see Wilber, 1996; Aurobindo, 1999.)

The polarised debates of the modern era

With the age of enlightenment and the growth of science, the centre of exploration of human identity shifted from the religious and philosophical domains to those of the physical and human sciences. Three of the key figures who laid the foundations for modern theories of human development were Gustav Fechner (1801–1887), William James (1842–1910) and James Baldwin (1861–1934). There has not been a human development theorist since that period who has not been influenced directly or indirectly by one or more of these three great innovators.

Baldwin was one of the first modern writers to realise that 'no consistent view of mental development in the individual could possibly be reached without a doctrine of the…development of consciousness' (Baldwin, 1902). He also liberated the western Christian view of the soul as a fixed entity, 'a fixed substance with fixed attributes', and replaced it with 'the conception of a growing, developing activity'.

Baldwin was the first modern psychologist to map the developmental levels of the growing human consciousness, from 'prelogical', to 'quasi-logical', to 'logical', to the 'extra-logical' and finally the 'hyper-logical', where human beings can transcend duality and achieve unity consciousness. He realised that these developmental levels had cognitive, aesthetic and moral dimensions, a realisation that would have a profound effect for later writers on moral maturity such as Kohlberg and Graves, as well as theorists on adult development such as Erikson, Keegan, Maslow and many others.

Baldwin was a key influence on the scientific explorations of Piaget, who shaped much of our understanding of childhood cognitive development. In turn, Piaget's work has influenced many of the psychotherapists who studied early infant development, from Klein to Winnicott to Stern, and to the intersubjective systems therapists such as Stolorow and Atwood. Theories of early development have more recently been deepened and expanded by research in neuroscience on the formation and development of the brain and its neural connections throughout the body.

Four core dilemmas have been much contested within and across the many disciplines of human sciences in the modern and early post-modern era.

1. *The human being is an autonomous being and their development is driven by their inner drives, versus the human is developing in reaction to their environment*

   From the mid-19th century, two basic groups of theories emerged. On the one side were the biologists, geneticists and early psychoanalysts, who saw the individual as an autonomous system but determined by their genetic inheritance and their inner drives and mechanisms. In the other camp were the behaviourists, Marxists and many Darwinian evolutionists, who tended to place the source of the action in the environment and saw the individual as responding to it. Both were operating from a scientific paradigm of linear causality but located the causality at opposite ends of the spectrum. Neither was embracing a more integrative exploration of how the individual and their social system co-created each other.

2. *Individual identity is innate and the work of the individual is to uncover it, versus the identity is something that each person needs to create for themselves*

   Appiah (2005:17, 107) distinguishes between 'essentialist' ideas of identity and those that see the self as something that the individual creates. Essentialist approaches posit that the essence of an individual is innate, it is something we are uniquely born with. Often it can become buried under layers of social adaptation, and the work of the individual in psychotherapy is to peel back these layers and discover the 'true self'.

The 'other picture, the existentialist picture, is one in which... existence precedes essence: that is, you exist first and then have to decide what to exist as, who to be, afterward' (Appiah, 2005:17). In this approach, creating the self and one's identity is a lifetime's work. Many of these approaches see the individual as self-creating – the self, created by the self.

3. *Identity is unitary, versus identity is multifarious*

There has been a great deal of literature about the importance of authenticity and being 'true to oneself' and many psychotherapists have written about the importance of uncovering the true self (Winnicott, 1988). Even the work of psychosynthesis, with its focus on sub-personalities and developing the higher self, posits a unitary higher self as opposed to the many lower sub-personalities (Assagioli, 1965). Others see identity as naturally ever changing and being different depending on the context or others it is engaging with.

4. *Self as a noun, versus self as a verb*

Much of our language talks about the self, my self, her identity, and by so doing makes the self an object, an entity that has material form. However, Buddhist teaching and process scholarship (Bateson, 1972; Ryle, 1967; Whitehead, 1939) would suggest there is no such thing as the 'self', but rather we all live in an ever-moving flow of life and the self is a temporary pattern of engaging.

Transcending the polarities: an integrative approach to self-identity

To move beyond these polarising positions, we would offer the following propositions:

1. *The self evolves in relation to its physical and genetic inheritance and the contexts it inhabits*

The long-running debate between nature and nurture continues to rumble on but we view it as a very outdated false either/or dilemma.

We inherit certain predispositions, which take form in the human relational and family context during our early years. As we enter the verbal and social years of our childhood, we co-develop our identity and personality within our community and cultural contexts. The culture provides the language, verbal and non-verbal, and the modes of approval and disapproval that shape us. Many of the beliefs and attitudes that make up our identity are absorbed consciously as well as unconsciously from those around us. We are shaped by our contexts and to a lesser extent we shape our contexts. As Appiah (Appiah, 2005:107) suggests, 'We do make choices, but we don't individually determine the options among which we choose.' This suggests that the individual may build their self, but they do not get to choose all the materials.

2. *The self has many layers*

In the same way that neuroscience has showed that our brain contains many layers of processing – some we share with reptiles, some with all mammals and some more distinctly human – so the self can be seen to have many layers.

Proto-self. As an individual we have a self-regulating system that maintains our body's homeostasis and health; the brain continually monitors the various bodily processes and creates a neural mapping which is constantly updated and creates neural connections across many parts of the brain. Damasio (1999) calls this the 'proto-self', for it is non-conscious but crucial to survival.

Experiencing self. This is internally and externally focused and is the brain's pre-verbal or non-verbal account of how the organism's own state is affected by engaging with an external object or internal memory. Damasio sees a critical role for emotion in the formation of the core self. Emotions are complex patterns of chemical and neural responses that create connections throughout the brain and the whole body and have specific regulatory and survival functions. Damasio distinguishes emotions from feelings, for feelings he sees as 'a mental image' of an emotion. Core consciousness happens through pulses, each pulse triggered by an interaction with an object or an internal recollection from memory or an imagined image of the future. The experiencing self not only involves many other parts of the brain as well as the neo-cortex, the limbic brain and the amygdala, but also neural pathways throughout the body, especially the large clusters in the gut and the heart.

Narrative self. According to Capra and Luisi (2016:270), human reflective consciousness (what some describe as self-reflection) 'emerged in evolution together with the evolution of language and of organized social relations. This means that human consciousness is inextricably linked to language and to our social world of interpersonal relationships and culture. In other words, consciousness is not only a biological but also a social phenomenon.' Language as used here is not just verbal language but includes all forms of non-verbal language, such as gesture, movement, sounds and signs. Daniel Kahneman (2012) in his best-selling book, *Thinking, Fast and Slow*, distinguishes between the 'experiencing self' and the 'reflective self' which is similar to the narrative self. The experiencing self is our moment-to-moment consciousness, whereas the 'narrative self' is reflective and preflective – turning past experience into an integrated story and creating stories about possible futures.

It is the narrative self that mostly is listened to in psychotherapy, telling its stories about what has happened and its fears about what might happen in the future. As Harari (2015:295) writes, 'the experiencing self remembers nothing. It tells no stories.'

Some writers like Gazzaniga (2011) in his book, *Who's in Charge?*, and McGilchrist (2009) in *The Master and the Emissary*, associated these two selves with the different hemispheres of the neo-cortex, the left hemisphere being the narrating self and the right hemisphere being the experiencing self, but others have shown that the brain cannot be so easily divided into separate functions.

The pattern that connects internally and externally

We are not suggesting that we each have three selves or that these selves are separate systems, rather that these are three different processes that all humans are constantly engaged with. These three processes are very different but not separate, for each is constantly affected by, and affecting, the other two. All three aspects of self are not bounded by the skin, but are co-created in dynamic relationship with a) those close to us (the relational world of Chapter 7); b) the social, community and cultural contexts we are part of and are part of us (the systemic worlds of Chapter 8); and c) the ecological world we inhabit and which flows through us (the eco-systemic and spiritual worlds of Chapter 9).

We are, at the same time, self-authoring and socially constructed. It is all too easy as a psychotherapist to see all ways of behaving and thinking as being aspects of the individual's personality or pathology, and underestimate or even be blind to how they may be part of their family, social, regional or ethnic culture (Ryde, 2009).

Individuality is multifarious but seeking coherence

If we look at our own lives, we can recognise that we behave very differently at different times and in different settings. Also, we have different states of being and moods in our experiential self and different and ever-changing stories and constructions in our ways of making sense of our lives and who we are. Our identity is a product of what has come before as well as our aspirations for our future. It is created by the dynamic interplay between the individual and the many contexts, relational, social and ecological, they exist within. Drawing on social psychologists such as Breakwell (1986, 2012), Vignoles *et al.* (2006) and Jaspal and Cinnirella (2010), we view the individual in the midst of these many currents as constantly seeking:

- continuity – across time and situation

- distinctiveness – uniqueness or distinctiveness from others

- self-efficacy – feeling confident and in control of their life

- self-esteem – feelings of personal self-worth

- belonging – maintaining feelings of closeness to and acceptance by other people

- meaning – finding significance and purpose in their life

- coherence – establishing feelings of compatibility between interconnected identities.

These principles are similar to Siegel (2010), who uses the acronym FACES to show how identity needs to be *Flexible, Adaptable, Coherent, Experimental* and *Stable*. This process of integration is at the core of human meaning-making and psychological health. However, it is not just an internal process, for as we will show in the next chapter, health is relational, social and ecological, not just personal.

Other writers and scholars (Tajfel & Turner, 1986; Turner *et al.*,1987; Jetten, Haslam & Haslam, 2012; Gergen, 1999, 2001) have shown that our sense of identity has many socially constructed levels:

1. The individual level where people define themselves as individuals compared with other individuals and in terms of personal identity.

2. The social level where people define themselves and act in terms of their membership of a specific group (compared with relevant outgroups and in terms of social identity).

3. The human-centric level where people define themselves and act as part of the wider human species.

To these human-centric identities, we have added a fourth which is critical for our times:

4. The eco-centric level where we sense ourselves as fully participating in the more-than-human world of the ecology and an eco-self develops.

As we shall see in the stages of development below, this links to the evolution and maturation of our consciousness through the following stages:

- *Non-differentiated* from the world around us.

- *A proto-sense of self* which incorporates our environment and caregivers as part of us.

- *Intersubjective relational* – self in dynamic relationship to others.

- *Socio-centric* – our identity formed by and in relation to the families, roles, communities and cultures we inhabit.

- *Human-centric* – moving beyond identity with our own roles, tribes, communities, gender and ethnic groupings to seeing all humankind as kindred.

- *Eco-centric* – experiencing identity as participative with the wider ecology which surrounds us and flows through us.

These levels of development of consciousness fundamentally change our sense of our identity, but are neither linear nor inevitable. The potential for them is within us all, but the realisation of them requires the co-creative forces from without and within. Some people will never open up to the later forms of consciousness, others will open to them early in their life and then close them down and never return or return only in later life. For some, all aspects of consciousness are simultaneously available, and, like faces of a prism, can provide parallel perceptions of the same experience. These levels of consciousness permeate our narrative, experiential and bodily proto-self (see above).

I, myself and me

When 'I' talk about 'myself', there is the 'I' that is constructing and telling the story and 'myself' that the story is about. The 'I', like the author of a play, is hidden from the view of the audience, but can be sensed through their different plays. There is also the 'I' that is acting in the world and a 'me' that is the object and recipient of others' actions. Wilber (2000:33–35) usefully describes the difference between the *'proximate self'* (what we experience as our 'I', our subjective being, through which we see the world), and the *'distal self'*, what we experience as our 'me', a self we can objectify and see. He shows how the 'I' at one level of development becomes the 'me' at the next level, as deeper levels of reflection and self-witnessing open up. Later in the book we will show how this is a central process in the psychotherapy endeavour and in human development.

There will always be a level of awareness beyond that which we can see or name, as anything we can see or name is an object within that awareness. We will come back to this at the end of Chapter 9, when we will briefly touch on 'non-dual' awareness.

Nine stages of human development

Many models have talked about the seven ages of being human, including Shakespeare's famous speech from *As You Like It* where he describes the 'seven ages of man' (sic). With recent scientific findings on the importance of birth and pre-birth, we have added an eighth stage at the beginning of the cycle. Also, with the dramatic change in longevity and the increase in time people have after traditional retirement, we have inserted a new ninth stage, of Eldership and individuation (before the last stage).

Each stage has cognitive, physical, behavioural as well as psycho-social challenges and we will try and integrate approaches from each of these fields. For each stage, we have chosen to highlight the theory of the writers who we see as being most informative and developed in providing an understanding of this stage.

Stage 1: Pre-natal, peri-natal and post-natal development

Development starts from conception and pre-birth and through to the birth or peri-natal transition that lays down 'schemata' or 'organising principles' that will shape our personality and development for the rest of our lives. The psychiatrist and birth researcher, Frank Lake (2007, first published 1966), and later the American infant psychotherapist William Emerson (1996), would point out, when we trained with them, that for most people the most overwhelming and, for many, the most traumatic experience of their lives was their birth process, which confronts the emerging child before a good deal of the brain has been formed, especially the neo-cortex and the hippocampus, so the child has no way to make sense of this experience. Birth trauma, although dismissed or ignored by most of the later psychoanalytic tradition, was first written about by the Austrian psychoanalyst and contemporary of Freud, Otto Rank (1932). Later, Frank Lake's contemporary psychiatrist, Stanislav Grof (2016, first published 1975), developed a model for understanding in greater depth the kinds of effects that birth can have on our later lives. His model has four distinct stages of birth, or what he calls basic perinatal matrices (BPM) that give rise to different kinds of trauma (as well as positive experiences), and that have different kinds of effect on our future development.

1. *Basic Perinatal Matrix I (BPM I)* is activated before the birth process starts while we have not yet started to make the journey down the birth canal. Experience of the womb can be of a warm nurturing place or one full of bad feelings, if the mother's anxiety has been so overwhelming that cortisol has entered the child through her bloodstream.

2. *Basic Perinatal Matrix II (BPM II)* is when the baby has started on the journey down the birth canal, but the cervix is not yet open. If the cervix does not open easily at this point, it can be traumatising for the baby, particularly if the oxygen supply is compromised, as the flow of blood from the umbilical cord can be reduced. The baby may experience panicky feelings, potentially leading to feelings of claustrophobia and other fears and terrors in later life.

3. *Basic Perinatal Matrix III (BPM III)* marks the point in the birth process where the baby comes through the birth canal. This can feel thrilling, but can also feel violent and terrifying, particularly if the

umbilical cord gets caught round the neck of the child or methods such as suction or forceps are used to extract the child. A fixation at this stage can lead to thrill seeking or love of violence in later life.

4. *Basic Perinatal Matrix IV (BPM IV)* characterises the point in the birth process where the baby has left the womb. This may be associated with feelings of expansion and the presence of the holding mother, calming fears of this unknown experience. Loud noises, bright lights, no holding presence and/or a too early cutting of the umbilical cord can catapult the baby into terrifying feelings which are very traumatising.

Grof (2016, first published 1975) originally discovered these four basic perinatal matrices when using psychedelic (LSD) therapy with patients suffering from mental disorders in Europe and the United States. Later he developed 'holotropic breathwork' as a method for re-contacting the very early implicit memories, still lodged in the body-mind, to both reveal and heal the various birth traumas. These approaches were taken up and further developed by both Lake (2007, first published 1966) and Emerson (1996). Thomas Verny (1995) also provided more detailed research of the experiences the foetus and emerging baby can go through in the womb.

Stage 2: Early infancy

This stage is so critical to laying the foundations of physical and mental health, it has been greatly focused on by psychotherapists such as Freud, Klein, Winnicott as well as many later schools. More recently, neuroscience has shown that many parts of the brain and the architecture of the neural pathways only develop post-birth through interpersonal relationships with primary caregivers. Jean Piaget (1955, 1977), who spent much of his life studying the cognitive development of children, described this as the 'sensorimotor stage', as the baby is developing their sensory perceptions and their bodily motor skills.

We believe that the psychoanalyst Daniel Stern, building on the work of those who went before him, as well as more recent research into infancy, gives the best map of this territory. He researched infant development through the detailed observation of mothers with their babies (Stern, 1985, 2018), much as Winnicott had before him. His observations and subsequent writing occurred before the developments in neuroscience had shed much light on how the infant sense of self develops, and he comes to many similar conclusions. His work builds on Winnicott but differs from him in an important way: Stern (2018) regards development as enveloping earlier stages rather than these being left behind, thus earlier developmental stages are still within us as adults. He also pushes back the age at which a sense of self develops – even from birth – earlier than previous theorists, including Winnicott and Klein, thought.

Originally, Stern outlined four stages of infant development: 'the emergent', 'the core', 'the subjective' and 'the verbal'. Later (2018), he added two more phases: 'the core self with another' between the core and the subjective stages, and 'the narrative self', which we believe is critical in identity formation, and this was included in the stage of childhood.

The *emergent* sense of self relates to Winnicott's notion of 'going on being' (Winnicott, 1969) in which the infant has a sense of continuity of being from moment to moment, with a physical and mental sense of cohesion. Stern says this develops from birth to two months. This developing sense of self is facilitated by physical contact with the mother, particularly skin-to-skin contact.

The *core* sense of self starts to develop, in Stern's view, between the ages of two and seven months. By this time, the infant has developed enough 'organising subjective perspective' to engage others, particularly the mother who helps the child to self-regulate. Stern regards the baby as being 'intensely social' during this stage but that the 'other' is there to help the child self-regulate. S/he needs this relationship in order to be confident of being soothed when experiencing uncomfortable sensations like hunger, pain and tiredness. At this stage, the (m)other is essential as it is she who can understand the needs of her baby and meet them as much as is possible. Like Winnicott, Stern regarded the mother as potentially more able to attune to her infant than others, though he also studied mothers who were not able to attune to their babies and speculated that they had not been attuned to themselves. (This we will look at further in the next chapter when we explore early attachment patterns and trauma and the mark they leave.) In more collectivist cultures, the baby is likely to have many close relatives who hold and attune to the needs of the baby so that no one person is left with the responsibility of making this all-important provision. It is important to remember that these stages were devised within a particular social context and are shaped by them.

In his later work, Stern added a fifth stage between the core self and the subjective self, an intermediate level which he called 'core self with another'. From about three months, the baby starts to feel themselves to be part of their family where a 'framing environment' is able to regulate the baby's engagement with the world.

The *subjective* sense of self is developed during the first six months. The relationship with the (m)other becomes more intersubjective at this point, in that the baby is aware of the reality of the existence of others who can at once have their own separate life while being able to understand and share the baby's subjective world. The baby learns that they are separate but that they can be known and understood by others. The mother no longer simply attunes to the baby's needs but develops 'vitality affects' where she copies the rhythm and 'shape' of the baby's emotional communication but translates it into a different form. For instance, a loud 'ah!' from the baby could be mirrored by a movement that has the same shape and energy, maybe with a different sound like 'oh!' In this way, the mother both attunes to the baby and takes the communication in a different direction. This game gives immense joy to the child, as does a game of 'peep bo' which demonstrates that someone who has disappeared can return.

The *verbal* sense of self emerges during the second year of the infant's life with the coming of language creating 'a new domain of relatedness', but one which 'moves relatedness onto the impersonal, abstract level intrinsic to language and away from the personal, immediate level' (Stern, 1985:77). Stern considers that the ability to know the other in a direct way tends to be lost with the ability to symbolise that comes with the development of a verbal sense of self. He points out that the verbal sense of self is so powerful that it tends to dominate the others and cuts us off from more direct experiencing (Stern, 1985, 2018). It must be remembered, however, that the subjective sense of self is still available to us, though child-rearing practices tend to stress and reward the verbal sense of self.

Stage 3: Early childhood

Erikson divided childhood into two phases, calling the first 'initiative versus guilt', where the child explores their world, the environment surrounding them, what they can do with objects and how to play with others. But in this exploration, they discover parental and carer limits, or those imposed by a sibling. They are admonished when they do things that others do not like and can feel bad and guilty, or frustrated and angry. Learning to be creative and express one's will, alongside discovering physical and social limits and boundaries, is essential to this phase.

Stern (2018), whose understanding of infancy we described above, later added a sixth stage of infant development, which he termed the *narrative self* and saw developing around the age of 3–4 years old. In this stage, the child starts to 'interpret the world of human activities in terms of story plots... psychological explanations embedded in the structure of a narrative' (Stern, 2018:xxiv–xxv).

For Piaget, this was the stage of the pre-operational thought. Piaget noted that children do not yet understand concrete logic and cannot mentally manipulate information. Children's playing often includes 'pretending' at this stage. However, the child still has trouble seeing things from different points of view. The child's play is mainly symbolic and involves manipulating symbols.

Stage 4: Later childhood and latency

Erikson's second stage of childhood (Erikson, 1950) develops around the time that the child is coping with school (aged 5–12 years) in pre-puberty and is concerned with 'industry versus inferiority'. Here, the child is trying to master physical, creative and cognitive competencies as well as managing interpersonal and peer-group skills. The child can take pride in achievements and grow in confidence or feel inadequate and inferior to others and withdraw from areas of achievement. For Piaget (1955), this is the *concrete operational stage*: which he saw as happening from ages 7 to 11. Children can now think logically (they understand reversibility) and can classify, but are limited to what they can physically manipulate. They are no longer 'ego-centric' and start to become 'sociocentric' (Piaget, 1955).

Stage 5: Puberty and adolescence

Adolescence brings new and fresh challenges. Whereas in childhood individuals had to find ways of living and being accepted in their own family, in adolescence they have to find a way of beginning the separation from family, via their involvement with a peer group. In the early years of this stage, this involves finding a gang or group that you want to belong to, and which will accept you – a difficult challenge in its own right. This sometimes involves leaving other friends behind or managing conflicts between the ways of behaving in one's gang and those behaviours that one has learned as part of one's family.

Within the peer group, the challenge is to fit in and stand out – having something different to offer and to be recognised for it in order to be accepted becomes all-important. Often it is in this stage that later valency for social roles (Belbin, 2010) is laid down.

As the peer group evolves, issues of sexual identity become more pressing – will I be accepted if I don't fit into the peer-group norms of sexuality, can I pair off with another member of the peer group or someone outside it and still be accepted?

Throughout adolescence comes the challenge of dealing with a changing body, as your adult shape starts to emerge from within you. Breasts form, facial and body hair emerges, male voices change. Hormonal cycles arrive with the onset of menstruation in young women and testosterone surges in young men.

Adolescence is also the age of experimentation, trying out different interests, roles, ways of behaving, attitudes and beliefs. It is like trying on clothes to see if they fit, noticing how others respond to them – wanting approval from peers and the right degree of shock in one's parents.

This description of adolescence is one that those from the western world are familiar with. In many other less individualistic cultures, adolescence is a time of developing skills for adult life, but young people may be expected to stay closer to the family and play an important and socially assigned role in family life as well as that of the community (Laungani, 2004:41). Maybe this stage is the one where there is most difference between cultures.

Erik Erikson (1950) described this stage as 'identity versus role confusion'. Piaget showed how in this stage, the adolescent aged 11–16 is cognitively entering the *formal operational stage* of abstract reasoning. At this stage, they can develop abstract thought and utilise metacognition. Along with this, the children in the formal operational stage display more skills oriented towards problem solving, often in multiple steps. For Piaget, this is the last stage of cognitive development and in later stages, this formal operational cognition just becomes broader and deeper. More recent writers comment on and extend this model, as we shall see below.

Stage 6: Early adulthood

If we had a privileged, western upbringing, then in adolescence we can quickly move up the Maslow pyramid of needs while still being materially supported by our parents, family or community. We can have our survival and safety needs provided for us, our needs for affirmation and love from a mixture of family and peers satisfied, and we can spend time on self-actualising, discovering who we are and who we want to be. However, on leaving home, or going to college, we are suddenly faced with the challenge of standing on our two feet, financially and materially. We return to the bottom levels of the Maslow hierarchy. We need to earn money, find somewhere to live and people to live with. We need the approval of bosses to stay in a job and to get promotion, and we need to make good working relationships with colleagues who are not of our own choosing.

In this period, the young adult faces the challenge that Erik Erikson describes as 'intimacy versus isolation'. There is internal and external pressure to find a 'life partner', and, as many friends settle down and some get married and have children, others can feel isolated and left out.

Again, this is the pattern in the western world. In many other cultures, husbands and wives are chosen by families and the individual remains part of the family economy, albeit playing a more important role within it. In some cultures, young women go to join their husband's family, thus losing the support of their own kin. Within these more collectivist cultures, the idea of 'independence' does not have the same meaning as in the western context.

Stage 7: Mid-life

Erikson described this stage as facing the challenge of 'generativity versus stagnation'. Generativity refers to 'making your mark', creating or nurturing things that will outlast you as an individual. It is the period when you have achieved credibility in your chosen area of work and have the energy to make your unique contribution. Peter (Hawkins & Smith, 2013a:60–61) describes this stage as moving from 'accumulation' when we are trying to prove ourselves, 'get on' and be approved of, to 'full leadership', where the core question becomes: 'What is the difference I want to make in the world?' (Hawkins & Smith, 2013a:61). For others, this stage can produce feelings of stagnation, of being 'stuck in a rut', trapped in a relationship, work or family role that feels constraining and unfulfilled. For some, what is termed a 'mid-life crisis' can lead to a radical change in work, taking up a new interest, having a sexual affair, going travelling or going back to new studies. These, in different ways, are routes out of stagnation to rediscover a vitality in life. Others can become depressed or turn to alcohol or drugs (prescribed or not prescribed) and sink into the slough of despondency and depression.

Success can also be a trap, where we attain all we set out to achieve in the outer world of work, family, home, possessions and have lost our inner subjective self and sense of meaning in what we do and what we own. In his book, *The Principles of Psychology*, William James says:

The self of a man is the total sum of all that he can claim as his, not only his body and his psychic power, but his clothes and his house, his wife and his children, his ancestors and his friends, his reputation and his accomplishments, his land, his sailboat and his bank account. All these things give him the same emotions. If they grow and prosper, he feels triumphant. If they disappear and come to vanish, he feels diminished and from this concludes: It is clear that between what someone calls 'ME' and what he calls 'MINE', the line is difficult to draw. We feel and act in relation to certain things that are ours in the same way that we feel and act in relation to ourselves. (James, 1890:291)

We can also become devotees of the 'Age of More' (see Chapter 2).

For others in this stage, their careers may be taking off and becoming more complex. They may have moved from carrying out simple tasks, to leading a team, to running a whole organisation. Post-Piagetian writers on cognitive development have shown how this requires 'post-formal operational' cognition (Commons & Richard, 1984) that can move from systems thinking, to meta-system thinking, to paradigm thinking. We shall return to this in Chapter 8, as we see these post-formal operational levels as essential for the integrative psychotherapist.

Stage 8: Individuation and eldership

Erikson, in his classification of the stages of psycho-social development, went straight from the challenges of mid-life to those of old age. This, we believe, is a product of his time, when there was far less time between the average time of retirement and the decline towards death. In the last 50 years this has changed dramatically, with many more people living into their eighties, nineties and even past 100. Some people have more years of so-called retirement than they do of working life!

We have talked elsewhere about the important stage of eldership (Hawkins & Smith, 2013b), which has been a far more developed concept within indigenous tribes of humans but has become lost in white western societies. Eldership is the stage when the core focus moves away from making one's mark in the world, and now embraces the concern of how to enable others to make a difference. It is the stage of mentoring those who come after you, teaching in the widest possible sense of that term, of grandparenting, and bringing your acquired skills and wisdom to support endeavours in your community. Some of our clients say, 'This is the time for me to give back', 'I now have time to help others.' It is still a time of making a difference, but now this difference is made through others, by walking behind them to support their endeavours, not leading from the front.

The challenge of this stage is to retire, but still to be useful. The challenge of navigating the course of leaving a full-time role that may have provided your security, sense of purpose, ready-made community and feelings of importance, is now to create these for yourself. Some retire quickly into reduced horizons, while for others this is a time to develop a rich 'portfolio' new career, a mixture of paid work, volunteer work, community roles and new creative activities.

Jung also wrote about the stage of individuation which he saw as coming in mid-life, but with the recent demographic changes, this is often now focused on this stage of eldership. Individuation was a time to step back from concentrating on your strengths and core capabilities, to focus on other aspects of yourself that had become left behind and enshadowed by your strengths. Jung talked about powerful animus-centred men developing their anima, their softer, caring and nurturing sides, and anima-focused women discovering their animus power and ability to lead. Some people in this stage learn a musical instrument, join a choir, take up art or writing that they have not touched since school days. Others focus on their physical well-being, neglected in the busy days of work and bringing up a family.

For some, this stage is the time when a spiritual focus re-emerges and, for some, the beginnings of what Bateson (1972) termed 'Level III learning' where experience is no longer punctuated by the 'I'. As we will see later in the chapter, this form of learning also opens up the possibility of developing 'higher', 'post-conventional', 'transpersonal' levels of consciousness that Ken Wilber (2000) describes as 'causal', 'subtle' and 'non-dual' (see below and Chapter 9).

Stage 9: Acceptance, facing death and dying well

Erikson's final stage of psycho-social development was facing the challenge of ego-integrity versus despair. He described ego identity at this stage as 'the acceptance of one's one and only life cycle as something that had to be' (Erikson, 1950:268), and later as 'a sense of coherence and wholeness' (Erikson, 1982:65), which means to be able to accept one's life for what it is and has been with all its faults and failures, as well as its successes and achievements. At this stage, many people rework their life story or narrative to find ways of giving it shape and coherence across the many different phases they have lived through.

The other task of this stage is facing one's own mortality. Woody Allen is reported to have said, 'I am not afraid of death, I just don't want to be there when it happens.' But death is not an event, it is a process. This process can be viewed as the last few days, months or years of one's life, or it can be understood as a process that exists throughout life. Certainly, from our sixties onwards we become increasingly aware of losses at the physical, mental and social levels. For each of us this comes differently – it may be diminution of sensory capacity, of seeing, hearing, smelling and so on; a decline in physical strength and ability; a gradual loss in memory capacity; the loss of friends and family who die before us.

In western societies, there has been a strong taboo about death. Death has been sanitised and medicalised – seen as something to be avoided at all costs and as the opposite to life, rather than as a core aspect of life. In most human societies throughout the ages, one would have had intimate contact with death and dying, have seen siblings die in infancy or childhood, lost one of your own offspring in birth or childhood, been present at the death of parents or elders. Today, in many, but not all, societies, with the extraordinary success of humans in diminishing infant and childhood mortality, increasing life expectancy, and more and more people dying in hospitals, care homes or hospices, death has been moved to the margins of life. This has come at the price of an increase in fear and anxiety about death and dying (Gawande, 2015). The psychiatrist and existential psychotherapist Irvin Yalom draws on the ancient teaching of the Stoics, who taught that 'learning to live well is also learning to die well, and that, conversely, learning to die well is learning to live well' (Yalom, 2011). St Augustine wrote, 'It is only in the face of death that man's self is born' (quoted in Montaigne, 1965:63). This sentiment is echoed by the poet T. S. Eliot in his *Four Quartets*, by Tolstoy in his novels *The Death of Ivan Illyich* and *War and Peace* and Prospero in Shakespeare's *The Tempest*. One of our own spiritual teachers, Fazal Inayat Khan, would say that the degree to which you can embrace death is equal to the degree to which you can fully embrace life.

Yalom (2011:36, 37) shows how we may be awakened by death at many stages in our life through:

> grief at the loss of someone you love, life threatening illness, the breakup of an intimate relationship, some major life milestone, such as a 'big' birthday, cataclysmic trauma, children leaving home, loss of a job or career change, retirement, move to a retirement home, or through powerful dreams.

We should not leave it to the final stages of life to learn from or be awakened by death. The Koran encourages us to 'die before we die', and the Sufis teach the path of 'Fana', learning to let go of attachment to one's identity, a process of 'unselfing'.

Moving through the stages of development

These stages in one way of looking are linear and age related, but through other lenses are openings to different forms of consciousness, some of which are simultaneously available, or arrive out of sequence. Examples of this would include a young person having a near-death experience or becoming the family's economic bread winner.

Through another lens we all face the challenging transitions from each stage to the next. In some societies, there are formalised life-transition rituals to help individuals transit. From another perspective, we do not leave the previous stage of development behind. We may incorporate it successfully within the next and current stages in our life, or parts of it may remain as unfinished gestalts,[1] or as unmet needs which regularly reappear throughout our life, particularly at later transitions. Often our reactive feelings and behaviours, or difficult psychological patterns that we take to psychotherapy, are unsuccessful and unconscious attempts to complete these unfinished transitions and stuck patterns (see Chapters 7 and 11).

As we mature to more complex levels of consciousness, we envelop and include the previous levels. Thus all development is envelopment (Stern, 2018). Wilber (2000:19) describes the healthy transitional process whereby, at each stage, there are three recognisable and repeated processes:

1. We *identify* with our current way of being and knowing (what later Bill Torbert (2004) would describe as our dominant 'action logic'). In this phase, we are not aware of it, as it is the lens through which we see and make sense of the world.

2. We *differentiate* from this way of being and knowing – we can stand back and see it, separate from it, and be critical of it. It becomes part of the 'me' that can be seen, rather than the 'I' that is looking.

3. We *integrate* it as one way of being and knowing available to us, but it is no longer framing and organising our experience or driving our reactive emotions and behaviour.

---

1 A gestalt is a 'whole' and in this context an 'unfinished gestalt' is experienced when a process is not completed.

Conclusion

In this chapter, we have described:

- A *proto-self*, nearly entirely unconscious that is organising many of the life-sustaining processes of our organism, our temperature, blood flow, hormonal flow, digestion, etc.

- A *core self*, or an *experiencing self*, which is embodied and responding, behaving, acting in relation to external and internal stimuli such as events, other people, the physical environment, everything that makes up our immediate context; and also reacting to memories of the past and images of possible futures.

- A *narrative self* or *reflective self-consciousness*, which creates narratives out of experience and constructs meaning. This third level of mental processing is always relational and social, as it utilises language and images, belief and values and stories from the many familial, social and community groups and cultures we are born into, develop within and later choose to belong to.

We have explored the question of where our identity, or self, resides. This question has kept theologians, philosophers and scientists busy for many, many years. Even now, some people think the individual soul is material and many scientists are searching for the self in the circuitry of the neural pathways, hoping that they can map the self in brain patterns, in a parallel way to the way that DNA was mapped. We have followed Bateson (1979, 1992) and Maturana and Varela (1980, 2008) in realising that mind and self are a process not a structure. They are an emergent and constantly evolving phenomenon, of a complex whole organism or holon. The self is not just self-created (otherwise we would need a second self, creating the self). The self is not the same as the stories we and others relate. It is always an ever-changing and forming pattern of internal and external connections while we are alive, and perhaps even after death. Even then stories about us continue to evolve.

We have shown that the process of individual development is always internally and externally dialogic. Internally, the proto-self, core self and narrative self are only separate in our conceptualisation, for each is permeating the other two, through constant flow between these named levels. So, we suggest that all illness and health is psychosomatic, as the body affects the behaviour and the mental processes of the mind, and the mind and behaviour continually effect the material bodily manifestation of the organism. Our identity and self continually co-evolve in relation to the human and more-than-human systems that we are part of, and which become part of us. Our identity is historically formed through the millennia of co-evolution on this planet and beyond.

Our identity appears to be multiple, both in the different ways we engage with life, in different times and contexts, and in the many different narratives of self we create, and others create about us, which may be congruent or discordant. But the living co-evolving process of the self is seamless and indivisible and it is always changing.

We are never an island, but rather nested within many complex systemic levels, which are also nested within us. We influence and are influenced by the social levels of family, groups, communities, nations, each with constantly co-evolving cultures within the more-than-human levels of our environmental niches. These comprise the many other living organisms with which we share our lives, and which partake in our habitats, as well as the physical and climatic systems of which we are part.

Our self is neither a material essence nor a 'true self' waiting to be uncovered from under all the 'false selves' and returned to; nor is it just something that is self- or socially constructed. Our self is to be found in what Bateson (1972) terms 'the patterns that connect', and our continuity of self lies in the way these patterns continue to develop, unweave and reweave over time.

However, we should remember that all of these notions of a self are constructions by our individual and collective minds. We have offered them here to free all of us from our current limiting assumptions, those that can limit the way we view ourselves and others, as well as the psychotherapy we receive and give. Our hope is that they do not become a new imprisoning palace of mirrors and of mental constructs, but a map to take us into the open air of fuller living and engagement. We remember the Buddhist teaching that reasoning and words show the way only at the beginning of the journey.

Having explored the nature of self and individuality, we now, in the next chapter, explore what makes an individual psychologically healthy or unhealthy and how psychotherapy contributes to the movement from illness to health.

CHAPTER 4

What Does it Mean to be Mentally Healthy and How Does Psychotherapy Help?

Introduction

In this chapter, we will explore the second set of questions we believe are essential for all psychotherapists and counsellors to address. In the last chapter, we asked these questions: what is an individual human being? What is the nature of the self? How does self-identity form and develop?

Practice as a psychotherapist of any school or approach is based on an assumption that our psychotherapy enables our clients or patients to improve their psychological health. This requires that we have some clear understanding of what constitutes psychological health and unhealth and how psychotherapy makes a difference. Therefore, in this chapter, we will build on the foundations of understanding human individuality by exploring what a psychologically healthy individual is and how we understand psychological illness or unhealth. Only then can we address the essential question: how does psychotherapy assist the move to greater psychological health?

To ensure that we keep this book and your reading of it dialogical and relational, as we discussed in the Preface, we invite you to engage with your current thinking about these three core questions, before we share how we see these key fundamentals from an integrative psychotherapy perspective.

Please complete the sentences below with three to five bullet points:

1. A psychologically healthy person is someone who:

    *   ....

    *   ....

    *   ....

    *   ....

    *   ....

2. A psychologically unhealthy person is someone who:

    *   ....

    *   ....

    *   ....

    *   ....

    *   ....

3. Psychotherapy assists the move to being more psychologically healthy by:

    *   ....

    *   ....

    *   ....

    *   ....

    *   ....

What is mental health?

We address the important question of what mental health is from a relational (intersubjective), systemic and ecological perspective, including ways of understanding human beings, which we will explore in detail in Chapters 7, 8 and 9. This perspective helps us avoid what Charles Taylor (1991) described as the 'monological fallacy' and Peter described as 'entity Thinking' (Hawkins, 2017a), which is the view that health and illness reside only within an individual or a bounded system. Instead, we see health as always being a dialogical interplay between the individual and their social, ecological and physical environment. From the history of public health, we know that some of the biggest contributors to improved health in whole communities have been: improving the sewage systems, providing clean drinking water, better hygiene among health workers and a good balanced diet. We also can see from current research that the health of individuals in parts of the world is now negatively affected by the decrease in urban air quality, the over-use of pesticides and the large amounts of sugar in processed food, leading to diabetes and then to heart attacks and strokes. Others have talked about psychological pollution, of being bombarded with fragmented information from multiple sources and the effects of screen time on individuals (see Chapter 2 and Greenfield, 2009, 2011). In other parts of the world, poor mental health comes from a different source: armed conflict and repressive regimes have, among other horrors, led to tragic loss of life, homes bombed, children not safe at home or at school and the necessity to leave home and culture to seek safety in other countries or refugee camps. These events have led to whole populations being severely traumatised and unable to form stable relationships or provide well for their children, physically and emotionally, thus passing on further trauma down the generations. In Chapter 2, we also explored the effect on mental health of the fragmentation of the containers within which we do our psychological processing, meaning-making and development.

In this chapter, however, we will first explore what a psychologically healthy individual is. Many western medical models and approaches define health negatively – that is, that health is the absence of illness, the removal of symptoms and afflictions. Another common idea of illness is that it is something 'we catch', the entering of the body by nasty germs, viruses or unhealthy bacteria, or something that happens to us by accident, such as cutting a finger, falling over and breaking a leg. Individuals in this popular construction are the recipients, the done-to, the victims, and they need a doctor or other healer to make them better.

Traditional concepts of mental illness were similar. People talked of mental afflictions and evil spirits, and one needed a shaman, priest or imam to carry out an exorcism, to cast out or remove the nasty spirit that had invaded you. Even in 20th-century psychoanalysis and humanistic psychotherapy, this concept partly lived on. The demons for Freudian analysts were not seen as coming from outside, but as having been created in your past, repressed down into the unconscious 'id', the cellar of your mind, where they could still disturb you in dreams, fears, compulsions or somatised symptoms.

Even in early humanistic psychotherapy your illness was often seen as created by what your parents had or had not done. This was famously portrayed in Philip Larkin's poem:

> They fuck you up, your mum and dad.
> They may not mean to, but they do.
> They fill you with the faults they had
> And add some extra, just for you.
>
> But they were fucked up in their turn
> By fools in old-style hats and coats,
> Who half the time were soppy-stern
> And half at one another's throats.
>
> Man hands on misery to man.
> It deepens like a coastal shelf.
> Get out as early as you can,
> And don't have any kids yourself.

We have quoted the poem in full, to recognise that in order to be mentally healthy we need to understand that we are not just the victim of bad or inadequate parents, for they may have been doing the best they could, given their own psychological inheritance and difficulties. Part of psychotherapy, as we will see later in this chapter, is not only to get in touch with feelings towards one's parents, but to recognise them as separate people in their own right, with their own struggles, and to be able to forgive them.

Defining mental health as the absence of mental illness was only overcome through existential, phenomenological and humanistic psychotherapy moving away from the medical model and having an increasing focus on the individual's potentialities and building on their strengths, rather than curing illness. This was further developed by the 'positive psychology' movement as we shall see below. But first, we must pause and look at the various elements that we term mental health.

The mind, the brain, the body, the relational and beyond

Daniel Siegel tells how, when he lectures to mental health professions around the world, he asks for a show of hands for how many have, in their training, attended a lecture where they were given a definition of the mind. He reports that, wherever he went in the world, the response rates were similar – 'only 2–5% of people in these fields have ever been given even a single lecture that defined the very foundation of their speciality – the mind' (Siegel, 2010:51).

Although, recently, psychotherapy has been greatly influenced by the exponential growth in discoveries in neuroscience and writings on the brain, it is important to realise that in psychotherapy we are involved with exploring and developing the mind of the client, and are not there to 'reprogram their brain', although there are a growing number of psychotherapies focused on that very aim.

It is important for psychotherapists to understand the difference between the brain and the mind and how the two are connected. Scientists have struggled for many years to try to understand this puzzling relationship. Even as late as 1994, Revonsuo and Kamppinen, as editors of *Consciousness in Philosophy and Cognitive Neuroscience* wrote, 'Even though everybody agrees that mind has something to do with the brain, there is still no general agreement on the exact nature of this relationship' (quoted in Capra & Luisi, 2016:252).

Even now, the terms 'mind' and 'brain' are loosely used and mean different things in different fields of study. Susan Greenfield, an eminent neuroscientist in Oxford, where she is Director of the Institute for the Future of the Mind, writes that 'the mind, one's own individual take on the world, can actually be the personalisation of the physical brain through tangible, physical mechanisms' (Greenfield, 2011:51). For Greenfield and many neuroscientists, the mind is the personalised brain, how we have developed and adapted our brain, laid down habitual neural pathways and created particular patterns of connectivity.

Gregory Bateson (1972) was a seminal thinker and polymath who broke away from the Cartesian notion of the mind being *res cogitans* – a thinking thing – to see mind, not as an entity, but as a mental process. He saw the mind or mental processes as existing in organisms long before they developed brains or higher nervous systems. He would provocatively ask:

'What pattern connects the crab to the lobster and orchid to the primrose and all four of them to me?' (1979:8) Once he arrived at a seminar and placed a lobster on the table and asked his students, 'If you came from Mars, how would you know that this was something that was once alive?' Bateson (1979:9) extended his understanding of the mind, to seeing it as existing in circuits of connection between organisms and between organisms and their environment. As he said in an interview with Fritjof Capra, 'mind is the essence of being alive' (Capra, 1988). His revolutionary new thinking in epistemology – how we think and understand the world – had major influences on family therapists, social psychiatry, theories of change and communication (see Chapter 8).

In parallel to Bateson's work, and later building on it, was the work of two Chilean scientists: Humbert Maturana and Francisco Varela, who developed the field of cognitive science, integrating biology, psychology and epistemology (Maturana & Varela, 1980:13). In his paper 'The biology of cognition' Maturana writes, 'Living systems are cognitive systems and living is a process of cognition. This statement is valid for all organisms, with and without a nervous system.' He goes on to say, 'Our cognitive processes differ from the cognitive processes of other organisms only in the kinds of interaction into which we can enter, such as linguistic interactions, and not in the nature of the cognitive process itself' (Maturana & Varela, 1980:49).

Maturana, with his colleague Varela, went on to develop what has become to be known as the Santiago Theory or the theory of autopoesis. Capra and Luisi (2016:257) give the best summary of the relationship between the mind and brain as perceived by the Santiago theorists:

> Mind is not a thing but a process – the process of cognition, which is identified with the process of life. The brain is a specific structure through which this process operates. The relationship between mind and brain, therefore, is one between process and structure. Moreover, the brain is not the only structure through which the process of cognition operates. The entire structure of the organism participates in the process of cognition, whether or not the organism has a brain or a nervous system.

More recently, others, including Sloman and Fernbach (2017) in their book, *The Knowledge Illusion: Why We Never Think Alone*, have argued that mind is not just dialogic, but collective and much of what we know is not inside our brains but collectively held between us and our communities and our living and material environment.

So how do we connect these different concepts of mind? Capra and Luisi (2016) offer a reflection on different types of neuroscience. The first is 'the neuro-reductionists', who attempt to reduce consciousness to neural mechanisms. The famous molecular biologist Francis Crick (1994:3) espoused this approach when he wrote:

> You, your joys and your sorrows, your memories and your ambitions, your sense of personal identity and free will, are in fact no more than the behaviour of a vast assembly of nerve cells and their associated molecules. As Lewis Carroll's Alice might have phrased it: 'You're nothing but a pack of neurons.'

The second group espouse 'functionalism', and this is very popular among both cognitive scientists and philosophers such as Daniel Dennett (1991). They build on the notions of writers like Ryle and Koestler who believe 'that mental states are defined by their "functional organization" – that is, by the patterns of causal relations in the nervous system' (Capra & Luisi, 2016:263). Mental states are not just patterns of neural connections but create wholes or holons, which are also created by the function they serve.

The third, 'small but growing group' (Capra & Luisi, 2016:263) are the 'neurophenomenologists'. They build on rigorous phenomenological examination of subjective and intersubjective lived experience, which we explore in many places in this book, and how this is paralleled in neural pathways and patterns. They also embrace complexity theory in order to avoid the reductionism of linear cause and effect explanations.

We would describe the first group as 'scientific materialists' who only acknowledge what can be objectively observed and empirically proven. The second group we see as 'system thinkers', but only the third group as 'systemic thinkers' (Hawkins, 2018b).

Daniel Siegel, neuroscientist and psychotherapist, led an interdisciplinary research group in attempting to define the mind. He arrived at the following definition: 'The human mind is a relational and embodied process that regulates the flow of energy and information' (Siegel, 2010:52).

He saw the mind as operating through the brain, but not contained within it, for he saw the mind as both embodied, operating through neural flows and other chemical and hormonal information flows throughout the body, and as embedded in relationships, with the flow of energy, emotion and information between people. From this foundation, Siegel (Siegel, 2010:9–11) built his Triangle of Well-Being.

Figure 4.1: The Triangle of Well-Being

We would build on this model, to see the mind as an emergent 'holon', a systemic whole that is organising and shaping the flow of information and energy throughout an individual's brain, body and social interaction.

Figure 4.2: The mind as an organising process

Further we would see the mind, as embedded not just in the relational field of interpersonal relationships, but also in the wider social field of family, community and ethnic culture. Then further out we see the mind as embedded in the co-evolutionary processes of *Homo sapiens'* inter-relationship with their environmental niche. These form the three levels of exploration in Chapters 7 'the relational', 8 'the social and systemic', and 9 'the ecological and spiritual'.

Figure 4.3: The mind as an organising process embedded in and beyond the body, brain and immediate relationships

What does it mean to be mentally healthy?

From what we have explored above, it becomes clear that to be mentally healthy, you also need a healthy body, a healthy brain and healthy relationships, but, as we will explore below, these are necessary but not sufficient. However, it is true that with certain levels of damage to the brain, body or social engagement, it is hard, but not impossible, to be psychologically healthy.

Rock and colleagues (2012) provide a very accessible model of The Healthy Mind Platter, to describe the key inputs an individual needs to maintain a healthy mind, based on the platter of vegetables and fruit we are encouraged to eat for a healthy diet.

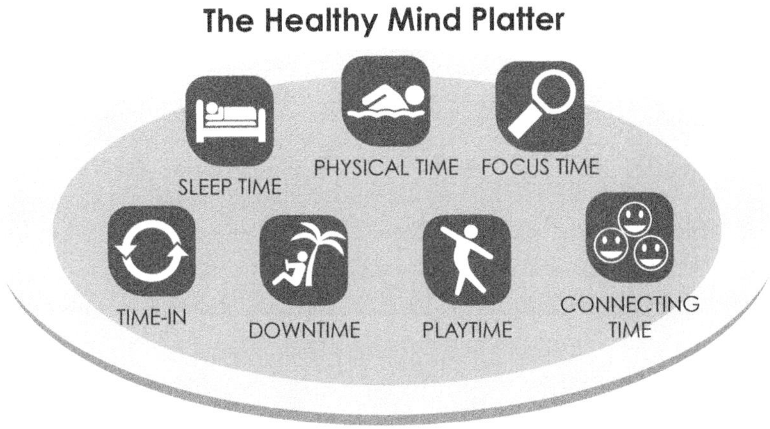

The Healthy Mind Platter

Figure 4.4: The Healthy Mind Platter for optimal brain matter

We find this very helpful, but once again would expand it, to include two other extensions of connecting time beyond the immediate relational, that is, 'social contribution time' and 'ecological connecting time'. We believe that, for a healthy mind, the individual needs to have a sense of purpose and an ability to contribute to their community, as well as a good quality connection to the ecological and natural world.

These nine inputs (7+2) provide the necessary ingredients and fuel for flourishing mental health, but how they are cooked and utilised by the individual becomes important.

Positive psychology began as a new domain of psychology in 1998, when Martin Seligman chose it as the theme for his term as president of the American Psychological Association. Other key developers of this field of psychology were Mihaly Csikszentmihalyi (1999), Christopher Peterson (2013), and Barbara Fredrickson (Fredrickson & Losada, 2005). Seligman and

Csikszentmihalyi (2000:13) define positive psychology as: 'the scientific study of positive human functioning and flourishing on multiple levels that include the biological, personal, relational, institutional, cultural, and global dimensions of life'. They focus, not on mental illness but on *eudaimonia*, the Greek word for 'the good life', and on the factors that contribute most to a well-lived and fulfilling life.

Seligman (2011) in his book *Flourish*, defined flourishing or positive individual health and well-being using the acronym PERMA, which stood for: Positive emotions, Engagement, Relationships, Meaning and purpose, and Accomplishments.

- *Positive emotions* are not just happiness and joy but also excitement, satisfaction, pride and awe, among others. These emotions are frequently seen as connected to positive outcomes, such as longer life and healthier social relationships.

- *Engagement* refers to involvement in activities that draw and build on one's interests. Mihaly Csikszentmihalyi explains true engagement as 'flow', a state of deep effortless involvement, a feeling of intensity that leads to a sense of ecstasy and clarity. The task being undertaken needs to call on higher skill and be somewhat difficult and challenging, yet still possible. Engagement involves passion for and concentration on the task at hand and is assessed subjectively and most completely when the person engaged is completely absorbed, losing self-consciousness.

- *Relationships* are essential in fuelling positive emotions, whether they are work-related, familial, romantic or platonic. Humans receive, share and spread positivity to others through relationships. They are important not only in bad times, but in good times as well. In fact, relationships can be strengthened by reacting to one another positively. It is typical that most positive things take place in the presence of other people.

- *Meaning and purpose* should address the question 'why'. Discovering and figuring out a clear 'why' puts everything into context, from work to relationships to other parts of life. Finding meaning is learning that there is something greater than one's self. Despite potential challenges, working with meaning drives people to continue striving for a desirable goal.

- *Accomplishments* are the pursuit of success and mastery, and sometimes can help us develop a sense of self-esteem and worthwhileness even when accomplishments do not result in immediate positive emotions, meaning or relationships. Examples of this include a young musician or gymnast practising for hundreds of hours, or an athlete or sportsperson spending much of each day exercising their skill, or an artist developing their craft.

All of these abilities are necessary for a healthy and fulfilled life but may be harder, though not impossible, to achieve if original attachment needs were not met in infancy and neural pathways not established at that time. Psychotherapy can be helpful in overcoming these difficulties. The same can be said for Parlett's five capacities. These were developed by our colleague and friend Malcolm Parlett (2015), who writes about psychological health coming as a result of developing 'whole intelligence'. He explores in depth five different aspects, which he first called 'capacities' and more recently 'explorations', of whole intelligence, while recognising that to be whole, they are indivisible and co-arise together. The five aspects are:

1. *Interrelating*: role-modelling and building a climate of deep respectfulness, acceptance of differences, building of trust; countering shaming, stereotyping, fears of 'otherness', and of un-constructive conflict.

2. *Responding to the situation*: awareness of the field, recognising different constructions of shared 'reality'; encouraging ownership; staying in the present; noticing what is being avoided; building resilience; exploring figure/ground; 'response-ability', finding one's leadership.

3. *Embodying*: slowing down and 'getting out of one's head'; encouraging sensory engagement; working with the felt sense; expanding awareness to the non-verbal, the non-human; the aesthetic qualities of the situation; recognition of fluctuating energy; acceptance of 'feeling data'.

4. *Experimenting*: encouraging playfulness, artful discovery, living with uncertainty, humour; discerning when the experiment is to enhance stability, coherence and lack of change; acknowledging that 'familiarity boundary – stretching is inherently shame/embarrassment inducing.'

5. *Self-recognising:* sharing of self-experience; slowing down and allowing time for integration; modelling non-judgemental approaches to others and their fantasies, choices, narratives; investigating values, habits, growing edges, life themes, self-organisation.

We are influenced by positive psychology (Seligman, 2011), whole intelligence (Parlett, 2015), the extended view of the mind as a process from Bateson (1972), Maturana and Varela (2008) and Capra and Luisi (2016), and by neuroscience from Siegel (2010) and Gerhardt (2015), in forming our own sense of what is healthy functioning. Our own thoughts and responses to the question about a healthy individual are also crafted out of our many years of experience and reflective supervision, in mental health, psychotherapy, coaching, spirituality and other fields, and also by deep questioning of the epistemology (ways of knowing) and assumptions that underlie not only humanistic and psychodynamic psychotherapy (Hawkins, 2017c), but the current dominant zeitgeist of liberal humanism (see Chapter 2).

We will explore key aspects of psychological health drawing on many different psychological and psychotherapeutic fields, traditions and schools. We see mental health as having several faces, which we can map on to Wilber's (2000) Integral Four Quadrants:

I Intentional (subjective) **An integrated coherent sense of self and life narrative**	IT Behavioural (objective) **Congruence**
We Cultural (intersubjective) **Healthy interdependence and relationships**	ITs Social (interobjective) **A sense of purpose and making a contribution to the wider world**

1 An integrated coherent sense of self and life narrative

We all have multiple selves, and our self-identity changes throughout our life, as we saw in the last chapter, but the ability to integrate these different selves, across both social contexts and time, is central to subjective mental health and well-being. One of the most valuable pieces of psychological research that has been undertaken during the time we have both been practising as psychotherapists is the discovery that the best predictor of parents' capacity to form secure attachment and healthy bonding with their own children is not whether they had a psychologically healthy or unhealthy childhood themselves, but whether they have developed a coherent life narrative about their own infancy, childhood and family life (Siegel, 2010:171–175; Gerhardt, 2015: 70). This involves being able to look back at one's own childhood, taking *implicit memories* that may be remembered physically and emotionally in the body and giving them *explicit* narrative form. Implicit memories, unlike *explicit memories*, have not gone through the hippocampus part of the brain that not only integrates the two hemispheres of the cortex, but helps join different parts of the body-mind to create integrated meaning. Difficult or traumatic implicit memories, which have not seen the light of mental awareness, can remain held in the body as what Christopher Bollas usefully termed 'the unthought known' (Bollas, 1987) and can re-emerge unbidden throughout life, when stimulated by difficulties, or when raising one's own children, or through dreams, or psychosomatic symptoms.

When one of us was working with disturbed adolescents, who had spent most of their lives in children's homes, one of the daily practices was to help the young people recount their day, as they lacked the ability to have any sense of continuity and often were drowning in their experiences of the moment, which were often retriggering earlier traumatic, implicit memories. They would narrate the story of their week and their time in the community, and only after that, start to build a narrative of their life.

2 Congruence

Much has been written about healthy individuals becoming 'self-actualising' and 'autonomous' (Maslow, 1972) and 'self-authoring' (Kegan, 1994). Elsewhere, Peter has critiqued the weaknesses of the authenticity literature and argued that it needs to be replaced by a theory of dynamic congruence (Hawkins, 2018c).

In dynamic congruence, the individual is able to create alignment between:

- what they say verbally and what their non-verbal gestures, body language and tonality indicate

- what they say they will do and what they actually do

- their values and beliefs and their actions

- how they see themselves and how others see them.

Unlike the notions of autonomy and authenticity, the congruent person can flexibly adapt how they are when relating to different people and in different social and cultural contexts, while still being congruent to their own pattern of self.

3 Healthy interdependence and relationships

When we were both in our twenties and in the early stages of our professional careers, we worked full time in mental health; Judy was head of occupational therapy in a London mental hospital and Peter was director of a half-way house therapeutic community, rehabilitating patients from psychiatric hospitals and psychiatric prisons. Both of us were part of the zeitgeist and dominant paradigm of the time, which was focused on moving people away from the large mental asylums, back into the community – one that involved the individual moving from institutional dependence to what was termed 'independence'. At the same time, the humanistic writers were defining health in terms of autonomy. Maslow (1972) and Rogers (1958) both argued that a healthy individual was someone who was self-actualised. Rogers (1961:196) wrote that self-actualisation was 'the development towards autonomy and away from heteronomy or control from external forces'. He (Rogers, 1961:196) went on to quote Angyal (the Hungarian born, American psychiatrist, one of the first to adopt a systemic view):

Life is an autonomous event which takes place between the organism and the environment. Life processes do not merely tend to preserve life, but transcend the momentary *status quo* of the organism, expanding itself continually and imposing its autonomous determination upon an ever-increasing realm of events.

We both began to realise that this framing of the mental health revolution and humanistic theorising were somewhat simplistic. None of us exists as an island complete unto ourselves. Even the Trappist monk, or Buddhist on a three-year isolation retreat is relating to an ecological world and an internal imaginary world, and is supported by, and dependent on, these relationships.

Donald Winnicott, Daniel Stern and others (see previous chapter) describe human development as moving from our early state of being merged with the mother, both before birth and in the early months post-birth, to a gradual healthy interdependence. We would see healthy interdependence as including not just being dependent on one other person, or one role, or one institution, but being able to draw on many resources, other people and groupings for one's well-being and development. Knowing where, when and whom to go to when you need help, be it medical, physical, mental, emotional or practical, is vital. It also involves being able to give and receive from others. Healthy interdependence and social interchange are critical for well-being. 'Considerable evidence suggests that being cut off from social contact with friends, family and other social groups is not just extremely upsetting, it can have significant negative consequences for health and even lead to early death' (Jetten, Haslam & Haslam, 2012:3).

We have worked with many people who are habitual givers, always needing to help others, and are very frightened of being the one who receives. They are frightened to ask for help as this brings with it the vulnerability of the other saying 'no', or first saying yes and then later abandoning them. Being always the giver or helper helps us stay in control. We also know habituated receivers, who feel they have nothing to offer others, or cannot even find the space to notice others' need. In our work in therapeutic communities, one of the healing factors was that everyone was required daily to be both a receiver and a giver, both practically through cooking for the community and doing the cleaning, decorating, gardening and so on, and psychologically through the groups and the community meetings – a circularity of caregiving.

4 A sense of purpose and making a positive contribution to the wider world

In the external realm, beyond intimate and family relationships, is the wider social and ecological world. We will show, throughout this book, that psychological health is not just a personal concern and how psychotherapy needs to avoid being lost in a narcissistic introspection. Mental health is also about having a sense of purpose and being able to make a positive contribution to the wider world. For some of our clients, this comes from the pride in bringing up their children, for others through their career and work, and for others through their contribution to their social or religious community. Meaning is not just an internal or a mental construct – for meaning to be genuinely meaningful, it needs to be enacted externally in the world.

5 Integration

In the middle of the four quadrants we have explored above is a fifth domain that connects all the others – the domain of integration.

Fritz Perls, the founder of gestalt psychotherapy, said the three most important things we need to do to become psychologically healthy were 'Integrate, integrate, integrate!' (Perls, 1969).

Jung, as we mentioned in Chapter 3, wrote extensively about how we need to individuate by integrating neglected, underdeveloped and shadow aspects of our self, and Freud showed how we need to integrate the repressed and denied parts of ourselves that are carried in the unconscious into the conscious ego (Freud, 1973).

So what does integration mean when seen from a relational, systemic and ecological perspective?

The word 'health' comes from the same root as wholeness, and holiness, so, in this sense, a healthy person is someone who has developed a sense of 'wholeness':

- between mind and body (Corsini & Wedding, 2008)

- that is coherent between multiple aspects of themselves (Assagioli, 1965) (see also Chapter 3 on identity formation)

- between their espoused values and beliefs and their actions

- between themselves and their ecological niche, living in co-creative interplay between themselves and the groups, communities and ecological environments of which they are part.

Integration is a process throughout life and is different at each level of development. At each stage, we have new psycho-social challenges (see Chapter 3) and in moving from one stage of development to a higher, more inclusive stage, we must not only unlearn and separate from the previous way of being and knowing, but also integrate it as one way of being within us (see Chapter 3).

Capra and Luisi (2016:337) see health as being 'in balance' and illness as being 'out of balance'. They apply this concept of balance at three levels: to the physical body and its many complex living processes; to the mind or mental process; and to the individual in relation to their social and physical environment. We believe that health is also creating a balance as well as a flow between the four quadrants we have outlined above, and a sense of meaningful integration between them.

Wholeness refers to the whole person or the individual's mind and body as a unit rather than as separate parts (Seligman, 2011). Integration refers to how we ensure that mind and body work together and how the individual integrates into the environment. Often people who come to therapy do not have these aspects of their life either in balance or flowing together. Psychotherapy's work is to help the client:

- integrate internally, facilitating them to integrate themselves and create a healthy evolving, integrating, narrative self

- find a balance and become self-regulating through the inevitable changes in life and development

- find a way of understanding and responding, rather than reacting, to their family, social and community contexts

- externally find a way of being in and part of the world (human and more-than-human), as well as separate from it, and make a positive difference to it.

Psychological illness

In the opening of this chapter, we showed how, in pre-modern times, psychological illness was often seen as an evil spirit that had entered into the person and needed to be exorcised. So-called mad people needed to be banished from the village or later incarcerated in large institutions, because otherwise we might be disturbed, catch their illness, or be driven mad by them.

Even today, psychiatry often treats people as if they are their symptoms. People talk about 'a psychotic' or 'a schizophrenic', 'a neurotic' or 'an autistic', rather than realise that these are social and linguistic constructions for making sense of particular patterns and ways of being and thinking. We always encourage seeing any person suffering from mental ill-health as a struggling human being who is trying to make sense of the world. We start from the belief that, although certain behaviours and ways of thinking may look mad or crazy to us, the individual is using the best way they know how to respond to their world.

Laing and Anthony (2010) and Foucault (2006) have applied the linguistic turn in post-modern philosophy to psychological illness. This has helped us understand how we reduce others by giving them a reified label of their symptoms. In Chapter 8, we write about the Milan school of systemic family therapists who sought to free themselves and their clients from the 'tyranny of linguistics' (Becvar & Becvar, 2008:239). This trap concerns these reifying labels. Fear of schizophrenia, for example, can lead people to see the label as the disorder and the person as the label. Ironically, this reifying of the label can become a way that sufferers are maintained in their distress, and it contributes to family dysfunction.

More recently psychiatry, psychology and psychotherapy have placed a great deal more emphasis on trauma, and an understanding that disturbed responses are often triggered by a traumatic event. Traumatic events might range from: a birth trauma, such as nearly dying in the birth process; an early rupture in the relationship between the baby and the mother; and living in a very disturbed family, with violence, addiction or schizophrenogenetic patterns of communication. But traumatic events are not just limited to childhood. Judy works as Director of Trauma Foundation South West, where the psychotherapy clients are traumatised refugees and asylum seekers. These clients' traumas range from: living in war zones; witnessing the murder of their partners and family; being victims of rape, torture and imprisonment; fleeing their home and community and making the terrifying journey to the UK; living isolated in a foreign country and experiencing officials who do not believe their story. This can create multi-levels of trauma – the events at origin, the trauma of the journey and the retraumatising events in the host country (for an example of this, read Chapter 14).

Adult trauma also happens in countries where there is less violence. Some of the many traumas that have turned up in our 'ordinary' psychotherapy practices include: a sudden death of a child, partner or parent and the subsequent bereavement; the loss of a previous religious belief that provided not only comforting sense to their life, but also a community of support; witnessing a stabbing in the street; being part of a major train or plane crash; surviving a terrorist bomb, in which friends died; being part of a very committed relationship that suddenly breaks apart, or part of an abusive and coercive relationship which the client finds impossible to leave.

Adult trauma, whether severe and dramatic or an everyday event, will often trigger earlier life events and developmental phases that had been adequately dealt with at the time, but not enough to lay the foundations that could withstand these new tremors. Judy notices in her work with refugees that the capacity to deal with the multi-level trauma is highly influenced by the strength that the individual has acquired from their early family relationships, community and religious beliefs.

'Pathology', as a word, comes from two Greek words: *pathos,* meaning suffering, and *logica,* meaning the logic or understanding. To study pathology is to attempt to understand the nature of the suffering of the other. One of the great psychotherapists who adopted this more compassionate and less labelling understanding of the word 'pathology' was Carl Jung. He wrote that: 'normality is a most relative conception' (Jung, 1935:210) and that it was achieved by a dynamic balance between the inner and outer worlds. Achieving this balance is central to Jung's approach to analytical psychology. He wrote:

> [The] main purpose [of analytical psychology] is the better adaptation of human behaviour, and adaptation in two directions (illness is faulty adaptation)...to external life—profession, family, society—and secondly to the vital demands of his own nature...to bring it to the right pitch of development. (Jung, 1981:92)

This led him to the realisation that there were two very different ways people could become so-called neurotic, or have a pattern of maladaptation either side of normality: 'collective people with underdeveloped individuality [or] individualists with atrophied collective adaptation' (Jung, 1935:7).

There are a number of key types of patterns of mental illness we believe it is important for psychotherapists to understand. Traditionally, the major distinction was between psychotic and neurotic patterns. Dan Siegel (2010) provides a simpler version of this distinction in his metaphor of the way that the river of integration flows through life and has two banks that people can be washed up on. He describes one as 'chaos' and the other as 'rigidity'. Chaos is one in which the brain is being flooded by images, feelings and compulsions, and cannot step back and integrate these. Rigidity is where the person has developed a fixity of thinking and behaving that restricts their lives, their relating and their development. Siegel goes on to explain how both types of pattern can be understood in terms of lack of horizontal or vertical brain integration, while carefully avoiding the suggestion that they can be reduced to brain malfunction. In our view, we are all as we are because of our genetic inheritance, our early and subsequent relationships and the influence of the society and ecology in which we live. The psychological conditions we mention below exist in this context and it should be borne in mind that we are all unique individuals within our relational, systemic and eco-systemic context and should not be labelled.

Psychosis

It is often said that those who have become psychotic have 'lost touch with reality'. Certainly, those with psychotic symptoms tend not to have the same reality as most others. Those who are diagnosed with schizophrenia develop symptoms such as delusions, which can be paranoid or grandiose, and hallucinations where they see, hear or smell things which are not apparent to others. Their thinking may also become 'disorganised'. Authors from the anti-psychiatry movement (Laing & Anthony, 2010; Szasz, 1961) have suggested that people who suffer in this way are in touch with a reality they cannot speak of and find symbolic ways of expressing it. They may literalise metaphors. For instance, someone who has become psychotic may literally, rather than metaphorically, see an elephant in the room, or believe that God has personally chosen them. Laing and Anthony (2010) regarded psychotic people as expressing something unsaid in the family system, which has led to some to blame parents for these disorders. While stress and distress may well be a trigger for psychosis, some have a valency for developing these psychotic states and there are neurological and chemical components to this. While psychotherapeutic methods have been used to treat psychosis, they are often not effective on their own and a mix of medication and psychotherapy is indicated.

Bi-polar disorder is another psychotic disorder that also leads to similar psychotic symptoms. Those who suffer from bi-polar disorder swing from feeling 'high' to very depressed indeed. When 'high', sufferers can be dangerous to themselves and others by doing inadvisable or delusional things like spending all their money or undertaking dangerous activities. When depressed, they are in danger of committing suicide, particularly as they are not open to reason. In both states, they may be influenced by voices telling them what to do.

Autism

Autism has a wide sweep as a condition, from people who are hard for others to contact at all, apparently living in their own world and not even able to carry out simple tasks, to much higher functioning individuals with what is now known as Asperger's syndrome. Although many people still clearly identify with it, Asperger's syndrome is no longer being used as an official diagnosis. They are now thought to be 'on a spectrum'. Autistic people tend to be very literal and find it difficult to understand nuance or metaphor, among a range of many other behavioural, cognitive and emotional difficulties, and so find the world around them baffling.

At one time, autism was thought to have been caused by cold, unresponsive mothers. As it became evident that mothers of autistic children differed in their responsiveness to their children, just as mothers whose children are not autistic do, this view changed. As autistic children might be harder to understand than others, it is sometimes thought that autistic people cannot love. This is far from the truth and they need and can love as much as anyone else (Soloman, 2014).

It is clear from neuroscientific research that the brains of autistic children are not neurally connected in the same way as others, though the reason for this is not clear. It is also evident that autistic children, who tend to have a better developed right than left brain, have abilities and capabilities that are not seen in neurotypical children and these abilities are now being recognised and appreciated, a fact that can vastly improve the mental health of those with autism who suffer from feeling different and 'lesser' than others. Psychotherapy with autistic people does not try to make them less autistic but helps them to live well in a neurotypical world.

Obsessive compulsive disorder

Obsessive compulsive disorder (OCD) is said to exist when someone feels driven to repeat certain behaviours such as checking, washing, scratching and tapping. This is often treated behaviourally, and this approach can be successful in managing these symptoms, particularly when the behaviour has become a habit that is no longer needed. If this is not the case, it may be more important to address the emotional motivation which leads to the formation of these symptoms. In our view, these behaviours are activated in some people when they are fearful and look for a way of keeping safe. The fear may come from re-activated early trauma or neglect, which has led the person to be easily alarmed. Their amygdala can become triggered in certain circumstances, and this leads to chemical and neurological changes that cause them to become hyper-alert. It is often important to soothe the alarmed brain before finding and working with any original trauma.

Addiction

It is hard for human beings not to think that more is better, and it can be argued that we are socially programmed to think in this way (see Chapter 2). As babies, we need to be attuned to in order to develop our brains and keep our bodies in balance. If these expectations are not well enough met, for whatever reason, we may develop an 'addictive personality', which looks for substances or experiences to try to soothe a hyper-alert brain and body. This seems to us to work initially but the strategy cannot be successful in the long run as more and more of the chosen addiction is needed to provide the desired effect.

Alcoholics Anonymous (AA) and other similar organisations/approaches have been very successful in tackling addictive behaviour, insisting on abstinence first and then facing the addict with the effects of their behaviour on themselves and others. It is very difficult to successfully provide psychotherapy without the person first giving up their addiction – particularly if it involves substances such as alcohol or drugs, as these change the chemical balance in the brain and any changes brought about by the therapy are easily altered when the substance is taken again. We usually suggest that people undertake a course of treatment with Alcoholics Anonymous or similar approaches before starting psychotherapy so they can better understand and resolve the deep-seated difficulty.

Eating disorders

Eating disorders are aligned to addictions and involve the over- or under-consumption of food (binge eating or anorexia nervosa) or sometimes both at the same time – overeating followed by vomiting. The chemical changes in the brain and body brought about by controlling food in this way soothe a brain that is finding it difficult to regulate the emotions or manage the complex life transition through puberty with its hormonal and body shape changes. Both food and the lack of food can trigger endorphins in the brain. Many people with eating disorders feel wracked with guilt by this behaviour but also feel extreme anxiety if they do not indulge in it. Body dysmorphia is also a common symptom where the person does not have a realistic idea of their size or shape.

As with addictions, treating eating disorders psychotherapeutically is very difficult, and behavioural help alongside is useful, such as setting targets and weighing. This can be counterproductive, however, if the person becomes too anxious when seeing they are losing or putting on weight. Sometimes this is a matter of life and death. An untreated eating disorder, particularly anorexia, can lead to the loss of their life as they have, in effect, starved themselves to death. The anxiety caused by changing eating habits is often extreme so psychotherapeutic work is often long term. Original neglect or trauma in babyhood should be approached carefully so as not to trigger overwhelming anxiety.

Personality disorders

Personality disorders are found in people whose whole personality seems to be imbued with troubling characteristics. Three common types are narcissistic, borderline and psychopathic/sociopathic. All of these find it hard to relate to and empathise with others. Narcissistic personalities tend to only care about their own needs, are self-obsessed and easily upset if life and relationships do not go their way. Borderline personalities tend to have an unstable sense of self which leads to erratic behaviour and impulsive actions. Their thinking is often inflexible, and they can be demanding and coercive in relationships. Psychopaths tend to be very antisocial and do not have enough empathy for others to establish healthy relationships or feel remorse. Sociopaths are similar but can sometimes relate to immediate people but do not have empathy for wider society, or groups of individuals.

Often these tendencies are just that – tendencies – rather than a complete description of someone's personality. However, the extent to which an individual does have these characteristics means that psychotherapy is difficult to lead to a satisfactory conclusion. Sometimes clients with these tendencies can be charming and compliant through the therapy, but it has not really touched them or their deeper patterns. It takes a very experienced therapist to see past this pretence and have the patience to work with them to a good conclusion.

Trauma

Trauma in infancy, childhood or later in life is now thought of as the main cause of psychological distress (Van der Kolk, 2015). When trauma is found in babyhood, it often means that the (m)other has not been able, for whatever reason, to help the child self-regulate and encourage the healthy laying down of neural connections to ensure that the child can emotionally grow and develop normally. When good enough attunement has been made to the child, they are in a good position to respond resiliently to trauma and stress later in life, though some later trauma may be so overwhelming it cannot be easily recovered from (see the section on attachment patterns).

Post-traumatic stress disorder (PTSD) is the name given to people who suffer trauma and cannot easily recover from it (American Psychiatric Association, 2013; Van der Kolk, 2015). Their brain finds it hard to get back to a sense of equilibrium. Trauma such as a serious car accident is often called a 'single incident trauma' and those who suffer from these events may vary in their ability to recover, depending on their initial experiences as a baby, and the severity of the trauma. Symptoms such as hypervigilance, flashbacks, headaches, nightmares and insomnia are common, as well as more general anxiety and depression. These are often treated by therapists who target the responses in the brain directly, for example using eye movement desensitisation reprogramming (EMDR), which has been successful in helping people with this disorder. Long-term psychotherapy is particularly indicated in cases of what is called 'complex trauma', often where there have been multiple traumas and these have retriggered trauma and loss in infancy or childhood.

Depression

To have times of feeling depressed is, of course, normal for human beings. An inability to feel depressed might, in itself, signal something amiss – maybe a disengagement from life and its travails. Less normal depression is sometimes called 'clinical depression' and can be diagnosed by having a number of common symptoms, which include low mood, sleep disturbance, feelings of low self-worth and loss of appetite. Many clients come to psychotherapy reporting that they feel depressed and it is important that the therapist hears what this means to them. Each individual's experience of depression can be different and may mean something dissimilar for each one. Depression can often be brought about by a relationship difficulty, a significant loss, or problems at work. Whatever the cause, the careful attention of the therapist is helpful. A feeling that life has no purpose or meaning may be the depression speaking but, as we say above, psychotherapy can also be about re-finding meaning, purpose and zest for life. Those with attachment difficulties early in life may be subject to depression, particularly as they may find it harder to make satisfying attachments in adulthood (see below).

Anxiety

Anxiety is also a normal state of mind and a survival necessity. A feeling of anxiety alerts us to something being amiss. Anxiety becomes abnormal when it is felt a good deal of the time with no particular cause. Many people live their lives with a low-level feeling of anxiety as a constant state. This is often caused by the sympathetic nervous system being constantly on alert. It is likely that people who suffer in this way were not helped to self-regulate by their carers early in life so that neural patterns do not work to switch off alerts when all is well, thus restoring the body to equilibrium and ensuring that the para-sympathetic nervous system is back in charge. The care and attention of the therapist can help this regulation as the brain does still have plasticity, though it is harder to make these changes later in life. Understanding the original difficulty and the brain processes can help the client develop a greater idea of their physical and behavioural patterns and by so doing create better emotional self-care and self-regulation.

The importance of early attachment and how this can play out later in life

Donald Winnicott was both a paediatrician and a psychoanalyst and spent many years studying children who had been traumatised through separation due to childhood evacuation from London and other large cities in the UK during the Second World War. He wrote extensively about the critical bonding between mother and child and the importance of the nursing triad (Winnicott, 1988) – the mother herself being supported by the father or other significant adult, in order that she could fully receive and process the child's emotions and be a 'good enough mother' (Winnicott, 1965).

Bowlby (1953) extended Winnicott's work in understanding the different types of attachment patterns between infants and their primary caregivers. He collaborated with Mary Ainsworth, who devised the Strange Situation Test in which babies come into a room with their mothers who then leave them briefly. Their response to their mother's return revealed how well attached the baby was to the mother. This research led to Bowlby describing four attachment patterns and shows how these may show up in later life (Bowlby, 1953:167–171; Siegel, 2010). The fourth pattern, 'disorganised attachment', was added later by Mary Main (Main & Solomon, 1986). The four different attachment patterns are:

- *Secure attachment:* research suggests this is present for about 60% of children studied. These infants show signs of missing the mother when separated, often by crying, but on being reunited actively greet them, often seeking some direct physical contact, and then quickly settle down. These are children of parents who are sensitive to the baby's communicated needs for connection, who can read the baby's signals and then effectively meet their needs.

- *Avoidant attachment:* demonstrated by about 20% of parent–infant relating. These infants show no signs of distress or anger when being separated and ignore the mother or actively avoid her on being reunited. Parent–baby observations show the primary caregiver as not responding to the child's signals in a reliable or responsive way and at times seeming to be indifferent to the child's distress.

- *Ambivalent attachment:* occurring in 10–15% of cases. The ambivalently attached infant can be suspicious and distressed when separated from the mother but, although the infant shows that he or she is trying to find her, is not easily calmed when they are reunited. Observation shows these parents to be sometimes responsive and attuned to their child and sometimes not.

- *Disorganised attachment:* occurs in about 10% of situations studied, but in 80% of high-risk groups such as children of drug-addicted parents. On reunion, the infant may look terrified; he or she approaches the parent but then withdraws from her, freezes or falls down on the floor, or clings and cries while simultaneously pulling away. Observations show at times a severe and terrifying lack of attunement, when the parent becomes terrifying to their infants, and when the parents themselves are also frightened.

Siegel (2010:xvii) writes:

> If parents are unresponsive, distant or confusing in their responses...their lack of attunement means that they cannot reflect back to the child an accurate picture of the children's inner world. In this case, research suggests, the child's mindsight lens may become cloudy or distorted... Or the child may develop a lens that sees well but is fragile, easily disrupted by stress and intense emotions.

Some of the early infants studied have now been followed up into early adulthood, and Hazan and Shaver (1994) developed the attachment theories into understanding adult patterns. What has been found as generalised patterns (clearly not true in every case) is the following:

- Adults who received *secure attachment* on the whole have satisfactory emotional lives with secure adult attachments and appear to meet their potential.

- Adults who received *avoidant attachment* tend to be distant and controlling in relationships.

- Adults who received *ambivalent attachment* are often anxious and insecure.

- Adults who received *disorganised attachment* have significantly poor mental health and find it hard to regulate their emotions. They often dissociate and are more at risk of PTSD if they experience a traumatic event.

These descriptions of attachment patterns can seem to encourage the idea that mothers are solely responsible for their baby's ability to develop healthy, well-connected brains and form satisfying relationships and fulfilled lives in adulthood. While it is clearly true that good enough attunement is extremely important for babies, mother and baby are in an intersubjective situation. For a variety of reasons, possibly genetic and/or pre-birth experiences, babies come into the world with differences. For instance, some may be generally calm or distressed, however well attuned the mother is. There are contributions on both sides and some mothers find it hard to discover a way to attune to their baby in spite of trying hard to do so. The baby may have a pain that cannot be soothed and cannot be taken away, for instance. This can set up a negative spiral that neither can control. This is particularly likely in the West, where the baby's carer may have long periods on her own with the baby (Gerhardt, 2015). In Africa, it is commonly said that 'it takes a village to raise a child'. There is greater recognition that one person alone cannot meet all the needs of a child and the primary carer needs support herself but the role of the father in supporting the mother to care for the child in Winnicott's nursing trial is not always possible and is often insufficient. If the conditions are conducive, mothers who have had their attachment needs well met in babyhood, and who are well enough supported, are more likely to create secure attachment with their babies.

How does psychotherapy contribute to greater psychological health?

Having explored psychological health and mental illness, we now come to the question about how psychotherapy, and in particular integrative psychotherapy, understands mental health.

The American Psychological Association, when addressing a definition of psychotherapy, says:

> Psychotherapy is a treatment that involves a relationship between a therapist and patient. It can be used to treat a broad variety of mental disorders and emotional difficulties. The goal of psychotherapy is to eliminate or control disabling or troubling symptoms so the patient can function better. Therapy can also help build a sense of well-being and healing.
>
> Problems helped by psychotherapy include difficulties in coping with daily life, the impact of trauma, medical illness, or loss, like the death of a loved one, and specific mental disorders, like depression or eating disorders. Psychiatrists and other mental health professionals can provide psychotherapy.
>
> One out of five Americans will experience a mental illness severe enough to require treatment at some time in their lives. Mental illnesses and emotional distress do not discriminate. They affect men and women of all ages, ethnic groups and socioeconomic statuses. These disorders impair how people feel, think, and act. They can interfere with how people function at work or school and affect their relationships with friends and family.[1]

Freud (see Chapter 5) is often quoted as saying, 'The aim of psychoanalysis is to relieve people of their neurotic unhappiness so that they can be normally unhappy.' However, he also importantly said that the aim of psychotherapy was to increase the human capacity to love and to work, which one of our clients echoed when he said, 'Everyone needs someone to love and something worthwhile to get up for each morning.'

For Jung, normality is finding one's needs being met in the situations of daily life (Jung, 1966) and, as we saw above, he understood the task of psychotherapy as being able to help the person achieve balance in their life between their internal and the external needs.

We believe that psychotherapy provides the following healing processes:

---

1   www.socalpsych.org/APA-psycotherapy.pdf

- An accepting, trusting relationship which can receive and recognise aspects of the client that were previously in their past so not recognised or received and therefore not mirrored back in ways that allow the client to recognise, own and integrate them.

- A relationship where the relationship itself can be an experimental laboratory for recognising one's patterns of relating, the emotional triggers and patterns that drive those ways of relating and the under-lying organising principles (unconscious beliefs and assumptions) that hold those feelings and ways of relating in place.

- An experimental laboratory where it is psychologically safe enough to experiment with new ways of being, to try them out, rehearse them and then reflect and receive support and feedback.

- A relationship which can survive 'relational ruptures' such as becoming furious with the psychotherapist, walking out of a session, forgetting to come, and discovering that they can still be there for the client, and survive the worst of the client's thoughts and projections.

- A place where the client can unlearn ways of being and thinking that no longer work for them and discover new ways. A place where they increase their positive mental health in the five areas mentioned above: an integrated sense of self, coherent living, a healthy interdependence, a sense of purpose and meaning and of making a contribution, and an integration across all these domains.

- A way for the client to deconstruct old self-narratives that they have created or have introjected from parents, siblings and peers, and gradually build a new integrating and evolving self-narrative that is 'Flexible, Adaptive, Coherent, Energized and Stable' (Siegel, 2010:70).

- A place to develop their 'emotional intelligence' (Goleman, 2009) and 'whole intelligence' (Parlett, 2015) by increasing their capacities for interrelating, responding to situations, embodying, experimenting and self-recognising.

- An opportunity to face the four existential challenges that confront us all: freedom and choice; aloneness; coming to terms with death; and creating meaning (Yalom, 2011).

- An opportunity to receive help and support in managing life transitions such as leaving home, committing to a life partner, having children, children leaving home, retirement and death of a loved one as well as dealing with how these life transitions can reawaken unfinished and unintegrated material from previous life transitions.

In Chapters 5 and 6 we will show how different psychotherapeutic approaches tend to focus more fully on one or more of these processes. In Chapters 7–9 we lay out our own focus and in Chapters 10 and 11 we show how this happens in the psychotherapy process.

Conclusion

In this chapter, we have explored how mental well-being is not the absence of disturbance or suffering, but the capacity of the human individual to create:

- an integrated coherent sense of self and a life narrative (subjective health)

- a coherence between their internal world and their actions and behaviour in the external world

- a healthy balance of separateness and belonging, healthy interdependence and fulfilling relationships

- a sense of purpose, thus making a contribution to the wider world

- an integration across all these four domains.

We have looked at how this requires constant quality inputs, including requisite sleep, play, physical exercise, down time, focus time, reflection and meditation time, what Rock and colleagues (2012) call 'in-time', relationship time, social contribution time and ecological and nature connecting time.

We have also explored how, in addition, we need the ability to face the psycho-social challenges of each life phase, and gradually develop our consciousness, managing the fulcrums between each stage.

Throughout this book, we will build on this, particularly in Chapters 7–9. In Chapter 7, we consider in depth the relational world; in Chapter 8, the social and systemic worlds of our family, community, region and global human family. In Chapter 9, we explore the ecological and spiritual worlds. But first we will revisit and reconsider the history of psychotherapy as it developed in the 19th and 20th centuries, from the perspective of what is now needed for psychotherapy to be 'future fit' for the challenges of the 21st century.

Part 2

The Roots: Revisioning the History of Psychotherapy

Introduction

Harari (Harari, 2015:59–60) tells us that: 'Changing the world begins by retelling the history and then reconfiguring the story.' This is true about developing psychotherapy approaches that are fit for the 21st century, with all the challenges we outlined in Chapter 2. It is also true for every psychotherapy relationship, where the client begins by retelling their story, but then must reconfigure and rework it into a healthier integrating narrative. This is the movement from the story creating them, to the client feeling they can create their own story and become self-authoring. As we will show later, this is only half the journey.

Stolorow and Atwood, whose pioneering work on relational psychotherapy we write about in Chapter 5, recount how they found that:

> psychoanalytic meta-psychologies derive profoundly from the personal, subjective worlds of their creators. This finding, which has a powerfully relativizing impact on one's view of psychological theories, led us inexorably to the conclusion that what psychoanalysis needs is a theory of subjectivity itself – a unifying framework that can account not only for the phenomena that other theories address but also for the theories themselves. (Stolorow & Atwood, 1996:181)

Our theories are the products of our own subjective experience and, importantly, also of our culture, our epistemology and ways of understanding the world, as well as the zeitgeist of the period we live in.

All new theorists are said to stand on the shoulders of the thinkers, researchers and practitioners who have come before them, but new theorists do not stand in the same place or the same time as their predecessors. Instead, they need to try to understand the thinkers who have come before them, but within the context of the place and time in which they were writing, as well as the writers' relationships with other thinkers and writers they were responding and sometimes reacting to.

Later, in Chapter 13, when we look at integrative psychotherapy training, we will discuss the importance of the process of understanding the psychobiography of other past and current theorists, not just understanding the theory from the lens of the personality of the theorist, but also their social, cultural, epistemological and spiritual contexts.

In these two chapters, we have made our attempt to 'reconfigure the story' and revision the history of psychotherapy, not in an objective way, but in terms of the streams of thoughts that have led us, in this place and time, to develop our integrative psychotherapy. There is so much psychotherapy history that we have had to be very selective and only include those who play some part in the roots or geological sub-strata of our own approach.

CHAPTER 5

The Historical Roots of Integrative Psychotherapy

Introduction

It is not for academic reasons that we now turn to history. We turn to history to find, explore and honour our roots as well as learn from them. Although integrative psychotherapy does not belong to a single 'school' of psychotherapy, it does have important roots that need to be in place for our practice to be healthy. These roots need to be planted in soil that is rich in nutrients and water, and the ground in which they are planted is important for the growth of our own blossoming as psychotherapists and psychotherapy communities. They give us stability, healthy development and rich fruiting. Our roots may not dictate how we grow but they are essential for that growth.

Each generation of theorists has come from a particular context and they are creatures of the time in which they wrote, so need to be seen as such. Many of our forebears did not practise as we would like to in our day, but they led the way and broke new ground for us. As Alcoff (2015:55) says:

> History doesn't excuse us, but it explains the conditions in which the interpretive process is occurring: what concepts I have at my disposal, how I am positioned vis-à-vis the 'deep rules' of my milieu, and, most importantly, what of my own history is at stake as I try to make sense of new events.

We learn by understanding where we come from and about where we are now.

For that reason, we need to honour those who came before us as well as break free from them. That is the aim of this chapter and the next one. In this chapter, we look at some of the important people who lived before the Second World War and who have contributed to our integration. Those who mostly worked after the war are covered in the following chapter. The reason for dividing the history into these two parts is because of a marked paradigm shift that happened around that time. This shift was found in the general culture, not just in psychotherapy. Before the Second World War, national institutions were generally accepted and there was more deference to authority. This meant that there was more general acceptance of the views of psychotherapy theorists from the schools they formed. Of course, there were exceptions but there was a tendency in this direction. Nevertheless, theory did develop over time and we are particularly interested in psychotherapy theorists who took psychotherapies into a more relational and systemic turn and how this affected theorising and practice. In order to think about how this happened, we need to understand how theories develop over time.

As in many other areas of study, such as philosophy or science, thinkers and theorists influence each other. This can happen within any particular field of study and even between fields. For instance, ideas from philosophy influence psychotherapists. Buber, for example, was a big influence on many fields of psychotherapy. Existential philosophers, such as Heidegger and Merleau-Ponty, have been extremely influential in certain psychoanalytic fields (Orange, 2010). Existential psychotherapy actually grew out of existential philosophy (Yalom, 1980).

The same process happens within and between schools of psychotherapy. Although there are apparently distinct 'schools', they do, in fact, merge into each other, even if they apparently are opposed to each other's stance. Some schools of psychotherapy see themselves as distinct from others, and others embrace these influences and describe themselves as integrative, as do the authors of this book. These usually integrate various specific approaches to form an ostensibly distinct integration (see Chapter 1). However, it may be truer to say that all approaches, however apparently discrete, are, to some extent, integrative as they do not live in a bubble and the zeitgeist throws up dominant ideas, as we will see below. As we show in Chapter 1, ideas about theory change and develop over time within the context of the contemporary world. Theory is never fixed, and ideas are not 'true' or 'false', but just ways of guiding us within the confines of present knowledge, so they should always be held lightly, with space to incorporate new ideas as they come to the fore.

All the processes that lead to changing ideas can be seen by examining our past, so, in order to understand the relational, systemic and ecological turn in psychotherapy theory and practice, we need to look through the history of the development of psychotherapeutic thought. As this is a chapter and not a complete book, this is necessarily a brief review of particularly influential theorists which led to the more relational work that is prominent today.

To return to the start of the history of psychotherapy that led to the relational turn, most histories start with Freud who has been called the 'Father of Psychotherapy'. This is part of a monotheistic and male-centric inspired view by Carlyle's way of understanding history in which he said, 'the history of the world is but the biography of great men' (Carlyle, 1841) – a history that portrays the human sciences as immaculate births out of the minds of great men, such as Freud, Marx, Darwin and Weber.

It is important to recognise the very influential work of 18th- and early 19th-century psychologists. Men like Hartley in England and Wolff in Germany were already using the term 'psychology' in the mid-18th century and were drawing on the thousands of years of studies of the psyche or soul that had previously been called philosophy or religion (see Chapter 3). Wilber (2000:xi) shows how the key figures of 19th-century psychology prior to Freud were Gustav Fechner (1801–1887), Karl Robert Eduard Von Hartmann (1842–1906) (who made popular the idea of the unconscious in 1859), William James (1842–1910) and James Mark Baldwin (1861–1934). All of these early psychologists connected back to the pre-modern philosophers and to ancient wisdom. Freud's role was to secularise psychology and to locate it in materialistic science.

Although psychoanalysts are direct descendants of Freud's work, the exponents of many other psychotherapies, particularly those that are humanistic, built their theories and practice on his work or have done so in reaction to it, as we saw above and will see below. Several influential humanistic psychotherapists, such as Fritz Perls and Wilhelm Reich, whom we shall explore in the next chapter, were originally psychoanalysts.

Psychoanalysis
Sigmund Freud (1856–1939)

It is interesting that Freud took precedence as the founder of psychoanalysis and has maintained a place in psychotherapeutic/psychoanalytic theorising that is not afforded to others, even though their theories may have more relevance to today's ideas and sensibilities. His ideas have been adapted, changed and added to since his lifetime but many theorists remain within the psychoanalytic family where they have more kudos than those, like Adler, who left it. Those who remain within the psychoanalytic fold are always at pains to show their psychoanalytic pedigree. Like many who started new movements, Freud is a towering figure, and in his lifetime at least, those who diverged from his theories were expelled from association with him.

It was not possible to remain a Freudian if you did a not espouse his views. This rigidity is typical of some charismatic founders of movements and is their strength and weakness. It is based on the idea of the heroic leader to whom unquestioning loyalty must be given – an idea that is more likely to be questioned today.

Freud was originally a neurologist and, as such, was consulted by patients who had 'nervous' disorders. Freud and his colleague Breuer were among the first, if not the first, to recognise the psychological nature of the symptoms that these patients exhibited. Freud and Breuer thought that the, often young, women who presented with hysterical symptoms suffered because of repression of a sexually conflictual nature. Middle-class culture in Vienna (as well as elsewhere in Europe) at the time was very circumscribed, particularly for women. It was expected that certain rules of behaviour were strictly adhered to and monitored, typically resulting in a stifling and restricted life. When Breuer first met Freud in the early 1890s, he had already developed hypnosis as a way of treating these patients and Freud worked with him on this at that time. Hypnosis was said to work with the 'unconscious mind', so Von Hartmann's important and influential idea of the psyche being largely unconscious was further developed by them.

As Freud's understanding of the sexual aetiology of hysterical conditions crystallised in his mind, he started to develop ideas about the centrality of sexuality in the development of the human psyche. He saw libido being channelled differently at each of five stages of development: the oral, anal, phallic, latent and genital. He believed that tension was caused by a build-up of libido and all pleasure was due to its release (Freud, 1938). At each of these stages, unconscious 'phantasies' held sway over the psyche, such as dependency at the oral stage, controlling and obsessive phantasies at the anal stage and the Oedipus complex at the phallic stage, which involved a phantasy for infant boys of killing the father and marrying the mother. Jung later proposed the 'Electra complex' as the girls' equivalent (Jung, 1918).

Alongside these theories, Freud developed a treatment practice in which the patient lay on a couch. Freud would sit out of sight behind the head of the patient who was encouraged, by the use of various techniques, to circumvent the conscious mind. These techniques included 'free association', remembering and recounting dreams and analysing 'slips of the tongue' (Freud, 1974).

Although the idea that the infant psyche seethed with sexuality was shocking to 19th-century European sensibilities, Freud in no way was making a critique of society's values. He regarded this developmental trajectory in children as natural, inevitable and instinctual in all societies and cultures. Furthermore, he did not regard the relationship of the clinician to the patient as being important. In fact, he sat out of sight in order to make his own presence have as little impact as possible. He encouraged psychoanalysts to be like 'blank screens' and to have 'evenly hovering attention' (Freud, 1912:109–120) with their patients so that the patient's unconscious mind could be projected on to it. He thought that by making the phantasies of the unconscious mind conscious, the 'complexes' which had developed would be resolved.

In 1912, Freud (1974) developed the idea of the 'transference' in which patients 'transferred' feelings and attitudes to initial caregivers on to the analyst, thus giving the analyst access to important information about the patient's unconscious mind. This was followed by the 'countertransference', which involved the analyst's attitude to the patient. These two linked ideas have been developed further by various theorists since then, both psychoanalytic and non-psychoanalytic. It was a seminal idea which was to bear much fruit in the years to come.

Freud wrote up several of his cases and these have become well known and demonstrate his work. In one of them, the case of 'Dora', the patient revealed that she had been sexually assaulted as a child by her father (Bernheimer & Kahane, 1985). Freud first thought that this was a traumatic event which caused the hysterical symptom of aphonia (inability to speak) that she had developed, but the negative and disbelieving response from colleagues to the possibility that the eminent father of this young woman could have behaved in this way famously led to his disavowal of the idea that trauma could result in this symptomatology. Instead, he ascribed these symptoms to phantasies which were thrown up by the unconscious mind. These were now not considered to be repressed memories but the patient's sexual phantasies which had no truth in actual experience.

Freud's assertion was that many apparently traumatic experiences of childhood, and, in particular, the reporting of sexual abuse, were not actual events but deeply unconscious phantasies which are inevitably part of the human psyche. This led to a huge source of disagreement both at the time and ever since (Gomez, 2005). It has only been in recent years that psychoanalysis has accepted that trauma is important in the aetiology of psychological distress. Other therapeutic disciplines have been much more ready to see the importance of traumatic events in making a considerable contribution to shaping the individual and, indeed, whole communities.

Freud was a pioneer in the development of 'talking therapies' which are still an important approach to helping distressed people today. He regarded the psyche as controlled by mechanistic energetic forces or instincts of the unconscious mind. These included the sexually orientated 'id', the rational and conscious 'ego' and the semi-conscious 'superego', which acts like a conscience and is largely introjected from the parents' or society's injunctions. This last gives his theory some sense of a wider system of influence, but on the whole, he did not think that the environment of the patient had much to do with these in-built factors and internal 'drives' that made up the psyche and the imbalance of which caused mental distress (Gomez, 2005).

As with many pioneers and originators of schools of thought, Freud had his adherents for whom any deviation from his original theory was heresy, while others developed the theory beyond Freud's original conception, acknowledging their debt to his original ideas but not feeling as if they had to adhere to the letter of the law.

Alfred Adler (1870–1937)

Alfred Adler was an early colleague of Freud's and did not consider himself to have been a pupil. The two disagreed on various matters of theory, including that sexuality was central to understanding human nature. A split therefore occurred between them. Adler was an early exponent of holism and called his kind of psychotherapy treatment 'individual psychotherapy'. His use of the word 'individual' here could be confusing. He used the word from the Latin *individuus*, meaning 'indivisibility' and thus emphasised the holistic nature of human beings in their connection with social lives. He is thus referring to the wholeness of each individual human and the wholeness of each individual within their social context. Although Adlerian psychology continues with many enthusiastic adherents, it has not been as influential as it maybe deserves.

Nevertheless, several of Adler's ideas have become influential, mostly for his inclusion of the social realm in psychological well-being and development. For instance, he thought birth order within a family was an important factor in influencing personality. Adler understood human beings to be 'meaning-makers' and that life is greatly enhanced if this meaning includes the social good rather than only considering the apparent needs of the individual. In his first book (Adler, 2009, first published in 1931:4) *What Life Could Mean to You*, he said:

> But no human being can escape meanings. We experience reality always through the meaning we give it; not in itself, but as something interpreted. It will be natural to suppose, therefore, that this meaning is always more or

less unfinished, incomplete; and even that it is never altogether right. The realm of meanings is the realm of mistakes.

His understanding that meaning is always a work in progress shows his influence from existentialists such as Nietzsche and Kant and was particularly influenced by Vaihinger and his 'philosophy of as if', where we act 'as if' we are what we think we are not.

This is reflected in his influential idea of the *inferiority complex* (Adler, 2013). This theory points out that we are all driven by making up for what we perceive as inferior in ourselves and act 'as if' this were not the case. However, an *inferiority complex* is found in people who are neurotically unsure of their own worth due to experiences in childhood which were particularly shaming. Those who have suffered in this way often over-compensate by stressing their achievements, thus forming a *superiority complex*. An inferiority complex usually has its origins in early life with parents who constantly criticise and do not support the fragile ego of the child. This is frequently reinforced by apparent failure in adulthood when the individual does not have the resilience to ride the setbacks that life inevitably produces. For this reason, Adler regarded a feeling of inferiority to be key in personality development as it drives our motivations in our life's journey to overcome that apparent inferiority.

Sándor Ferenczi (1873–1933)

One of Freud's early associates was Sándor Ferenczi. He was a close friend and colleague and would travel with him to give lectures in other places and countries. He was particularly enthusiastic in his wish to spread their ideas, not only to other medical schools but also to other disciplines such as social science, ethnography and literature. However, in later years, Ferenczi's ideas developed in a very different direction to Freud's, and this direction makes him an important influence on the therapeutic stance taken in this book and other relational approaches. Ferenczi's new theories resulted in a serious split with Freud which was very painful for them both. Freud's biographer, the English psychoanalyst, Ernest Jones, who was also part of Freud's original circle, reported that Ferenczi was mentally ill before he died, although this appears not to be true. He died of pernicious anaemia. This, along with a determination of many psychoanalysts to adhere strictly to Freudian theory and practice, meant that Ferenczi's work was largely dismissed and ignored for many decades.

Ferenczi's theories and practice have been increasingly recognised in recent years, as psychoanalytic and psychotherapy theorising have developed in ways which, to a large extent, he prefigured. Importantly, he regarded a warm and empathic therapeutic relationship to be of utmost importance in the psychotherapeutic process and criticised Freud's ideas of therapeutic 'abstinence' in which the analyst remains opaque to his patient and never shares his own thoughts and feelings. He regarded psychoanalysis to be a mutual endeavour between analyst and patient (Altman, 2015). Furthermore, he experimented with more 'active' techniques such as re-enacting situations that the patient found difficult (see section on Moreno in Chapter 6). Contrary to Freud, he thought that much psychopathology was caused by traumatic experience rather than it being an intrapsychic phenomenon and he tended to believe patients who had experienced sexual abuse rather than see these as 'phantasies' thrown up by a 'wish fulfilment'. His whole conception of therapeutic efficacy was to provide a reparative experience so that the patient would recover from neuroses. This was anathema to Freud and classical Freudians who thought of psychoanalysis as helping people come to terms with life as it is. Freud said that much was to be gained by 'transforming hysterical misery into common unhappiness' (Freud & Breuer, 2004, first published 1893).

Otto Rank (1884–1939)

Otto Rank was another theorist who criticised Freud for having sexuality so central to his understanding of human development. Rank thought this was unnecessarily restrictive. He thought that the birth experience was more formative (Rank, 2014, first published 1929). He also incorporated the focus on the body which became important to later psychotherapists. He, like Ferenczi, thought psychoanalytic methods to be too cold and unfeeling. Rank had been Freud's closest colleague and acolyte but was, like so many others, eventually rejected because of his criticisms of Freud and the way he diverged from orthodox Freudian theory (Karpf, 2015).

Carl Jung (1875–1961)

Carl Jung, a Swiss psychiatrist, was another early follower of and collaborator with Freud. Their ideas were markedly different, however, and a painful split occurred between them. A major difference concerned the nature of the unconscious. For Freud, the unconscious was a repository of unwelcome desires and wishes that stemmed from the energy of the libido. Jung's concept of the unconscious was much more positive. While Freud thought that making the unconscious available to the conscious mind was to release the energy of repressed and unacceptable emotions which led to neurotic symptoms, Jung saw the unconscious as having a much wider purpose and function. For Freud, the libido and the source of inner conflict was sexual in nature. This was not the case for Jung. For him the unconscious importantly included the 'collective unconscious' which is passed down through the culture and contributes to the richness of our inner life. Within the unconscious, we find the 'archetypes', universal patterns which can only be approached through archetypical imagery. The 'maiden' or the 'crone' are archetypal images, for example, but are not the archetype itself. These are given form and expression through the culture of the individual. Jung understood the purpose of our journey through life to be about living in a more fulfilled way by incorporating the imaginal which could be contacted through dreams and creative activities. He was therefore influential beyond psychiatry, psychology and psychotherapy to the fields of religion, literature, art and philosophy (Stevens, 1991).

While Freud focused on early development, Jung saw the whole of life as having important developmental tasks. Mid-life was particularly significant for Jung when the task of establishing yourself as an adult was complete and the individual could turn to more spiritual and creative matters (see Chapter 3). He thought that mid-life was a good time to enter into analysis so that the analysand could be helped to reflect on the purpose of their life at this stage. He understood this purpose to be to 'individuate'. This, for Jung, was to become a complete and whole individual, differentiated from the collective unconscious. Jung also wrote that our strengths have a 'shadow' side – that which is not yet incorporated into our conscious selves. He famously declared, 'the brighter the light, the darker the shadow'. He also said, 'Everyone carries a shadow, and the less it is embodied in the individual's conscious life, the blacker and denser it is' (Jung, 1938:131). An ostensibly very caring person, for instance, may have a shadow of anger and hate which is denied but appears in dreams and unbidden behaviour. Incorporating the shadow as part of individuation was seen as important.

There is a sense with Jung that he felt that human life was full of richness that is to be found in what he called the 'imaginal'. He saw the ability to symbolise and use images as key to mental health and psychological healing. He thought that our ability to live within this realm rather than reductively 'interpret' it was part of what he saw as important in life's journey. While much of Jung's work encourages a sense of living within a rich cultural and imaginal realm, which gives the sense of abiding in an interconnected world, his ideas about individuation suggest that our ability as individuals to crystallise out of that realm to become a separate human being was paramount for him and prefigured humanistic notions of self-actualisation (Edinger, 1996).

Melanie Klein (1882–1960)

One of the most important early developers of Freud's ideas was Melanie Klein. She had been in analysis with Ferenczi but moved to England at the invitation of Ernest Jones. Klein developed child psychotherapy while working in London. One of her most important contributions was to understand the importance of very early child developmental stages, far earlier than Freud had envisaged. Her view of the psyche was similar to Freud's in that she thought of sexual phantasies as a natural part of child development, albeit originating much earlier, from birth. She envisaged two important 'positions', rather than 'stages' – the 'paranoid/schizoid position' and the 'depressive position' (Klein, 2011). She saw that the psyche of the young infant was 'split' so that the fragile ego of the child could rely on the phantasy of a 'good breast' which perfectly met his/her needs while keeping it separate from the 'bad breast' which did not always appear when needed or did not produce the milk well enough. Of course, it is not possible for a mother to be perfect all the time, and this mechanism helps the child to cope with the ambivalence they would otherwise experience. Furthermore, at this stage, the child relates to the mother in parts – so the breast is considered to be a 'part object' – an 'object' being the one related to by the subjectivity of the child. Klein envisaged aggressive phantasies and intense feelings of hate in the young child, theories which many find unpalatable, but others like for their lack of sentimentality and their apparent closeness to experience. This theory reveals that she saw the early relationship with the mother as important in the child's development which prefigures the more relational view of later psychoanalysts such as Winnicott.

For Klein, the paranoid schizoid position is eventually replaced by the depressive position, with the dawning recognition that the mother is a whole human being and not in parts. This enables the child to recognise that a perfect mother does not exist. With this comes a sense of guilt for having attacked the 'bad breast' and a need to make reparation. This means that the child can now bear ambivalence and is capable of mourning the loss of the good breast (Klein, 1946).

Although Klein's ideas in many ways concur with Freud's mechanistic understanding of the psyche, they do start to suggest that relational factors may also be in play as the mother's response to the child's struggles will help them to resolve the conflicts that have arisen. Her notions of splitting and projection have been helpful in understanding some of the reason for conflict in human relating. Many conflicts, at any level – interpersonal, within a family, group, organisational or at a societal level – can be understood by the individuals or groups 'splitting' the 'other' from those they identify with which produces an 'us' and 'them'.

Donald Winnicott (1896–1971)

Donald Winnicott can be seen as the father of a more relational approach to psychotherapy. He was first a paediatrician and it was in this context that his intimate and extensive knowledge of children and infants arose. His journey to becoming a psychoanalyst began with being analysed by Melanie Klein and he was very influenced by her ideas. These were adapted in the development of his own approach. For instance, the 'depressive position' was changed to the 'stage of concern', thus emphasising the concern for the mother in having attacked her (Winnicott, 1965).

His theories about child development stressed the importance of the mother–child relationship. He saw the two as being merged from birth and gradually becoming separate. The mother, originally in 'maternal preoccupation', gradually and inevitably 'fails' the child, thus allowing a separate person to emerge with a strong enough ego to exist in the world. He saw the 'ordinary devoted mother' as 'good enough', thus supporting mothers that he saw in his clinics to feel able to cope with the exacting task of motherhood. He saw the father's role as supporting the mother and infant in what he called the 'nursing triad'. In what we think is the first reference to 'the myth of the separate mind' (Stolorow & Atwood, 1992), Winnicott said that there was 'no such thing as a baby'(Winnicott, 1960), as they exist in a completely symbiotic state. Only with sufficient support can a mother exist within this relationship, which is essential for healthy development. He understood the relational environment of the child as being key to healthy or unhealthy development and subsequently to a life which was, or was not, pathological.

His ideas on how psychoanalysis should be conducted were based on his understanding of the child. He thought that, in many ways, the therapeutic relationship should mirror the needs of the child that had been derailed earlier in life. He wrote much about the facilitating environment both for the child and for the patient. While Klein and Freud emphasised coming to terms with hard reality and learning to live with it, Winnicott emphasised the need for empathic understanding to allow the patient to make up for developmental deficits and allow the pathological ego to find a way to mature (Winnicott, 1988). Freud, Klein and Winnicott all thought that we use defence mechanisms to defend against injuries to our narcissism but, while Freud and Klein emphasised 'analysing' these, Winnicott believed that we develop a 'false self' which protects our 'true self' and we need to accept and understand this in order to let it go and the 'true self' to come to the fore.

Object relations

The British School of Object Relations grew out of the work of Melanie Klein and Donald Winnicott and a split in the psychoanalytic world in Britain at that time. Melanie Klein was an important theorist for British psychoanalysts but had differences with a classical Freudian view as shown above. Freud died soon after he moved to London (a move necessitated by the rise of Hitler), which left his daughter Anna to represent his views, and the two women – Anna Freud and Melanie Klein – were at loggerheads in the British Psychoanalytic Society. These became known as the 'Controversial Discussions' which, as a description, played down the rancour that was unleashed! The matter was finally resolved by splitting the two sides into different divisions which managed to co-exist within the British Psychoanalytic Society (BPS). A third was added called 'the independents' which comprised people who did not want to be identified with either one of these two groups. The independents took forward the object relations agenda that had started with Donald Winnicott and others (Gomez, 2005).

Object relations theory

Object relations refers to the idea that babies in infancy form their sense of self through their relating to others – most importantly with their initial caregiver, usually the mother. Important object relations theorists include, besides Melanie Klein and Donald Winnicott, Wilfred Bion, Harry Guntrip, Michael Balint and Ronald Fairbairn. Fairbairn interestingly came to these ideas separately. These theorists were working in the 1940s to 60s. A new generation of important object relations theorists, often thought of as belonging to the Relational School, included Christopher Bollas and Patrick Casement who worked in the 1980s and 90s. All these psychoanalysts belonged to the independent part of the BPS. American psychoanalysts are also important in this context, but we will explore these separately.

All these theorists made important contributions to the field, many in our understanding of human interaction and relationships. They took Freud's work further in understanding the importance of early childhood, particularly how we construct our sense of self through childhood experiences with parents and others and the way in which the relationship with the analyst mirrors and mitigates these experiences.

Bion developed the ideas of Klein, particularly her work on the defence of splitting and projective identification. He also developed important theories about group process (Bion, 1961) .

Ronald Fairbairn (1889–1964)

Ronald Fairbairn, a Scottish psychoanalyst who was mostly not in contact with London psychoanalysts, was the first to find that the libido was 'object seeking' rather than pleasure seeking as Freud thought. This encouraged a more relational approach to therapeutic work and saw the importance of attachment bonds before Bowlby, who is a leading theorist of attachment-based theories (see Chapter 4). He went on to explore the results of being securely or insecurely attached.

American psychoanalysts

Original American psychoanalysts emigrated to America from Europe, many of them Jewish and escaping Nazi persecution. Many creative thinkers arrived in America and made useful contributions to the development of psychoanalytic theory.

Franz Alexander (1891–1954)

Franz Alexander, an original follower and colleague of Freud, developed, with Ferenczi, the notion of analysis providing a 'corrective emotional experience' which was much disparaged, though later became fashionable again.

Karen Horney (1885–1952)

Karen Horney was another emigrant from Germany. Having been a member of the Berlin Psychoanalytic Institute, she later founded the American

Institute for Psychoanalysis. She is well known as an early influence on later feminist therapy by challenging Freud's notion of 'penis envy' in girls. She said that differences between the sexes are social rather than biological. She countered penis envy by suggesting that men developed 'womb envy' and this led them to compensate by developing other abilities instead. She also differed from Freud in her assertion that people develop over their lifetime rather than only in early childhood.

Behaviour and cognitive therapies

Behaviour therapy is built on behaviourism, a psychological method which focuses on objectively observable behaviour. It aims to study behaviour rather than any meaning the behaviour may have. Behaviour therapy, then, is more concerned to adapt or eliminate certain behaviours than to alter the meaning behind the behaviour. This can be seen as a polar opposite to psychoanalysis, which first explores the patient's psychological condition and sees behaviour as something that arises out of the twists and turns of their emotional and mental worlds.

Behaviour therapy was originally influenced by operant conditioning which seeks to modify behaviour by rewards or punishment. As it has an empirical approach, it is easier than in some forms of other therapy to set targets and evaluate if they are met. The goal of the therapy is clear – for example, if the presenting symptom of agoraphobia is no longer present, then it is clear that the goal has been met. In the case of agoraphobia, the patient can now go outside at will. The question of why the person became agoraphobic is not approached and, from a behaviour therapist's point of view, is irrelevant.

Not many practitioners of behaviour therapy have come to the fore as ground-breaking theorists. There are a few whom we think it important to mention.

B. F. Skinner (1904–1990)

B. F. Skinner laid out his principles in the book *The Behavior of Organisms* (Skinner, 1991, first published 1938), in which he shows how a stimulus from outside an organism (person) is reinforced or not and thus changes or adapts behaviour. Simple conditioning was described by Pavlov, whose dogs salivated when food was presented and the researcher rang the bell at the same time. After a short period of conditioning, the dog would salivate at the ringing of the bell even when there was no food presented. Operant conditioning, on which behaviour therapy is based, includes a third factor so there is 'stimulus-response-reinforcer'. For instance, a rat (or, indeed, a child) will press a lever only when a light comes on at the same time, if food only appears when the light is on. The behaviour is reinforced because when the light comes on, a reward of food is given. This principle is used in behaviour therapy to alter and then reinforce behaviour.

Skinner tried to account for more complex behaviour by a 'chain' of conditioned responses. Realising that this could not account for all complex behaviours, he also introduced the notion of 'rule-governed behaviour' where the organism adopts a rule from one set of conditioned behaviour and uses it across a wide range of behaviours.

Joseph Wolpe (1915–1997)

Joseph Wolpe was a behaviour therapist who introduced the notion of desensitisation (Wolpe, 1969). This is a technique which can be effective with phobias as it helps to desensitise the patient to their focus of anxiety. For instance, if a patient has a fear of spiders, she can gradually lose this fear by progressively approaching them. If she can do so without fear, then her lack of fear is reinforced. A spider will only be put before her when she has learned to tolerate one at a certain distance. She is then ready to approach the spider at a shorter distance until the conditioned response expires. Pictures of spiders which become gradually bigger and more apparently aggressive can have a similar effect. The same method can be used for other phobias such as agoraphobia.

Cognitive therapy

Cognitive therapy is a later development. This is built on cognitive psychology which focuses, not on behaviour, but on the person's cognition, the structure of their thoughts and how these form into basic beliefs, mindsets and attitudes of individuals which can limit their attitudes to, and involvement in, life. The limiting mindsets are explored and challenged in such a way that the patient can find more positive ways of seeing the world and can change their behaviour.

Cognitive behavioural therapy (CBT) has become very widespread and is a combination of the two. It is often successful in changing behaviour, is time limited and is verifiable through empirical research. It is often used in public services where there needs to be an 'evidence base' for the work and where there are financial constraints, so the short-term nature of CBT is attractive. It is often effective and useful in approaching single-issue difficulties such as specific phobias and can be a useful approach if used with people who have non-complex trauma, substance abuse, eating disorders and obsessive compulsive disorders.

George Kelly (1905–1967)

George Kelly has been given this place in the chapter though he may have taken issue with it himself as he felt his theories were in a category of their own. He is sometimes thought of as being similar to cognitive therapists in that he was concerned about the constructs people make of their experience; similar to humanistic therapists in that he thought clients should be seen from their own frame of reference; and similar to existential psychotherapists in that he was influenced by existentialism as no one frame of reference is 'the truth'.

He neither saw the individual as having internal drives (as in psycho-analysis), nor by their learning history (as in behaviour and cognitive therapy), but by their need to predict events by their own constructs. A healthy person can change their constructs when events challenge them but those who cannot do this become mentally unwell and need help to loosen the constructs they have made.

Conclusion

Having explored psychoanalytic and behavioural roots of our work, we can see that some have had more influence on us than others. You might like to reflect on how your own approach and beliefs have links back to some of these different previous theorists. For us, the more objectifying approach of the behavioural psychotherapists is less influential but it does have a place. As we will see later in the book, we do not see that we either have to start with behaviour to change our experience of the world, or start with how we experience the world and hope that it will lead to changes in our behaviour. This is an unnecessary either/or dichotomy that can be overcome, as we will see in Chapter 10.

We will now turn to the time, after the Second World War, when a distinct paradigm shift was experienced, as new models in science and epistemology started to impact on psychotherapy theory and practice.

CHAPTER 6

The History of Psychotherapy Since the Second World War

Introduction

There was a major paradigm shift both in thinking and psychotherapy after the Second World War, due in part to psychologists and psychotherapists having to come to terms with the traumas of both the war and the Holocaust and face up to the reality of the levels of depravity to which human beings could sink. Many of the leading psychologists of the time had been Jews. Some, like Freud, Klein, Reich and Perls, had fled Austria and Germany to avoid Nazi persecution, while others, like Frankl and Bettleheim, had endured and survived life in the concentration camps. The latter became interested in how some inmates of the concentration camps survived the horrors of both what they endured and witnessing the extermination of many of their compatriots, and many others psychologically suffered debilitating trauma. They drew on three other major paradigm shifts that had emerged in the middle of the 20th century, but which had roots back into the 19th century. The first was existentialism, whose roots go back to philosophers like Kierkegaard, Nietzsche and James. These philosophers reacted against Kant's 'panrationalism' (the notion that truth was based on rational logic or empiricism, as well as scientific positivism), with its attempt to capture all of life in a system of concepts, thus thinking that reality is accurately reflected in abstract thought. It was most fully integrated by Jean Paul Sartre (2001), a French philosopher who lived through the Second World War, and whose famous dictums include: 'Existence precedes essence' and 'We are our choices, within the limits of our given world.' The existentialist emphasised that the individual creates their own identity and reality within the given situations in which they find themselves.

Viktor Frankl (1905–1997) was Jewish, so when Hitler's Nazi army invaded Vienna, he was first sent to work in a Nazi-formed ghetto at Theresienstadt and later interred in Auschwitz concentration camp. He studied his own and his compatriots' ways of dealing with the horrors of the concentration camp experience. He wrote about this in his book *From Death Camp to Existentialism* (1961). He discovered that:

> when life is pared down to the sheer fact of existence and when nothing else has meaning, there is still the basic freedom, namely the freedom to choose the attitude one takes toward one's fate. This may not change the fate, but it greatly changes the person. (Frankl, 1969:108)

This fundamental experience shaped Frankl's development of what he termed 'logotherapy', where the focus is on how the individual creates meaning for themselves out of the givens of their existence. His later book, *Man's Search for Meaning*, published in 1959, became an international best-seller (recent edition, Frankl, 2013).

Existential and phenomenological psychotherapy

Rollo May, one of the great integrators of existential psychotherapy (May, 1969:11), defines existentialism as involving 'centring upon the existing person and emphasizes the human being as he is emerging, becoming'. One can notice the direct link here to May's colleague and humanistic psychotherapist, Carl Rogers, and Rogers's book, *On Becoming a Person* (Rogers, 1961).

The second important paradigm shift came from phenomenology that had first been developed by Husserl, elaborated by Heidegger and then taken up by Sartre, later still, the psychologist Merleau-Ponty and much earlier by the psychiatrist and friend of Freud, Binswanger. Phenomenological method starts with the therapist freeing their mind of all pre-suppositions as best they can, so they can meet each new client in their full uniqueness, rather than see them through the lens of their theories or beliefs. This involves deep empathic listening to try and understand the client from their own perspective, rather than from the therapist's own. Phenomenology also recognises that we *experience* the phenomena of the other, not just observe and listen. A great deal of communication is non-verbal and we receive the client through the resonance in our own bodily sensations and feelings; we partly discover the other in how they show up within us.

The third important paradigm shift of the mid-20th century was in science. In physics, this was pioneered by the quantum theorists such as Neils Bohr (1934) and Heisenberg (1958) and in biology by Bertalanffy (1968).

Their work marked the end of the era of Newtonian physics, which searched for the basic building blocks of matter and living organisms, and the beginning of the era in which life is seen as being built on relational interaction, which together creates complex systems that are more than the sum of their parts. These discoveries gradually built into 'general systems theory'. This applied systemic understanding to all levels of life, from sub-atomic particles, through plants, insects, mammals and humans, to groups, communities and eco-systems. In this new paradigm, co-creation replaces linear causality; the focus moves from studying discrete parts to focusing on patterns of connection that are always emergent and changing, and there is a recognition that you cannot know anything without changing it – you are part of any system you are studying.

Humanistic psychotherapy

Humanistic psychotherapy emerged as a 'third force' in psychology, with psychoanalysis and behaviourism being the other two (Cain & Seeman, 2006). The Association for Humanistic Psychology (AHP) was formed in 1962 by Abraham Maslow, Carl Rogers, Charlotte Buhler, Rollo May, Clark Moustakas and Virginia Satir. These various theorists, as well as others who were not present at the foundation of the association, had started to develop what became known as humanistic psychology about 20 years previously so that their work was already known and practised. Out of the AHP grew what came to be known as the human development movement. Unlike psychoanalysis, humanistic psychology held that human beings have a natural propensity to 'self-actualise' and reach an in-built potential if the conditions of life are conducive. It was founded, not in Europe, but in America and spread to Europe and other parts of the world from there. The cultural shift in time period and nationality no doubt explains some of the differences between psychoanalysis and humanistic psychotherapy. By the early 21st century, the two disciplines have come closer to each other's position, psychoanalysis becoming more relational and humanistic psychotherapy having become more professional.

Although many originators of humanistic therapies were academics, some tended to be radical in their approach and from its inception, humanistic psychotherapy or counselling could be apparently anti-hierarchic and even anti-establishment. The AHP coming into being in the 1960s is indicative of this approach as, at that time, young people began to question the values of their elders and were experimenting with 'alternative' lifestyles.

Humanistic work was typically practised by charismatic individuals who ran one-off but lengthy workshops and often had enthusiastic followers. These group leaders emphasised experiential experimentation and non-verbal action methods rather than 'talking about' experience. Although individual therapy existed in the humanistic world, there was a tendency for the work to be carried out in time-limited groups which fostered emotional intensity and confrontation. 'Breaking down' defences was cathartic and often part of the aim of these groups, thus allowing the individual to discover their 'authentic' self. This was useful for many but harmful and distressing for those who were too vulnerable to learn from it.

Many of the charismatic group leaders started schools of psychotherapy that still exist today. The main types are psychodrama founded by Jacob Moreno; gestalt therapy started by Fritz Perls; encounter groups, described and developed by Will Schutz; person-centred therapy founded by Carl Rogers; and transactional analysis founded by Eric Byrne. The body as well as the mind was recognised as important and certain schools of body psychotherapy arose. They were mostly influenced by Wilhelm Reich, an early colleague of Freud, who showed how the body was integral to the psyche. Important body-orientated schools included bioenergetics founded by Alexander Lowen and bioenergy work founded by Gerda Boyesen. These were not part of the original humanistic family but were embraced by them. The transpersonal was also recognised as important and the discipline of psychosynthesis, which was founded by Assagioli, was recognised too. In many ways, Assagioli was more a follower of Jung but was recognised as important in the humanistic field.

Each of these fields flourished, with new practitioners spreading the work internationally. Initially, more junior exponents of each field were taught through a form of apprenticeship and people were selected to do this who had taken part in the therapy, usually in a series of group experiences. When they had assisted for long enough, they started to take groups on their own. Although this method may seem a bit hit-and-miss, it did produce some excellent psychotherapists who further developed the field of psychotherapy.

By the 1980s, the exponents of humanistic psychology were keener to become more mainstream and each school professionalised their standards (Hawkins, 2017b). They devised and discovered more organised theory around their work and founded schools which taught the theory and practice of their particular therapeutic approach, often to a master's standard. Many of the UK courses available to students by this time became member organisations of the UK Council for Psychotherapy and increasingly became recognised by universities. Teachers would now be officially qualified in their particular discipline and would be experienced practitioners.

By the early 1980s, several schools became 'integrative'. We say more about integration in psychotherapy in Chapter 1. Suffice it to say here, integrative training tended to incorporate two or more different 'schools' of psychotherapy but, as we say in Chapter 1, integration is a more complex matter, also embracing an integration of the person as well as the psychotherapeutic method. Many, but not all, integrative schools included aspects of psychoanalysis in their approach, particularly object relations, as its greater relational position seems more compatible with humanistic therapies. Many founders of integrative approaches found the experiential and open-minded outlook of humanistic work to be enhanced if it was put together with psychoanalytic theoretical rigour and grounding in human development.

In the late 1980s, the humanistic and integrative section (now college) of the UK Council for Psychotherapy was founded and is now the largest of the colleges. This organisation has given humanistic theorists and therapists a base from which to collaborate as well as a platform on which to base quality standards and validated qualifications. Whereas humanistic psychotherapies were originally the 'wild child' of psychotherapy, they have now come of age and are serious contributors to psychotherapeutic theory and practice. No doubt something is lost in the original creativity and intuitive understanding but humanistic psychotherapy could not have survived in its previous form because of its insistence on anti-hierarchic structures in accreditation practices. Present insistence on validated qualifications would have thrown doubt on its legitimacy. Most humanistic therapists try, at the same time, to maintain the spirit of the founders.

Important figures in the development of humanistic psychotherapy are outlined here.

Jacob Moreno (1889–1974)

Jacob Moreno did not regard himself as a humanistic psychologist as he pre-dated this field by many years. He was also a social scientist and worked with social groups as well as individuals. Born in Romania, he was a contemporary of Freud and moved to Vienna at the beginning of the 20th century. He later moved to America. While in Vienna he created the 'Theatre of Spontaneity' from which grew the therapeutic method of psychodrama. He once met Freud at a lecture. He reported the meeting thus:

As the students filed out, he singled me out from the crowd and asked me what I was doing. I responded, 'Well, Dr. Freud, I start where you leave off. You meet people in the artificial setting of your office. I meet them on the street and in their homes, in their natural surroundings. You analyse their dreams. I give them the courage to dream again. You analyse and tear them apart. I let them act out their conflicting roles and help them to put the parts back together again.' (Moreno, 1972:5–6)

Psychodrama is an action-based method in which a protagonist is facilitated in exploring aspects of their life by acting them out, using other group members to become 'auxiliaries', in other words to take on other significant roles of people in the drama of their life. Moreno showed how a feeling connection between people, which he called *tele*, allows other group members to know how to play these roles with minimum briefing. Various methods that are now commonly used in humanistic psychology and elsewhere were first used by Moreno. These include role play, 'empty chair' technique, doubling, sculpting, sharing and warm-ups. All these, and more, were first used and invented by Moreno but he is seldom acknowledged and those who have used them more recently are often given the credit for their invention. He therefore influenced many action-based therapists including Fritz Perls, Will Schutz and Bert Hellinger. For Moreno, fostering spontaneity and creativity through the techniques he used was the most important therapeutic factor, as these qualities in individuals help them to live life well.

Abraham Maslow (1908–1970)

Abraham Maslow was one of the founders of humanistic psychotherapy. His concern was to understand human health rather than pathology. This idea led to him developing the theory he is best known for which is his 'hierarchy of needs' (Maslow, 1972). This asserts that the most basic of human needs have to be satisfied before others can be fully focused on. He first set this out in a paper called 'A theory of human motivation'. He regarded the purpose of life to be to meet the highest need, which is 'self-actualisation', but we have to meet the other needs first. This was set out diagrammatically as a pyramid, with the most basic at the bottom. Physiological needs are at the bottom of the pyramid, followed by safety, then love and belonging, then esteem and finally self-actualisation. In later years, Maslow added self-transcendence in which the person looks beyond their own sense of self to something spiritual or transcendent. Maslow was not a therapist himself but had a very great effect on most forms of humanistic psychotherapy, particularly Rogers's client-centred therapy.

Carl Rogers (1902–1987)

Carl Rogers was a very influential originator in humanistic psychology and psychotherapy/counselling (Cain & Seeman, 2006). He invented the terms 'person centred' and 'client centred' as he believed that the client is best understood from within their own frame of reference. He thought that the therapist should adopt three core conditions when relating to the client therapeutically (Rogers, 1961, 1965). These core conditions are ones in which the therapist shows empathy, congruence and unconditional positive regard. They allow the therapist to see the world from the client's point of view, creating a field which is trustworthy and consistent and provides a sense of acceptance, which can allow the client to change in a positive direction. Each individual creates a self-concept from within the experiential field in which they live and are raised. He regarded the condition of unconditional positive regard as essential for the individual to become self-actualised, which is why this quality is so important in a therapist.

Besides being a therapist, Rogers was a theoretician, He had 19 propositions (Rogers, 1961) which show how human beings separate out as individuals from their environment, how they devise a self-concept and what enabling conditions are needed for a healthy emotional life through a process of symbolisation. When certain experiences are not available to the person then they are not able to assimilate and integrate them and this can lead to distortions. Being understood from one's own frame of reference can lead to expanding the self-concept and greater mental and emotional health in which the person is integrated.

Rogerian therapy (also known as person-centred therapy) is still widespread today. He has been very influential, not only because his theory and methods are still practised today, but because his ideas are used in other humanistic and integrative theories as well as in coaching.

Fritz (1893–1970) and Laura Perls (1905–1990)

Fritz Perls founded gestalt therapy with his wife, Laura Perls, who is under-acknowledged for her role in its foundation. They were both born in Germany and fled Nazism to South Africa, where they were influenced not only by psychoanalysis, but also by 'holism' developed by Jan Smuts. Both developed gestalt therapy there having first trained in psychoanalysis. Fritz Perls's first book, *Ego, Hunger and Aggression* (Perls, 1992, first published 1969), was co-written with Laura but she was not acknowledged (Cain & Seeman, 2006). After ten years, they moved to America where they formed the New York Institute for Gestalt Therapy. Fritz moved to Esalen in later life.

Gestalt therapy is based in phenomenology, field theory, dialogue and gestalt psychology (Yontef, 1993; Resnick, 1995). Clients are encouraged to bring awareness to their present experience and the contact boundary between themselves and others. Neuroses are caused by gestalts not being 'finished' and occur when this awareness is not acceptable to the person, maybe because it is found to be shameful by important figures in the person's life. An uninterrupted gestalt cycle involves having an experience which leads to action, is integrated and then completed. For instance, I see an apple, feel hungry, reach out for it, eat it, acknowledge its taste and a feeling of satisfaction and then turn to other matters in my life. If I fail to eat the apple because I think it would be greedy to do so or it doesn't belong to me, there is an unfinished gestalt. A gestalt is a complete experience when the 'figure' and 'ground' are both seen and acknowledged. For instance, the apple in the above example is the 'figure' and the 'ground' is that it does not belong to me. I can complete the gestalt by going into a shop and buying one.

Field theory is another important influence on gestalt therapy. In field theory individuals are not seen as existing separately from their environment but as part of an interacting field of experience (Hycner & Jacobs, 1995; Parlett, 1991; Yontef, 1993).

Fritz Perls saw no reason for gestalt therapy students and practitioners to have an academic theoretical basis or for research to be carried out. Although many centres were formed, his main focus was on giving one-off demonstrations of his work. The more academic aspect of gestalt therapy was left to Laura and others, particularly Erving and Miriam Polster. Splits in the field, which were prevalent, are now much reduced and the need for the development of both theory and practice is acknowledged.

Other key developers of gestalt therapy include Ed and Sonia Nevis, who founded the Gestalt International Study Center in Wellfleet, Massachusetts; Gary Yontef (1981), who developed dialogue as a methodology in gestalt therapy; and Malcolm Parlett (1991), who developed field theory in gestalt therapy.

Eric Berne (1910–1970)

Eric Berne is the founder of the humanistic psychotherapy called transactional analysis. He was, for several years, a student of psychoanalysis but developed his own form of therapy having been refused admission to the San Francisco Psychoanalytic Institute. His thesis was that people were best analysed by exploring their social transactions rather than the individual unconscious mind. He described three ego states: *child, adult* and *parent*, which, in some ways, are similar to *id, ego* and *superego* (Berne, 1967). Besides using simpler language, Berne thought each ego state was formed at the point of transaction with others, rather than being co-existing states of the psyche. Each person exhibits any of these ego states in their relationships to others, and from these, forms certain 'transactions' with them. A person taking on the ego state of parent tends to elicit a child ego state from others, for example. Child to parent and parent to child ego states, he described as 'crossed' rather than the adult to adult transactions which are more straightforward. Interactions between people were often described as *games*, as these unconsciously play out a desired response from the other. He gave these games jokey but memorable names such as 'Ain't it awful' and 'I'm only trying to help you'. The latter is typically played by therapists and social workers! Berne's contention was that people often had a characteristic way of manipulating others which he called their 'script'. The job of the therapist was to uncover these scripts and games so that the individual would have more choice about how they interact and understand where these came from, which was often childhood.

Berne thought that we have four possible life positions: I'm okay, you're okay; I'm okay, you're not okay; I'm not okay, you're okay; and I'm not okay, you're not okay. These life positions will inform how games are typically played. This theory was popularised by Thomas Harris in his book, *I'm Okay, You're Okay*, which was based on Berne's theory (Harris, 1995).

The transactional analyst Stephen Karpman (Karpman, 1968) developed the popular and useful idea of the 'drama triangle', which describes a prevalent triangular game in which the roles of *victim, persecutor* and *rescuer* are played out in conflictual situations. The roles in this game are often exchanged as the victim becomes the persecutor, until someone breaks the game. While caught in this game, conflicts cannot be resolved. This useful theory is often employed in helping professionals who are not transactional analysts (Hawkins & Shohet, 2012).

Berne's book, *Games People Play* (Berne, 1967), became very popular with both professionals and the general public. It is also sometimes put together with other therapies in an integration and taught to other professionals, such as social workers, to enhance their work.

The revisioning of psychoanalysis

At this time of rapid growth in existential, humanistic and transpersonal psychotherapies, there also emerged a number of key writers and theorists revisioning different forms of psychoanalysis and psychoanalytic psychotherapy.

Jacques Lacan (1901–1981)

The French psychoanalyst, Jacques Lacan, became hugely influential, not just in France, and particularly to post-structuralist philosophy. He dismissed the object relations school of psychoanalysis and insisted that it was important to 'return to Freud'. He regarded linguistics as part of his new conceptualisation of Freud's theories and stipulated that the unconscious was itself 'structured like a language'. He was influenced by and influenced the linguistic turn in post-modern philosophy and had an effect on other psychotherapists who became interested in narrative in psychotherapy. Feminist thinkers have both utilised and criticised Lacan's concepts of castration and the phallus. Some have interpreted his work as opening up new possibilities for feminist theory, arguing that Lacan's phallocentric analysis provides a useful means of understanding gender biases and imposed roles, while other feminist critics accuse Lacan of maintaining the sexist tradition in psychoanalysis.

James Hillman (1926–2011)

James Hillman was the director of the Jung Institute in Zurich from 1959 to 1969 and later developed a new movement called archetypal psychology. He wrote many influential books, including *Re-visioning Psychology* (Hillman, 1975), emphasising the role of myths and fantasies for making a necessary connection to the soul. He saw connecting with the imaginal realm as our most fundamental human need compared with our more superficial ego needs.

Relational psychoanalytic psychotherapy

In the 1990s, psychoanalytic psychotherapists developed more relational forms of the work which gained central significance within this field.

They acknowledged that the major therapeutic agent making psychotherapy effective is rooted in the relationship between client and psychotherapist or psychoanalyst. This did not just concern the method of paying attention to and working through transference and countertransference phenomena, but the therapeutic nature of the relationship itself was newly attended to and conceptualised. This move brought the psychoanalytic closer to the position of humanistic therapists. Many of the relational psychoanalytic psychotherapists were importantly influenced by the work of Donald Winnicott and they in turn provided a development of his work. Important theorists include Patrick Casement, Christopher Bollas, Robert Hobson, Thomas Ogden, Susie Orbach, Valerie Sinason, Stephen Mitchell, Robert Stolorow, George Atwood and Donna Orange. Some of these we consider later in the book, but here are two of the most influential ones.

Patrick Casement

Patrick Casement wrote several very influential books, including *On Learning from the Patient* (Casement, 1985), *Further Learning from the Patient* (Casement, 1990a) and *Learning from Life* (Casement, 1990b). Casement espoused the view that the patient is constantly 'telling' the therapist, unconsciously, what they need, and he showed how psychotherapists could learn to listen in new ways and even more carefully to their patients. He understood that, through dreams and other unconscious means, clients are continuously communicating their needs to the therapist. This process is particularly active when patients tell stories that contain an unconscious message in their subtext in much the same way that dreams have many layers open to the therapeutic search for meaning. For instance, if the client tells you that they went to a meeting and they were annoyed because their companion was late, it may also be an unconscious message about the therapist being late to the last session or their fear that the therapist might be late in the future. He thought that the patient's unconscious always knew what they needed and that empathetic responses conveying accurate understanding of these needs were most therapeutically productive.

Christopher Bollas

Like Casement, Bollas emphasised the role of unconscious communication in psychotherapy. He saw human beings as searching for their own 'idiom', their own means of expression, and he wrote several influential books, including

The Shadow of the Object (Bollas, 1987), *Being a Character* (Bollas, 1992) and *Cracking Up* (Bollas, 1995). He developed the idea of the 'unthought known', which describes how something may be known from experience but somehow 'displaced' – not yet brought into consciousness to be reflected on and assimilated.

Transcultural and culture-specific approaches to psychotherapy

Insofar as psychotherapy is interested in understanding and addressing psychological disturbance in clients, it can ignore and be blind to cultural biases. Andrew Samuels has for decades championed the place of the societal, cultural and political in psychotherapy and has written much on the subject, including *The Political Psyche* (Samuels, 1993). He and Judy started an organisation called Psychotherapists and Counsellors for Social Responsibility (PCSR) to highlight these issues. Three types of therapy have grown up to address cultural biases in the UK – feminist, intercultural and pink therapy.

Feminist therapy

It is noticeable that there is a dearth of female theorists in this history, although the great majority of practitioners are women. Humanistic psychotherapy, perhaps most open to feminist explorations and concepts, has far fewer female theorists than psychoanalysis. This is still true today. We saw above, for example, the way that Laura Perls was sidelined.

Feminist therapy integrates theory from social science to psychotherapy. It seeks to help women understand their cultural position within society and empowers women to find their own voice free them from being enthralled to the internalised oppression imbibed through cultural injunctions regarding women's roles and position in the social world. There is no one founder of feminist therapy but Susie Orbach, with her influential book *Fat is a Feminist Issue* (Orbach, 2010, first published 1978), has become widely recognised. She and and Luise Eichenbaum founded the Women's Therapy Centre in 1976 which is still operating to promote women's psychological and social liberation. Jean Baker Miller, who wrote *Towards a New Psychology of Women* (Baker Miller, 1987), was an important figure, as was Juliet Mitchell who sought to reconcile Freudian theory with feminism, explored in *Psychoanalysis and Feminism* in 1974 (Mitchell, 2000, first published 1974).

Intercultural therapy

Intercultural therapy is another type of therapy that has come into being in response to the 'white' cultural bias in western societies and within psychotherapy that affects clients. If there is a dearth of women recognised as important theorists, then that is even more the case when it comes to therapists who are not white. The early psychoanalyst Masud Khan was Pakistani by birth and achieved a significant status in the world of London psychoanalysis. He was a protégé of Freud's daughter, Anna, but was a controversial figure who socialised with patients and students and espoused anti-Semitic leanings.

Jafar Kareem importantly instigated and developed intercultural therapy and started an interest group for intercultural therapy at the UK Council for Psychotherapy. His book *Intercultural Psychotherapy*, which he wrote with Roland Littlewood, was ground breaking (Kareem & Littlewood, 1992). It was under his influence and as part of that group that one of us (Judy) became interested in this area and subsequently researched and wrote about the meaning of whiteness in psychotherapy (Ryde, 2009). Jafar Kareem also started the Nafsiyat Intercultural Therapy Centre, which promotes and provides psychotherapy across cultures and in 20 different languages. Lennox Thomas, Aida Alayarian, the gestalt therapist Faisal Mahmood and the group analyst Fahad Dalal are all-important figures within intercultural psychotherapy in the UK.

Intercultural therapy seeks to ensure that cultural bias does not interfere with the therapy process, to understand and research cultural differences between client and therapist so that they can be addressed in psychotherapy. It also aims to ensure that psychotherapy is open to and provided for those who are predominantly from non-white society.

Pink therapy

Pink therapy was founded by Dominic Davies in the UK to promote the understanding of gay issues in psychotherapy and provide access to therapy for people identifying themselves accordingly. It holds a register of gay and gay-friendly therapists to ensure gay people do not have prejudiced therapists and, in particular, can avoid psychotherapists who seek to 'cure' them of their sexual orientation as seemed implicit in early psychoanalytic literature. The book *Pink Therapy* by Dominic Davies and Charles Neal has been very influential (Davies & Neal, 1996).

Conclusion

In these two chapters, we have provided a brief history of some of the influential theorists and innovators in psychotherapy over the last 150 years. Some of the pre-modern roots were covered in Chapter 3. How these strands of history feed into the relational, systemic and ecological turns in psychotherapy will be the work of the next section. We have therefore intentionally left out from this chapter the great innovators in family and relational systems therapy and the early thinkers in ecological approaches to psychotherapy; they will be covered in later chapters.

Inevitably, we have been very selective and mostly included the writers and psychotherapists who have had an influence on our own thinking and practice. We invite you to think about who else you would include as nurturing the roots of your thinking and practice and how you would describe their contribution to the psychotherapy stream of development.

Part 3

The Three Epistemological Stems or Strands

Introduction

Having looked at the history of psychotherapy in the last two chapters, both pre- and post-1945, in this section we will outline the three main elements that we see as being at the foundation of 21st-century integrative psychotherapy.

Through the history we have seen two important but gradual awakenings in psychotherapy. First, that you cannot separate an individual from the many levels of context that they are part of, and which are part of them. In individual psychotherapy, metaphorically, there are not just two people in the psychotherapy room, for each brings with them their family, communities, cultures and ecology, because these are intertwined into the very fabric of our being and shape the lenses through which we see the world and the language in which we construct our narratives.

Second, that we cannot observe, study or engage with another individual through a quasi-empirical scientific approach, sometimes referred to as the medical model. We only know the other in and through the context in which we meet them, in and through the relationship we co-create with them and in and through our subjective ways of making sense of the encounter.

These awakenings have necessitated psychotherapy to engage with other human sciences in rethinking our epistemologies. We all have an epistemology and make sense of the world through it. It is the basic frame through which we perceive, know and interpret our experience. In some ways our core epistemologies are similar to Piaget's 'schemata' (1955, 1977), Kelly's 'construct grids' (1955:219, 266), and Stolorow and Atwood's 'organising principles' (1996). They are not just how we frame meaning-making, but also the lens through which we perceive.

The three strands we explore are: the intersubjective relational, the systemic and the ecological. As we have shown in the historical overview, and will explore further in the next three chapters, these three epistemologies have their roots in the mid- and late 20th century, but they only started to be incorporated into psychotherapeutic approaches in the late 20th and early 21st century. Intersubjectivity, along with relational and dialogical concepts, was integrated into intersubjective and interpersonal psychodynamic psychotherapy, relational gestalt therapy and a number of other integrative psychotherapy and counselling approaches. Systemic concepts were developed in many disparate fields and first applied in family, couple and community psychotherapy in the second half of the 20th century. Ecological conceptualisations have emerged from the growing awareness of our total interdependency on the more-than-human world, and the ecological crisis that our planet now faces. The introduction of this into psychotherapeutic understanding has been all too slow and carried out by small, often separate, groups in the 1990s and early 21st century. Some early so-called ecological approaches to psychotherapy such as the work by Bronfenbrenner (1979) and Willi (1999) were merely extensions of human-centric systems approaches and not radically embracing the inextricable interconnection and interdependency of the human and more-than-human world.

To date, we are not aware of any substantial work to integrate these three critical epistemologies into a fully integrated approach to psychotherapy, which we believe is essential to address the challenges of our changing times (see Chapter 2). In many ways, these are not separate stems, but perhaps better portrayed as strands. They do not have solid, separate materiality and do not lend themselves easily to measurable quantification. Rather, they are processes of perceiving and knowing that have recognisable and distinctive qualia (qualitative properties of experience). Although these qualia distinguish them from each other and other ways of perceiving and knowing the world, they are also embedded in each other. Any relationship creates a relational living system that develops a life of its own. Any system has recognisable patterns of relating between its various parts, as well as showing repeating ways it engages with, and co-creates, its immediate environment. Every system has its own ecology and is embedded in a larger ecology. This ecology does not just constitute the outside world of the individual but flows through every organism and relationship and system within it.

In exploring each of these strands, we will be elucidating some key principles for integrative psychotherapy that at one level they all share, but which they each look at through different lenses:

- The need to include a broader perspective on what we are seeing, listening to and empathising with in psychotherapy.

- To understand that whatever we are focusing on is interconnected with and interdependent on the wider systems within which it is nested, and the systems that are nested within it.

- To understand that the larger systems we are nested within are simultaneously nested within us.

- To understand that there is a difference between systems thinking that is centred on expanding what we are focusing on, and systemic engagement which is about the consciousness through which we are perceiving whatever we are focusing on – the lenses through which we are looking, and the ways we are making sense of our perceptions.

There is a great deal of confusion about what is meant by the terms 'systems', 'systems thinking' and 'systemic'. This is because systems thinking has emerged from many different and contrasting fields, including mechanical engineering, cybernetics, nuclear physics, biology, theories of holons and holism, networks and so on. Each of these fields tends to use the terminology differently.

We believe it is important for psychotherapy to move to a more systemic way of thinking, perceiving, acting and being, but to do so it is essential to be clear about what we mean by systemic.

The first important distinction we would like to offer is the distinction between the use of the term 'systems' to refer to what we are looking *at*; and using the term 'systemic' to refer to where we are looking *from* and how we are engaging with the world.

In the first dimension – what we are looking at – we can easily recognise that a whole has attributes that do not belong to the sum of parts. If you take apart and disassemble a bicycle or an animal, many of the most crucial functions of the whole are immediately lost.

Second, we can recognise that any system we look at has systems within it and in turn is part of larger systems. Atoms have protons and electrons and a nucleus within them, and in turn are parts within a larger system called a molecule. Teams are made up of individuals, and in turn are part of a function, which is part of an organisation, which is part of a business eco-system, which is part of a sector, which is part of human activity, which is part of the wider ecology. Everything in the universe, as far as we can know, exists within interconnected nested systems.

If we think about this further, we start to realise the next principle, that of interconnection and interdependency:

So long as the smaller systems are enclosed within the larger, and so long as all are connected by complex patterns of interdependency, as we know they are, then whatever affects one system will affect the others. (Berry, 1983:46)

Yet what we normally look at, think about and talk about are separate things. Our very language names things as being separate. We tell our children 'that is a tree', 'that is a leaf', 'that is mistletoe growing out of the tree, but is not part of the tree'. Part of the way our left hemisphere neo-cortex works in order to analyse the world and solve problems is to break things down into their constituent parts, to create boundaries. To make sense of the world we apply the analytic scissors to create cuts in the seamless web of life (Bateson, 1972), but we then forget that it is our own thinking that has created the cuts and the boundaries. We think the cuts and boundaries exist 'out there' in the world.

If we now turn to how we know and make sense of the world, what philosophers describe as our different epistemologies, what we have described above is just one epistemology, one way of knowing. This is 'entity thinking' (Hawkins, 2017a), where we turn the world into separate objects to be studied. This is useful for freezing life, to analyse particles and parts, but not for studying the interconnection of living systems, nor for understanding the reality of flow and co-creation between nested systems.

The second level of epistemology is to see the world intersubjectively (Stolorow, Attwood & Orange, 2002) and as socially constructed (Gergen, 1999, 2001). From this way of knowing, there is a recognition that I only know another through: a) how they show up in relationship to me (not how they are with others when I am not there, or in other settings; and b) through how I make sense of them inside myself.

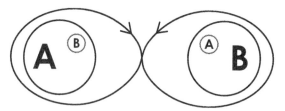

Figure I.1: The dialogical listening flow – each party listening to the other externally and internally

This recognises that we cannot know the other truly objectively, only intersubjectively.

This concept is not new and has been known in more collectivist cultures for many years (Ryde, 2009). It is beautifully expressed in the southern

144

African concept of Ubuntu – 'I am because you are.' Martin Luther King also eloquently echoed this in the context of the Civil Rights Movement in North America in 1964, when he said:

> All I'm saying is simply this: that all life is interrelated, and in a real sense we are all caught in an inescapable network of mutuality, tied in a single garment of destiny. Whatever affects one directly, affects all indirectly. For some strange reason, I can never be what I ought to be until you are what you ought to be. And you can never be what you ought to be until I am what I ought to be. This is the interrelated structure of reality. (Rieder, 2013)

The third level of epistemology is the inter-systemic, which recognises that every system we are studying, we are studying from within our own systemic position. This also has two aspects. First, in one sense we are part of any system we are studying, and inevitably have some effect on that system. From both the early Hawthorne experiments in factories (Landsberger, 1958), and the work of nuclear physicists such as Bohr (1934) and Heisenberg (1958), we have learned that whether we are studying human groups or sub-atomic particles, we are influencing that which we are researching. Second, we bring with us all of our ways of thinking, framing, language and making sense that are part of the systems we are nested within. Not only are we nested within the beliefs and mindsets of our family, community, psychotherapy training, culture and species, but they are nested within us, and form the lenses and filters through which we perceive the world.

The fourth level of systemic perceiving is the eco-system. As we will explore in Chapter 9, 'deep ecology' is not just a matter of widening our gaze to recognise the 'more-than-human world' that is all around us, but also looking from a place that recognises that the ecological is not separate from us. It is the ground of our being: it flows through us, it is in the air we breathe, the food we eat and the elements we are made from. This is the principle of a co-abiding, participatory, holographic universe – a paradigmatic shift in our worldview from 'separateness' to 'inter-being' which fundamentally transforms our sense of place and purpose within the mind of nature. 'Inter-being' was a term created by the Buddhist monk Thich Nhat Hanh (1997) and we use it as a term indicating how the ecology resides in us and we dwell within the wider ecology, and likewise our family and our community reside in us and we reside within our family.

Mind is entwined within matter at every level of inter-being, all particles, all cells, all bodies, all teams, all organisations of nested systems, immersed within deeper systems of inter-being, all sharing the same immersion within the mind of nature and the constant co-evolution of creation (Weber, 2017; Bateson, 1979).

The fifth level of epistemology is 'non-dual', which is the practice of returning our awareness to partake in the indivisible oneness of being, a way of being and perceiving taught by many spiritual teachers from diverse traditions and places throughout the ages. In the current time, there has been an upsurge in both religious and secular non-dual teachers. Non-dual practices can help us to realise that any system we study is a conceptual creation, and to ween our tendency to focus on things and to participate in flow. Elias Amidon (2014) describes non-dual awareness thus:

> 'nonduality' and 'nondual awareness' are names that refer to direct recognition of the clear light of timeless awareness that is the matrix of all apparent existence. This clear light is beyond being; it cannot be known as an object of knowledge or named accurately, though it is ever present. Direct recognition of the clear light does not belong exclusively to any tradition or spiritual view. It is our common inheritance.

By creating a grid of these two dimensions – the level of system we are looking at, and the place of being we are looking from, or epistemology we are looking through, we can clarify what we are referring to when we use the words systems, systems thinking, systemic and systemic being.

	Level of focusing *Epistemology*				
Level of system being focused on	Attempted objective observation	Intersubjective/ Social-construction/ Relational	Inter-systemic	Eco-systemic	Non-dual
Individual					
Interpersonal relationship					
Family, group or team					
Wider organisation or community					
Species					
Gaia (the whole planet system)					

We would use the term 'system' for the divisions we create in the first column and only use the term 'systemic' for the horizontal dimension of ways of perceiving and knowing. Level one is objectifying and therefore non-systemic, and the second level relational and intersubjective and therefore not fully systemic. In the fifth level of the non-dual, all sense of division and separation dissolves and so also, for this level, the systemic and the dynamic between nested systems is irrelevant. Thus, only levels three and four can be seen as truly systemic.

To tentatively part populate the grid merely to illustrate the interconnections, we would offer the following, while recognising the danger of labelling or trying to box in approaches that inevitably transcend these boundaries. Our suggestion is where these approaches are mostly focused and the most dominant epistemological approach they focus through.

	Level of focusing Epistemology				
Level of system being focused on	Attempted objective observation	Intersubjective/ Social-construction/ Relational	Inter-systemic	Eco-systemic	Non-dual
Individual	Medical model traditional behavioural and psychoanalytic psychotherapy	Recognition of the creative counter-transference			
Interpersonal relationship					
Family, group or team	Systems approaches to family therapy	Systemic approaches to family therapy and teams	Intersubjective systems psychotherapy		
Wider organisation or community	Sociodrama. Therapeutic community approaches				
Species	Psychoanalytic anthropology				
Gaia (the whole Earth planet system)					

Our integrative psychotherapy approach is mainly centred in the dark grey shaded areas but is paying attention to the light grey areas that are inevitably part of the field. We have included the non-dual and personally believe that it has much to offer to the necessary shift in human consciousness, but its application to psychotherapy needs another whole book.

As you read the following chapters, we invite you to reflect on your own ways of viewing the world and how these are challenged by these different ways of perceiving and knowing. Rather than wait to read how we apply this to our work in the following part, please pause after each chapter and consider how using this particular frame of reference might change how you would view a particular relationship with a client or with your psychotherapist, and from this new perception, how you might engage differently.

Alternatively, depending on your style of learning, you might like to read Part 4 on practice and then come back to Part 3 to understand the principles that flow through the practice.

CHAPTER 7

The Relational Turn in Psychotherapy

Introduction

Since psychotherapy has been in existence, research has persistently shown that the relationship between psychotherapist and patient/client has been the all-important factor promoting its effectiveness (Lambert & Barley, 2001). Many of the readers of this book will have been, or presently are, patients/clients in psychotherapy of different orientations. You may like to reflect on and consider what have been the most important and changing factors for you in the psychotherapy you have received. There may be many different aspects of the work that were important to you and you felt to be life-changing, or you may recall particular moments which have been most significant and led you to important realisations. Judy remembers, for example, a psychotherapist who she was seeing interrupting something she was saying to point out a fox playing with her cubs just outside the window. They watched this touching scene together for at least five minutes before resuming as if nothing had happened. The warmth and contact of that shared event comes back to Judy as an important moment in their work together.

As human beings, we are social animals. We come into being within relationship, and disturbance in our relationships causes us the greatest distress, particularly disruptions with original caregivers (see Chapter 4's section on attachment), but also with significant others throughout our lives and, indeed, with our psychotherapist. Most people who seek psychotherapy cite a difficult relationship as the reason for coming into therapy, whether it be a disturbance or break-up with a partner, disruptions in relationships with other family members, difficulties with bosses and colleagues or problems with forming satisfactory relationships in the first place. Even issues that are ostensibly not about relationships – such as addictions or depression and anxiety – usually turn out to be rooted in relationship difficulties. It would be hard to imagine a psychotherapy situation in which relationships were not at all relevant.

The outside world enters the psychotherapy space in the form of relationship problems, just as, inevitably, we bring with us our cultural world. Judy once had a client who, after several months of therapy, had not mentioned her small daughter. When Judy realised this, she could see that, far from being unimportant, the space left by this little girl was highly significant. It was also significant that it took months before Judy noticed this absence.

As psychotherapy developed as a discipline, it became clear to people from many schools of psychotherapy that, to be truly human, we need other human beings to relate to us, to know us and thus bring us into the world (Gerhardt, 2015). Although this has been intuitively known for many decades, neuroscience now shows us that our very sense of self is made, and brain pathways marked, through our close contact with others (Gerhardt, 2015; Siegel, 2010). The quality of these early attachment patterns of relating have a great effect on us and, where our original caregivers were unable to attune to us, or where our environment was marked by traumatising events or interactions, this can have a very damaging effect, leaving us with grave difficulties throughout our lives (see the section on attachment patterns in Chapter 4).

The transference relationship is an important aspect of the inter-relationship between client and psychotherapist for considering how the client's relational world enters the psychotherapy room. Although (classical) psychoanalysts originally thought of transference as giving clues to the internal world and original relationships with the client's caregivers, it also helps the psychotherapist to see how the client relates to important others in their present life. Malan usefully saw this, and called it the Triangle of Conflict (Malan, 2007, first published 1995). It shows how the relationships with the therapist ('in here'), parents ('back then') and present persons ('out there') are connected with 'in here'.

Therapist ('in here')

Present persons ('out there')   Past persons ('back then')

Figure 7.1: The Triangle of Conflict (from Malan, 1995)

When any one of these are spoken of, then all three are invoked. As integrative psychotherapists, we do not privilege any one of these three positions, but see all as important, so that focusing on one or another is equally valid and productive. Even more central is focusing on the patterns that show up along the three sides of the triangle, to discover the relational organising principles of the client that underpin their ways of engaging with others.

For integrative psychotherapy, as with many other psychotherapies, the relationship between psychotherapist and client is fundamental to the work (Erskine, 2015; Finlay, 2016; Gilbert & Orlans, 2011). Although Freud did not value the relationship with the psychotherapist as an important therapeutic factor, this has been reconsidered in more recent years. Gerhardt, the psycho-analytic psychotherapist who brought information from neuroscience to bear on child rearing and psychotherapeutic practices, said that Freud had:

> inadvertently stumbled upon the most potent formula for change [because] talking to others, forming a relationship with someone who listens to how you feel, is the major element in unblocking the emotional plumbing and in formulating new, more effective emotional strategies. (Gerhardt, 2015:226)

Within psychoanalysis there has been an ambivalence about how far the 'real' relationship (as opposed to the transference relationship) with the psychotherapist is important to the efficacy of the work and how far the relationship is only useful as a tool for understanding the client's life. Regarding the 'real' relationship as important may be considered as straying too far from Freud's thought for it to be readily taken up. However, since Winnicott's explorations, the implications for the relationship between client and therapist have become increasingly clear. The realisation that being understood by your therapist is all-important for the patient and most likely to facilitate a good outcome for therapy has gathered pace. Now many psychoanalytic psychotherapists regard themselves as 'relational' in their approach, which has generated something of a paradigm shift in the field. Jean Baker Miller proposed that feminism necessitated a more relational approach in her co-written, ground-breaking book, *Toward a New Psychology of Women* (Baker Miller, 1987), while Robert Hobson first developed the 'Conversational Model' of psychotherapy (Hobson, 1985). Others who developed a more relational approach to psychotherapy include Karen Maroda (2004), Stephen Mitchell (2000) and the 'intersubjective systems theorists' including Robert Stolorow and George Atwood (Stolorow & Atwood, 1992, 2014); Atwood and Stolorow (1993) and Donna Orange (1997) whose work we discuss below.

Humanistic psychotherapy has not always regarded the therapeutic relationship as central, though Carl Rogers, discussed in various chapters in this book, did regard the core conditions for therapy to be the ability of the therapist to relate to the client with authenticity, empathy and unconditional positive regard (Rogers, 1990). There has been a relational shift in gestalt thinking as well, which puts the intersubjective relationship at the centre of the work and understands this to be the healing factor for the client (Hycner & Jacobs, 1995).

Petruska Clarkson (1995) devised a model which showed five aspect of the therapeutic relationship. Peter was in dialogue with her in developing this model. These aspects are:

- The working alliance.

- The transference/countertransference relationship.

- The reparative.

- The person-to-person or I/thou relationship.

- The transpersonal.

We have re-worked this model and developed it further and now propose nine aspects of the therapeutic relationship that, we believe, are essential to the relational strand of integrative psychotherapy and – taken together – constitute the richness of the psychotherapeutic encounter and enable it to unfold. Having named these components of the therapeutic encounter we will explore each of them in more detail.

1. *A joint endeavour.* Psychotherapy is a joint endeavour in which the client, the psychotherapist, their relationship and the client's life world are all involved.

2. *The relationship as a container.* The relationship between the therapist and client sets the frame for psychotherapeutic work. The relationship is the container in which relating occurs.

3. *Meeting as whole persons.* In the psychotherapy relationship, both parties meet as whole persons. This comes before having two people with different roles – the psychotherapist in their role and the client bringing a collection of symptoms, problems or issues. From this foundational meeting of whole persons, psychotherapists feel their way into the client's field of experiencing.

4. *The creative countertransference.* The psychotherapist knows the client through the creative countertransference: the therapist's subjective responses and reactions to the client.

5. *Understanding the world from the client's perspective.* Psychotherapists need to try and understand the world from the client's perspective. They attempt to see, hear and feel their world as the client senses it.

6. *Knowing the other through relating as persons.* Psychotherapists know the other through their relating as persons.

7. *Finding a co-created feeling language.* In forming a relationship, the psychotherapist and client pay attention to language and take time to co-create a joint, unique feeling language, through which they can meet at depth and co-create new meaning.

8. *Collaborative inquiry through generative dialogue.* Psychotherapy is a collaborative inquiry in which the dialogue uncovers and creates meaning.

9. *The healing relationship.* The psychotherapeutic relationship is healing in and of itself. While creating a safe enough environment, it is, at the same time, a place for experimentation. It aims to be reparative, restorative and healing by unfolding and extending the client's potential.

1 A joint endeavour

It might be thought that psychotherapy is an endeavour carried out by the psychotherapist with the client being the customer or object of the activity. Our contention is that it is a joint endeavour in which the client, the psychotherapist, their relationship and the client's life are all involved.

Clients may, for instance, think of the psychotherapy as 'my therapy', one which they attempt to use to help them improve their lives. The psychotherapist may think of the therapy as something they are doing *for* the client. They may think of themselves as using their professional expertise to further the well-being of the client. Or they may protest that the therapeutic endeavour is neither of these but arises in the relationship between them. Or the process may be thought of as improving the life-space of the client. Our contention is that the psychotherapy encompasses all four places – the client, the psychotherapist, their relationship and the client's life – and the process of the psychotherapy is an inquiry embedded in all four.

The life-worlds of both client and psychotherapist inevitably enter the therapeutic space as we carry our lived experience with us in the form of our 'organising principles' (Stolorow & Atwood, 1992). The life-space includes not only our family, community and working life, but also the systemic cultural and inherited space they sit within (as we will explore in Chapter 8). We also include the relationships of human beings to their ecology (which we will explore in Chapter 9). All four aspects are involved in this endeavour in an intricate dance of interdependent relating. The 'organising principles' of all are connected in one web of mutual influence. All four will be affected and changed through successful psychotherapy.

2 The relationship as a container

If these significant relationships are to be explored in depth, it will be made possible through the 'container' of the psychotherapy in which it occurs. Without a safe container the kinds of reflecting we do together would become unmanageable (Gray, 2014). The relationship container needs to be built on a good working alliance, which creates the room for fighting, laughing, crying, silence and all manner of other feelings and actions. So, what is this container? It is a working alliance formed by the reliability and regularity of the time allotted, the appointment time, the place where the therapy occurs, the rituals of meeting at the door and settling down to the work and negotiating the financial payment which provides a mutuality of energy exchanged. Although many of the practicalities are set unilaterally by the psychotherapist, they are freely agreed by clients who would not undertake the work if these did not suit them.

Other aspects of the frame, such as how the two participants greet each other or say goodbye, happen within the context of the relationship. For instance, I (Judy) have two clients who are refugees. One (Rachel) enters the room without looking at me. She crosses the space without speaking and arranges her bags on the floor around her, gets out her water bottle, settles into the chair and then looks at me. I sit still while this happens, often looking down at my hands. The other one (Gajanan) greets me from the door, I rise from my chair, greeting him too, and we both sit down together. When it is time to leave, Rachel gathers up her things without looking at me and silently leaves. I do not stand. At the end of his session, Gajanan thanks me for my help, we both stand, and he leaves, looking back at me to say goodbye as he opens the door. Both these clients have become comfortable with silence and they are usually the ones to break it.

All these small co-created rituals and common understandings about how the work is framed help psychotherapists and clients to stay steady in the work. They help the psychotherapists not to be overwhelmed or resentful of the energy they need to generate for this feeling work. It helps the client to *feel into* themselves and share what emerges, and therefore becomes possible, with their psychotherapist. The client knows that the psychotherapist can carry on with the work because the frame is safe and secure (Gray, 2014). The client learns that it is so because it is consistent over time and the therapist is there to come back to, week after week, not wiped out by the feelings that have been 'shared'.

3 Meeting as whole persons

For integrative psychotherapists, as well as those of most other approaches, it is important to relate to patients/clients as whole people and not just the issues that they bring to the consulting room. Most often, clients will approach us with an issue that they want help with. It is important to take this seriously as this is what has alerted them to their need for this special kind of help. Their symptoms, problems and issues are part of the field of our relating and nothing therefore is irrelevant. These may be the first things we need to hear from our clients and attend to at depth. Our clients would soon leave if we had an attitude of not being interested in why they sought us out.

However, we are not *just* a 'role', and our clients have come to us because we are psychotherapists. They have sought us out as professionals to help them and that is why they have come to see us, rather than a friend. A client would soon leave if she told us, for example, that she had been estranged from her daughter for several years and we said something like, 'Well, how awful! I had something similar myself a few years back and I have a friend whose daughter refused to speak to her for months. There is a lot of it about these days.' This would be a response that a friend might make, not a psychotherapist, and it would not help to resolve the issue for the client. The psychotherapist would start by showing, not just telling, the client that they know how painful that must be and then ask her to tell them more about it. At the same time, the psychotherapist would not expect that this is all that is important about the client and all that she needs to bring to them.

It would be likely that the presenting issue of the client, being estranged from her daughter, would be resolved in the next few weeks or months, either by the two starting to speak to each other or by the client letting go of her need for her daughter to contact her. In the course of the sessions, she would begin to open up to the psychotherapist, and they would develop a 'feeling language' (Hobson, 1985) (see below) to find a way to be together so that she could reveal herself in her world within the container of the relationship (see Chapter 10).

4 The creative countertransference

The psychotherapist is also helped to provide consistency by reflecting on, rather than reacting to, the feelings and spontaneous ideas that arise in them in response to the client. These responses are usually known as the countertransference. The countertransference, as first noticed by Freud, was seen as something to be avoided (Stefana, 2017). We all are children of our time and he was no exception. He was influenced by the latest ideas in science and medicine and was concerned to show that psychoanalysis was an objective, empirical scientific discipline and not, therefore, influenced (or distorted) by the relationship between analyst and patient. While later analysts thought that the countertransference aspect of the transference relationship was a useful tool (Heimann, 1950) in understanding the unconscious of their patient, Freud regarded it as obstructing the analysis. He thought it showed a lack in the analyst and that they had not been fully 'analysed'. The transference relationship refers to the way that a patient will 'transfer' feelings that were engendered in early childhood and often later authority figures on to the analyst. For Freud, it was important that students of psychoanalysis were analysed themselves so that they would be free of their own neuroses and able to see their clients clearly, unaffected by a countertransference – the reactive feelings that flow from the analyst to the patient. He saw that the unanalysed or a poorly analysed analyst might unconsciously project their own wishes on to patients, thus encouraging patients to compliantly meet them rather than resolve their own conflictual and neurotic patterns.

Paula Heimann (1950) was the first psychoanalyst to suggest that counter-transference could be used creatively as a tool to understand the transference relationship and the unconscious of the patient. By understanding your own responses and reactions as analysts, you could gain important insights into the patient's process. Analysts were then at pains to distinguish between the neurotic countertransference that arose out of the unconscious needs of the analyst and the 'diagnostic' countertransference that helped the analyst to understand the patient (Holmes, 2014).

For today's integrative psychotherapist, noticing how our responses to the client create reactions that distort and derail the therapeutic work is a useful way of understanding our client. Exploring this in order to find a way of responding rather than reacting unthinkingly is an important part of supervision, as is demonstrated in modes 4, 5 and 6 of Hawkins's Seven-Eyed Model (Hawkins & Shohet, 2012) (see Chapter 11).

If we again take the example of the client whose daughter is estranged from her, the psychotherapist may have an unhelpful response, because she has a similar situation with one of her own children. She might therefore see her own situation as being the same as the client's (rather than the situations having similar aspects). The psychotherapist's painful feelings will be brought to the surface and may lead to her wanting to soothe the pain of the client quickly rather than explore the difficulty. This could lead to various unhelpful reactions. For instance, it could lead to her wanting to push her own solutions; or to steer her away from this issue as it is too painful; or see it as more intractable than it is; or be too envious of the client to allow any progress. Alternatively, she may catch her countertransference reactions and reflect on them in supervision and in her own thoughts. By these means she could understand the way the client is unconsciously trying to push her to collude with her own hurt feelings. She might, for example, see that the client wishes her to think that all children are inevitably 'bad', selfish and neglectful. Using the creative countertransference, the psychotherapist can begin to better understand and respond to the client, rather than unhelpfully collude (Casement, 1985).

5 Understanding the world from the client's perspective

To carry on with the example above, the integrative psychotherapist will feel their way into the client's world, using all their available senses to be present for the client. In entering this world, the psychotherapist will lean into the world of the other as it is presented and emerges in their mutual relating, without expecting it to be just like their own experience. In this way, the psychotherapist learns of the 'organising principles' (Stolorow & Atwood, 1992) that structure the client's perceptions and the client-in-her-world as well as gradually clarifying the 'organising principles' of the psychotherapist–client relationship. We now know from neuroscience that the brain has 'mirror neurons' which respond when we are with others and give us a real felt sense of their feelings and emotions (Gerhardt, 2015; Van der Kolk, 2015). If the client has been estranged from her daughter, how does the client–daughter field of relating feel; what is the colour, shape, rhythm, timbre, pitch of their relating? How does this impact on, or get played out in, the therapeutic relating? This deep contact with the client's felt sense will provide a platform for exploring together the world of their relationship and enable them to come to fresh understandings.

6 Knowing the other through relating as persons

It is because of the deepening relationship between client and psychotherapist that we can come to know our client at existential depth. Our knowing of the other is not just the circumstances of their exterior life, though we come to know that too, but the felt reality of what it is to be this other person. This knowing arises in the context of the psychotherapist's own field of experience. Our knowing of the other person is rooted in the context of sharing the psychotherapy's orbit. We know the intersubjective togetherness of us. We cannot know someone separately from our own knowing and experience. We are not separate selves but intersubjectively configured (Stolorow & Atwood, 2014). To carry on with the example above, the client's estrangement from her daughter is different when within the psychotherapist's field of knowing than, say, that of her husband. In either case, it is a meeting of two sets of organising principles that allow new sense to be made of the world. The meeting configures new organising principles which become joint ones where client and psychotherapist meet.

The intersubjective systems theorists (Orange, Atwood & Stolorow, 1997; Stolorow & Atwood, 2014) are particularly important in helping us to understand this within the psychotherapy relationship. They point to a difference between themselves and other psychoanalytic theorists who use the term 'intersubjective' (Stern, 1985), as they do not regard such close interdependence simply as a developmental stage, one that is reached when there is sufficient maturity to know that it is possible for others to understand and relate to our subjective experience. Rather, they regard intersubjectivity as an ontological state, a universal 'given'. They do not regard human beings as having 'separate minds' but as being part of each other in an indivisible universe. They explain it in this way:

> The assumptions of traditional psychoanalysis have been pervaded by the Cartesian doctrine of the isolated mind. This doctrine bifurcates the subjective world of the person into outer and inner regions, reifies and absolutizes the resulting separation between the two, and pictures the mind as an objective entity that takes its place among other objects, a 'thinking

thing', that has an inside with contents and looks out on an external world from which it is essentially estranged. (Stolorow, Atwood & Orange, 2002:1)

Given this reality, they regard the 'self' as something that is found anew within our relating. The 'me' that relates to my sister is different from the one that relates to my boss. They assert that our 'organising principles', which are built up through many and different relational/intersubjective experiences, interact with the 'organising principles' of others, thus making fresh configurations at each meeting. It is within this context that they say the therapeutic relationship happens 'in the space between analyst and patient' (Stolorow, Atwood & Brandchaft, 1994:52).

An important concept here is the intersubjectivists' particular understanding of the unconscious. They describe three kinds of unconscious: the dynamic, the unvalidated and the pre-reflective (Stolorow & Atwood, 1992). The *dynamic unconscious* consists of the 'experiences that were denied articulation because they were perceived to threaten needed ties' (Stolorow & Atwood, 1992:33). In other words, these are experiences which may seem to threaten our bonds with others – particularly primary caregivers on whom our very existence, both physical and emotional, relies. This is more like the Freudian unconscious in that it consists of that which we as individuals cannot accept, such as hateful and destructive feelings and impulses that we would rather deny.

The *unvalidated unconscious* consists of the 'experiences that could not be articulated because they were never made conscious through the requisite validating responsiveness from the surround' (Stolorow & Atwood, 1992:33). Stolorow and Atwood say that our potential is present at birth but needs what they call 'validating responsiveness' to come fully into being. This idea is quite common in psychotherapy theorising. Winnicott, for instance, suggests that we are born with potential that is only brought out by a 'facilitating environment' (Winnicott, 1965:300, 1971:105). We are therefore unconscious of what we have never had confirmed or reflected back to us by others, but might still come to know it, if we are given more conducive circumstances.

The *pre-reflective unconscious* is a particular contribution these theorists have made to our understanding of the unconscious. They do not describe 'things' of which we are unconscious, but this level of being involves the 'organising principles' that unconsciously 'shape and thematize a person's experience' (Stolorow & Atwood, 1992:33). These principles are soaked up naturally from our cultural milieu as we grow up, particularly from caregivers, but carry on being co-created within our systemic and ecological environment throughout our lives. This means that the organising principles, and therefore the pre-reflective unconscious, of both client and psychotherapist will change and reconfigure within the psychotherapy relationship and the experiences both are party to. While this is true of all our life's experiences and relationships, the therapeutic relationship gives an opportunity to reflect on this and make the process more conscious. Gradually, we are less at the mercy of our early organising principles. We can recognise our own organising patterns as they arise in the relationship and let go of our attachment to them.

In this way, the intersubjective systems theorists help us more fully to understand how we come into being through our relationships.

7 Finding a co-created feeling language

One of the first people to recognise the importance of this aspect of relationship in psychotherapy was the psychiatrist, Robert Hobson. He did not belong to any particular school of psychotherapy but studied Jung in his early working life. His writing could easily be claimed by psychoanalytic and humanistic psychotherapists, but he developed his own model – Hobson's Conversational Model. In his ground-breaking book, *Forms of Feeling* (Hobson, 1985), he laid out his model and gave many examples from his work. He was a big influence on both of us early in our career, through his book and his teaching in person.

Hobson thought that it was important for patient and therapist to find a 'feeling language' together – one that arose out of their relationship. What arose therefore did not 'belong' to either. This 'feeling language' would help them to communicate in a conversation which could seem to be inconsequential but led to a deep contact between the two. It is clear from his work that the sensitive and careful attention paid to his patient and their everyday language is the healing factor. His ability to hear his patients in specific detail through their communications with him prefigures much of the work that comes after him, particularly the intersubjectivists, although he is not much recognised for this. He was one of the first, if not the first, to emphasise that the therapy happens in the 'space between' the psychotherapist and patient. For instance:

> A feeling-language is constantly created, modified and endowed with value, within a unique developing relationship. It involves processes which we habitually separate as 'thinking', 'emotion' and 'action'. Such watertight

compartments are inappropriate to an experience which is apprehended as a 'whole'; an experience that is created in the space between persons. (Hobson, 1985:7)

He regarded the *how* of what was said as much more important than the *what*, so that the importance in seemingly trivial conversations could be understood. He gives an example of talking about cricket to a new patient and points out that this is not merely about forming a rapport but about discovering a mutuality and feeling language with which painful and significant communications can be made. He points out that, in a conversation, we are constantly modifying what we say in the light of the other person's non-verbal response, so we are not talking *at* or *to* them but with them.

It is interesting that Hobson uses the term 'conversation' rather than 'dialogue'. It has a less technical feel than the word 'dialogue'. Hobson knowingly uses this term as he regards the minutiae of everyday talking to contain what needs to be communicated and, by finding a feeling language together, real intimacy can be found, and healing or resolution of the patient's difficulties made possible.

Hobson was writing and developing his ideas somewhat before the American intersubjective systems theorists but their books were published around the same time (*Forms of Feeling* 1985, *Contexts of Being* 1984) and with no obvious connections made between the two, although their ideas were very similar. Hobson did not use the term 'intersubjective' and was not apparently influenced by existential phenomenology, as were the intersubjective systems theorists, but came to very similar conclusions. Intersubjective systems theorists such as Robert Stolorow, George Atwood, Bernard Brandchaft and Donna Orange (Stolorow *et al.*, 2002) regarded the therapeutic relationship as all-important and as arising *between* the two participants. It is quite possible that neither knew of the other's work – they did not refer to each other – but we are sure that Hobson would have agreed with intersubjective systems theorists when they asserted that the nature of reality was intersubjectively configured, that we are all interconnected within a contextual intersubjective field. Hobson's writing is more explicitly placed within the frame of reference of the actual conversations he had with his patients. His writing is less couched in philosophical terms and feels warmer, more available and experience-near. Although he was writing at the same time (mid-1980s), he was older than the intersubjective systems theorists and his one book came out of a great many years of experience. He was born in 1920 and died in 1999, whereas intersubjective systems theorists are about 20 years younger and are still working.

Hobson was determinedly not constrained by any particular 'school' of psychotherapy. Maybe this was facilitated by being a psychiatrist by basic training and able to use influences from many sources. His obituary in *The Independent* in August 2018 says he named his influences as: 'Wordsworth, Coleridge, Jung, Rogers, Popper, Harry Stack Sullivan's interpersonal psychiatry, Aubrey Lewis's rigorously scientific psychiatry, his fellow-stammerer, Nye Bevan, and the American learning theorists' (Shapiro, 2018).

From the perspective of integrative psychotherapy, it is interesting to note that theorists do not have to know of each other to come up with similar ideas, though they usually do so around the same time. No doubt this is because their approach to theory arises out of the zeitgeist and the contextual field in which they write.

Another approach, which is similar to intersubjective systems theory, is dialogic gestalt theory. In fact, some psychotherapists are part of both schools (Hycner & Jacobs, 1995). The intersubjective perspective opens naturally from gestalt psychotherapy because of its espousal of field theory (Lewin, 1935, 1952:42). Clarkson and Mackewn describe the 'field' as: 'all the coexisting, mutually interdependent factors of a person and his environment... All aspects of the person and of his field are interrelated, thus forming a whole or a system' (Clarkson & Mackewn, 1993:42) and Yontef says:

> The field is a whole in which the parts are in immediate relationship and responsive to each other and no part is uninfluenced by what goes on elsewhere in the field. The field replaces the notion of discrete, isolated particles. The person in his or her life space constitutes a field. (Yontef, 1993:125)

Parlett adds that:

> The essence of field theory is that a holistic perspective towards the person extends to include the environment, the social world, organizations, culture. The more assiduously we can navigate the various field theory maps, the more we are likely to perceive and recognize the indivisibility of people from their surroundings and life situations. (Parlett, 1991:74)

Dialogic gestalt therapists, such as Hycner and Jacobs, built on field theory and the philosophy of Martin Buber (2004). Richard Hycner writes: 'At the heart of this approach is the belief that the ultimate basis of our existence is relational or dialogic in nature: we are all threads in an interhuman fabric' (Hycner & Jacobs, 1995:6).

As we have shown above, it seems that both intersubjectivists and dialogic gestalt psychotherapists see the self as existing within relationships and that their work is concerned with understanding whatever arises in that meeting. This understanding is not merely an intellectual exercise but is how we come to an ever-deeper awareness of the subjective experience of the other.

8 Collaborative inquiry through generative dialogue

Collaborative inquiry is a term used for a form of qualitative research but can also be used for psychotherapy. A collaborative inquiry needs two equal members both exploring and investigating the complex field they find themselves in. In psychotherapy, the two are equal in their humanity but different in role. The psychotherapist is being paid and has been trained at length to undertake this work. The client has come for help and it is their experience that is being explored. But in another sense, they are equal partners in the endeavour and exploration and the experience of both is equally valid.

The term 'dialogue' is used to describe a special conversation – one in which the exploration and mutual understanding is more important than the outcome or who is 'right'. What is more, when in a dialogue, we lose our attachment to *needing* to be right. Out of this special way of relating, new meaning can arise. It both uncovers and co-creates new meaning. This is different from a discussion (which is related to the words 'percussion' and 'concussion'!) or debate or negotiation, where two opposite points of view are battled out and one 'wins', or there is a compromise (Bohm, 1996; Buber, 2004). Collaborative inquiry, both as a research methodology and as a means of joint exploration, uses dialogue in the course of its research, undertaken in the spirit of equality and open inquiry (Reason & Bradbury, 2001).

Integrative psychotherapy is a form of collaborative inquiry that both 'uncovers' and 'co-creates' new meaning. To understand how this happens, it is useful to understand the difference between our 'experiencing self' and our 'narrative self' (Kahneman, 2012) (see Chapter 3). The 'experiencing self' is constantly in the present moment and alive to our present experiences through our senses. The 'narrative self' creates an ongoing 'story' of our lives. Each self is created using different parts of the brain (Siegel, 2010). So, when we say that 'meaning' is uncovered, we are referring to the emergent meaning in our experiencing self that, through the psychotherapy, becomes more conscious in the newly emerging 'narrative self'.

To say the dialogue uncovers meaning implies that meaning is already there to be found. This could be a meaning that is readily available to the psychotherapist and client. For instance, in the case of the client who was estranged from her daughter, it could be important to know that the client held long and deep belief that families should be 'present' for each other. The psychotherapist would need to reflect on whether or not she shared this belief. She would not need to give voice to this, but it would be necessary to know it, in order to understand her own responses.

Besides this conscious, but possibly unexpressed, belief, the psychotherapy might uncover more unconscious ideas about how families should behave. In this case, the client might unconsciously think that her daughter is in mortal danger if she is outside her sphere of protection. It may be that the client's daughter had a dangerous accident when playing at a friend's house or that the client herself had been in a dangerous situation when *her* mother was not paying attention. This could be an 'unthought known' (Bollas, 1987), which is an emotionally embodied experience, but not yet incorporated into the client's narrative self. If this is uncovered in the psychotherapy, it can be thought about and the roots of it discovered, leading to a fresh understanding, and a new development in the narrative self arises.

In the course of the psychotherapy, new meanings will be co-created, thus forming new, and maybe more generative, stories in the client's narrative self. For instance, a new meaning could arise that mothering can include giving space to our children to discover life for themselves, that letting go of our children is part of our parenting of them. These newly discovered meanings may help the client to move on with her life without undue anxiety or resentment about her daughter. This may or may not allow her child to resume her relationship with her mother. The client may need to mourn the loss of her child while being unattached to the idea of her returning.

9 The healing relationship

The psychotherapeutic relationship is not just a means to get to know a client and vice versa; it is, in itself, healing. We know from neuroscience, as well as intuitively, that we are formed through relating. Babies have been described (Winnicott, 1964) as being full of potential that is not yet actualised, so that, given the right conditions, they will realise their full promise. This is a nice description but it needs adding to. The constant back and forth of relating is what our sense of self is actually made of. We come into being within relationship, both literally through how relating shapes the way neural connections in the brain are formed – and metaphorically. To understand these processes is of course very important to generate the hope that healing will occur in the psychotherapeutic relationship, particularly for those whose quality of parenting has been poor, leading to insufficient or destructive relationships. Casement (1985:82) writes of the 'unconscious hope' of patients who demonstrate, through their behaviour, what has been lacking in their experience of being parented, in the unconscious hope that their psychotherapist might pick this up and provide what is needed.

This need for healing is, to some extent, true of us all. None of us is without difficulty. This coming-into-being through relating does not stop when we leave infancy. All our relationships help to form us, but a therapeutic relationship may be particularly important in healing past damage, as it is focused on the needs of the individual within their context. Psychotherapy can both repair aspects damaged by destructive relating and bring into life potential aspects as yet undiscovered. Maslow (1972) and Rogers (1961) thought of these as 'potentialities' and Stolorow and Atwood (1992:33) regard them as belonging to the 'unvalidated unconscious' as it refers to aspects of being that have never been validated. These were not brought into being in the relationship with caregivers, as we saw above. Psychotherapy can provide another chance of awakening, reflecting on and validating those dormant aspects of the self.

In the case of the client who was estranged from her daughter, she may have had a cold and distant relationship with her own mother, for example, and this led her to look to her daughter for warmth and intimacy, which the daughter fought against and felt suffocated by. The therapeutic relationship may not only explore these things, but provide some of the closeness, warmth and understanding that were not available to her as a child. This might free her in relation to her daughter. The freeing up of that nexus of relating could allow the daughter to come back in or, if she does not, frees the mother to accept this and to carry on with her life.

Conclusion

The co-created and complex relationship between psychotherapist and client is constantly forming and re-forming during the therapy as new meanings, memories and life events enter the therapeutic space. We cannot be continually aware of all of these aspects simultaneously, but our own reflections in and around the work and the reflecting we do in supervision allow the possibility of gradually taking them all into account. We may even discover new forms of relating to add to those we described. These help us to structure our thinking and navigate our way through what are sometimes the choppy waters of relating in open and undefended ways.

The intersubjective relationship, one that arises in the space between psychotherapist and client, allows for phenomena that arise within the space to be seen and taken into account. It means that the dichotomy of whether something 'belongs' to the psychotherapist or the client is not an issue; it belongs in the relationship, the co-created space between them.

In the next chapter, this thinking is pushed further so that the psychotherapy is understood, not just intersubjectively, but also systemically.

CHAPTER 8

The Systemic Turns

To draw a boundary line between a part which does most of the computation for a larger system, and the larger system of which it is a part is to create a mythological component, commonly called a 'self'. In my epistemology, the concept of self, along with all arbitrary boundaries which delimit systems or parts of systems, is to be regarded as a trait of the local culture – not indeed to be disregarded, since such little epistemological monsters are always liable to become foci of pathology. The arbitrary boundaries which were useful in the process of analyzing the data become all too easily battlefronts, across which we try to kill an enemy or exploit an environment.

Bateson, 1992:202

Introduction

In the last chapter, we explored how we can only know another partially and intersubjectively. We know them through how we recognise them inside us and feel their feelings through empathic resonance and mirror neurons. In this chapter, we will go beyond the relational turn in psychotherapy to explore the second stem or strand in our trilogy, the systemic turn. As Bateson points out in the quote above, the brain and the individual are inseparable, or as Dan Siegel (2010) so neatly puts it, the mind is embodied. Siegel also goes on to say the mind is embedded, in our relationships, with our family, friends, communities, social groupings and our culture. The individual belongs to these wider systems, but they also flow through the individual.

In this chapter, we will explore five paradigm shifts in understanding psychotherapy.

1. *From parts to wholes.* This built on the work of many 19th-century scientists in quantum physics, biology, and chemistry, which led to the development of 'general systems theory' (Bertalanffy, 1968). It recognised that 'whole systems' were more than the sum of their parts and encouraged a move away from studying mental health symptoms towards an understanding of the person as a whole, their thinking, feelings, patterns of behaviour and interactions. In leading-edge psychotherapy, immediately after the Second World War, this systems view was combined with a growing interest in 'holism' and the existential and phenomenological focus on the whole person.

2. *Your mental health is not your own.* This recognised that you can only understand an individual person within their social and cultural context. We will explore how the experience of working with the mental breakdown of many soldiers in the Second World War, the beginnings of social psychiatry and the growth of group and family therapy lay at the root of this second systemic turn, where mental illness and mental health were seen as dynamically co-created between the individual and their familial, social, community and organisational contexts. Many therapists, having embraced this second systemic shift, turned their focus from treating individuals separately to working with group therapy, or treating the family system, or focusing on the health of the hospital community. If the first systemic shift recognised the person as a complex system that could not be reduced to its parts, the second systemic shift recognised that the individual could only be understood in their ongoing interactions and exchanges with their social contexts.

3. *You are part of many systems and they are part of you.* This recognised that none of us are just part of one system. We belong to many systems – our original and current family, our local community, the organisations we work for, the church, social organisations, sports clubs, our culture and so on. It also showed how these many complex systems permeate and form us, as much as, if not more than, we permeate and form them (Finlay, 2016).

4. *You are part of, and affect, every system with which you interact.* This recognised that any therapeutic work with an individual creates a new systemic context. The therapist is part of the therapeutic system and has to be aware of themselves, the context and the relationship between them and the client, as these are all aspects that are co-creating what emerges (see Chapter 7).

5. *Embracing the systemic dance across the nested systems.* The fifth systemic turn recognised that every system we are nested within is itself nested within a larger system, which itself is nested within an even greater system. As Wendell Berry, the great American farmer philosopher, beautifully showed, we all live within 'a system of nested systems: the individual human within the family within the community within agriculture within nature' (Berry, 1983:46). This brought with it the realisation that what had been learned about the systemic co-creation between the individual and the group; the individual and their family; the individual and the kaleidoscope of systems they inhabit; and the individual and their therapist, could also apply at the systemic interfaces, right up and down the many levels of nested systems. This fifth systemic turn brings the focus on the systemic dance that echoes across all the levels of nested systems and the systemic interfaces.

Systemic turn 1: From parts to wholes

'Holism' comes from the Greek word *holos*, which means 'all', or the 'whole' and has been applied to understanding humans, with the perspective that human behaviour should be viewed as a whole integrated experience, and not as separate parts. The movement emerged as a reaction to the reductionist approach in science, which worked on the principle that you could understand something by reducing it to its constituent parts and then look for simple principles of linear causality. The empirical reductionist adopts Occam's Razor (Gauch, 2003) to discover the constituent parts and the simplest causal explanation based on the belief that the simple is the source of the complex. For the holist 'the whole is more than the sum of the parts' and the whole cannot be understood by reducing it to its constituent elements.

Some of the earliest thinking in this area came from evolutionary biology, which understands whole organisms, not by studying their parts but by their patterns of connection, and the way they integrate and develop. In the late 1920s, Bertalanffy wrote:

> Since the fundamental character of the living thing is its organization, the customary investigation of the single parts and processes cannot provide a complete explanation of the vital phenomena. This investigation gives us no information about the coordination of parts and processes. Thus the chief task of biology must be to discover the laws of biological systems (at all levels of organization). We believe that the attempts to find a foundation

169

for theoretical biology point at a fundamental change in the world picture. This view, considered as a method of investigation, we shall call 'organismic biology' and, as an attempt at an explanation, 'the system theory of the organism'. (Bertalanffy, 1972:411)

Organismic biology created a shift in biological thinking but became even more impactful as it developed into general systems theory. Later, Bertalanffy wrote:

If the term 'organism' in the above statements is replaced by other 'organised entities', such as social groups, personality, or technological devices, this is the program of systems theory. The Aristotelian dictum of the whole being more than its parts, which was neglected by the mechanistic conception, on the one hand, and which led to a vitalistic demonology, on the other, has a simple and even trivial, answer – trivial, that is, in principle, but posing innumerable problems in its elaboration. The properties and modes of action of higher levels are not explicable by the summation of the properties and modes of action of their components taken in isolation. If, however, we know the ensemble of the components and the relations existing between them, then the higher levels are deliverable from the components. (Bertalanffy, 1972:411)

This idea was taken up by the psychoanalyst and psychiatrist Foulkes (1948), who revealed how the healthy organism functions as a whole and can be described as a system in dynamic equilibrium. He saw this whole organism as constantly adjusting to its context, or 'total situation', not just passively, but with creativity (Foulkes, 1948). He would later go on to apply this thinking beyond the individual to the systemic life of groups (see below).

Another great early thinker in holism was Jan Smuts, a lawyer, biologist, Field Marshal, President of South Africa and the only man to be party to the peace treaties that ended the Anglo-Boer War, the First World War and the Second World War. He was a man of action as well as a deep thinker on the essence of life and evolution. His book, *Holism and Evolution* (Smuts, 1926), set out to provide a new foundational concept for our understanding of the world, and to show that life and mind 'are in their own right true operative factors and play a real and unmistakable part in determining both the advance (of mind and life) and its specific direction' (1926:15). He wrote to oppose scientific materialists who he saw attempting 'to reduce life and mind to a subsidiary and subordinate position, as mere epiphenomena, as appearances on the surface of the one reality, matter' (1926:8).

Smuts built on Darwin's evolutionary theories and suggested that evolutionary development moves constantly in the direction of growth, continually creating more complex whole systems.

His ideas became critical in the development of Adlerian psychotherapy, gestalt psychotherapy, psychosynthesis, and more recently Wilber's integral psychotherapy. Alfred Adler used Smuts's *Holism and Evolution* for his university lectures in Vienna (and had Smuts's book translated into German). He described Smuts's holism theory as 'supplying the scientific and philosophical basis for the great advance in psychology which had been made in recent years' (Blanckenburg, 1951:81). Assagioli (Assagioli, 1965:14) describes Smuts's holism as one of the most 'significant and valuable contributions to the knowledge of human nature and its betterment'.

Smuts considered the human being as the latest and most evolved manifestation of holism in the known universe. For Smuts, this 'self-realisation' of the 'holistic movement' manifests in the human realm as a movement towards greater freedom, and to be a free person is the highest achievement of which any human being is capable.

> The Whole is free, and to realize wholeness or freedom in the smaller whole of individual life represents not only the highest of which an individual is capable but expresses also, what is at once the deepest and highest universal movement of Holism. (Smuts, 1926:312)

His ideas also influenced existential and phenomenological psychotherapists. Rollo May (1969:11) defines existentialism as, 'centring upon the existing person and emphasizing the human being as he is emerging, becoming'. He also writes about overcoming the psychoanalytical tendency to see the human being as driven by internal drives and the behaviourist tendency to see them as reacting to external stimuli. To overcome this false dualism, he and Maslow proposed that, like all other aspects of evolution, human beings are constantly evolving, discovering how to fulfil their potentiality and develop themselves as a meaningful integrated whole. This requires the psychologist or psychotherapist to be interested in the whole person, not only their thinking, but also their feelings and emotions; not only their narratives, but their lived and embodied life.

This was taken up by Rogers in his notions that we are always 'becoming a person' – a movement towards wholeness, integration and self-actualising. This, he argued, required a therapist who was also fully present in the wholeness of their being, so that there was 'a humanistic, personal encounter' in which the concern is with an 'existing becoming, emerging, experiencing being' (Rogers quoted in May, 1969:91).

In this systemic turn, psychotherapy is a meeting of two living humans, both evolving towards a wholeness of being and living. The interest of the psychotherapist is in the whole person, not just their symptoms or difficulties, but their actualities and their potentialities; not just their behaviour or their unconscious drives, but their complex patterns of thinking, feeling and doing.

The danger, if we remain at this first shift towards systemic thinking, is that we reify the individual as a distinct entity and a closed system. Like a great deal of liberal humanism (see Harari, 2015; Hawkins, 2017c), we end up focusing on individual well-being as the goal and purpose, not just of therapy but of all life. Psychotherapy is then in danger of strengthening the narcissistic ego with its human-centrism. This may have its place in some stages of individual human development. However, what life is calling out for is that human beings wake up and learn how to move beyond human ego focus to systemic eco focus. If the individual is to thrive, their family and community need to thrive and for the family and community to thrive, the wider state has to be healthy and thriving; for the one human family to thrive and be sustainable, the wider more-than-human world has to be healthy and thriving (see next chapter).

Systemic turn 2: Your mental health is not your own

Even when we view the individual holistically as an evolving organism, this must entail dropping any notion that the individual can be understood by trying 'objectively' to focus on their parts, their drives or their complexes. In that case, we would still be seeing the individual as a closed system, an entity that has a life that exists separately from the many ongoing and constantly changing relational engagements that are an essential aspect of their lived world.

During and after the Second World War, a number of young psychiatrists and psychoanalysts were involved in treating mentally ill soldiers. In the First World War, these soldiers were referred to as 'shell-shocked'. Now, in the Second World War, they were described as 'battle-shocked' or suffering from 'war neuroses' (Harrison, 2000). The assumption was that those most exposed to the pressures and explosions of the frontline of battle were the ones most likely to 'break down' mentally. However, they tested this hypothesis and found that some army units that were under the most severe pressure actually had low levels of mental illness, and some others, with less frontline pressure, had higher levels. The units with high levels of neuroses also had high levels of fighting among themselves, drunkenness, going absent without leave and other forms of difficult behaviours. From this, the researchers developed the notion that there were healthy and unhealthy army units, and if someone was placed in an unhealthy army unit it would bring out their latent unhealthiness.

Several experiments were run to see if this process could be reversed. They wondered if, by creating a healthy 'therapeutic community', where all staff and patients were engaged in managing and attending to the health of the community, this would bring out individuals' latent healthiness. Experiments at Northfields Military Hospital in Birmingham and Mill Hill in London laid the foundations for therapeutic community principles later to be applied in psychiatric hospitals, such as the Henderson Hospital in Surrey, the Littlemore Hospital in Oxford and Fulbourn Hospital in Cambridge. The same principles were then applied to half-way house therapeutic communities for people returning to the community from mental hospitals, in drug and alcohol addiction treatment centres and in prisons. This therapeutic community movement had an enormous influence on the growth of the social psychiatry movement, group therapy, family therapy and the treatment of individuals in their social and community context, as well as the training of psychotherapists, with a strong developmental impact on the world of organisational development and social ecology.

At the heart of these developments is the awareness that mental illness does not just happen within the individual but comes from the dynamic interaction of the individual with their family, community and/or organisational context.

Foulkes, who took part in the second Northfields experiment, developed group analysis and became fascinated by the relationship between individual formation and group formation and development. Foulkes started out as a psychoanalyst from Frankfurt and Vienna, but he was always interested in the wider social context, influenced by the Frankfurt School of social philosophy and the sociologist Norbert Elias, and later by general systems theory. His key theoretical concept was the group matrix that belonged to the group as a whole, something different and beyond the mere sum of its members or component parts. Something new and separate from its parts is claimed to emerge when individuals relate to each other as members of a group. He defined the group matrix as 'the hypothetical web of communications and relationships of a given group' and as 'the common shared ground which ultimately determines meaning and significance of all events and upon which all communications and interpretations, verbal and non-verbal, rest' (Foulkes, 1964:292).

Foulkes posited two aspects to this group matrix: the first was the foundation group matrix, influenced by past family, social and cultural experiences and language; the second was the dynamic group matrix, emerging through the interactions and the relationships live in the group. Both of these aspects of the matrix, which he called transpersonal, he saw as radiating through the individual group members, including the group leader. The lines of force may be conceived of as passing right through the individual members and it may therefore be called a transpersonal network, comparable to a magnetic field (Foulkes & Anthony, 1957:258). Hence, he saw the group matrix as playing an active role in both forming and restricting the development of the individual members and their meaning-making. For Foulkes, the group provided a powerful container in which the individual could be helped to explore their interface with a larger social system, understand how they both contributed to creating the group and the group matrix. This becomes part of their formation and sense-making.

In parallel to Foulkes's development of the group matrix in the UK, Kurt Lewin (1952) was developing 'field theory' in the USA. He believed that human behaviour could only be understood as a function of the interaction between an individual and their psychological understanding of both their physical and social environment. Like Bertalanffy (1960, 1968) and Bion (1961), he tried to capture his breakthrough insight in a mathematical equation: $B = f\,(P, E)$. (B) stands for Behaviour including action, thinking and valuing; (P) for the person and (E) was for the person's particular environment. Thus, the equation can be translated as: 'behaviour is a function of the interaction of the person and their environment' (Lewin, 1935).

The environment included the family, social groups and culture that the person was immersed within as well as their physical environment. Lewin's thinking has had a huge influence on many fields including psychology, sociology, organisational development and, in particular, on the work of the National Training Laboratories in Bethel, Maine, which pioneered 'T' groups. In psychotherapy it is considered by some key theorists as one of the core pillars of gestalt psychotherapy (Yontef, 1981; Parlett, 1991). Lewin's theories provided a new way of viewing collective behaviour, not just in small groups, but also behaviour in larger organisations. The group, or organisation, could be seen as having a life of its own, with its own norms, dynamics and culture, which, although initially co-created by founding individuals, could continue beyond their participation as a group or institution. It could be seen, not simply as the sum of the individuals or other units who make up the group, but as an entity that could be quite different. Groups could, for example, have their own norms, and the dynamic processes of the group were not necessarily predictable from understanding the life-space of individuals (Saxe, 2010).

Ronnie Laing, the Scottish psychiatrist, studied people diagnosed with schizophrenia and looked at how their so-called mental illness could be seen as the best strategy they could find to respond to living in a crazy family. Laing wrote:

> In over 100 cases where we studied the actual circumstances around the social event when one person becomes to be regarded as schizophrenic, it seems to us without exception, the experience and behaviour that gets labelled schizophrenic *is a special strategy that a person invents in order to live in an unliveable situation.* (Laing, 1990:95, italics in the original)

Laing was very influenced by the work of Gregory Bateson and his colleagues. Bateson had been part of the beginnings of cybernetics (the study of the interface between man and machines) at the end of the Second World War, and when he came to study mental illness and particularly schizophrenia, he posed the question, how would you program a computer so that it became schizophrenic? After much deliberation, Bateson and his group decided that you would have to give it two equally important but totally contradictory commands. From this, they developed their double-bind theory of schizophrenia (Bateson, 1972).

Gregory Bateson was also the main influence on the development of systemic family therapy, both through the Palo Alto centre of which he was the director, and the Milan school. One of Bateson's many great contributions was to emphasise the centrality of communication, both verbal and non-verbal. This came from his early pioneering work in anthropology with the Naven people in Papua New Guinea and the family and child rearing patterns in Bali, where he worked with his wife and fellow anthropologist, Margaret Mead. However, his understanding of communication took a whole new turn after the Second World War, through his dialogues with Wiener and the other key thinkers that made up the Macy Conference, from which originated the study of cybernetics. Cybernetics is both the study of the interaction of humans and machines and the application of the understanding of computer network systems to the comprehension of human interaction. From this, Bateson recognised that although western human language was mostly linear in its construction, with a subject, doing something through the verb, to an object, human communication was circular and comprised complex circuits of communication, with co-subjects constantly affecting the next communication of the other. He used a simple but profound distinction that communication was information that made a difference.

Bateson's work was taken up by the Palo Alto Mental Research Institute he directed. This group, including Jay Haley, John Weakland, Paul Watzlawick and Don Jackson, developed many imaginative approaches to psychotherapy in general, including such concepts as paradoxical interventions, meta-communication and prescribing the symptom (Watzlawick, Beavin & Jackson, 1967), but their main contribution was to couple and family therapy.

Their work was enthusiastically taken up by a group of family therapists in the Centre for the Study of the Family in Milan, including, Maria Selvini Palazzoli, Guilana Prata, Luigi Boscolo and Gianfranco Cecchin. They later became known as the Milan school and importantly saw families as a system made up of several important sub-systems – the spouse system, the parental system and the sibling system – each with its own communication patterns and unwritten rules, as well as patterns of connection between the sub-systems. To help the family, they believed you needed to help them change their patterns of communication, not just communication through the spoken word, but communication through behaviour and actions and non-verbal behaviour. They reframed illness from residing in the identified patient and their named disorder and relocated it in the recursive circuits and pattern of communication between individuals and sub-systems. They did this through circular questioning, eliciting members' perceptions of the situation and each other – where the perspectives and answers of every family member were taken as equally valid, as well as systemically limited, that is, coming from the perspective of their place in the system.

Salvador Minuchin's structural family therapy has many similarities with the Milan school. He worked in Israel, Philadelphia and New York, both clinically and as teacher and supervisor of other family therapists. Minuchin encouraged structural family therapists to enter or 'join' the family system in therapy in order to understand the invisible rules that govern its functioning, map the relationships between family members or between subsets of the family, and ultimately disrupt dysfunctional relationships within the family, causing it to stabilise into healthier patterns.

The cul-de-sac and danger of just pursuing this systemic turn 2 is that a number of people started to see the individual as the victim of the madness of their family or of society. The schizophrenic became a hero fighting against the madness of their family or their hospital (see the film *One Flew Over* the *Cuckoo's Nest*). The 'outsider' (see *L'Etranger* (Camus, 1942) and *The Outsider* (Wilson, 1956)) becomes the hero fighting the madness of society (see May, 1969; Maslow, 1972). This just perpetuates a splitting dynamic, this time with the individual as the 'good' one.

Systemic turn 3: You are part of many systems and they are part of you

Many of the applications of the thinking of such theorists as Bertalanffy, Bateson, Lewin and Foulkes allowed new understandings to be formulated of the relationship between the individual and a particular social entity that they were part of, whether this was a family, group, community or organisation.

However, the lived reality of the clients arriving for psychotherapy, and indeed for all of us, is that we are members of many systems, both historically and in the present. This may include our family of origin, and other families we have been part of, including multiple places of work, membership of multiple social groups such as sports clubs, religious organisations, hobby groups, educational classes, internet-based networks and so on. Not only are we members of many systems, but these various groupings have a life within us; their 'matrix' of norms, values, dynamics and cultural patterns permeate our ways of being and thinking, and we become in part enculturated.

Charles Taylor (1964), the Canadian moral philosopher, argues that we are all 'dialogically constituted', and the material out of which our identities are shaped is provided, in part, by what others might call our culture. He calls it our 'language' which is 'not only the words we speak, but also other modes of expression, whereby we define ourselves, including the "languages" of art, of gesture, of love and the like' (Taylor, 1991:32). We may, in part, be authors of our lives, but the material comes not just from our genes but from the many cultures of which we are part.

Thomas Fuchs (not to be confused with S. H. Foulkes, the group psychoanalyst mentioned above), is a German psychiatrist and phenomenological psychotherapist, who argues that psychotherapy needs to focus on the complexity of the patient's 'Lebenswelt' or 'life world.' This entails how an individual lives in relationship to their 'lived space'. He defines this important concept of lived space as:

> the totality of the space that a person prereflectively 'lives' and experiences, with its situations, conditions, movements, effects and its horizons of possibilities – meaning the environment and sphere of action of a bodily subject. (Fuchs, 2007:426)

He goes on to say that each person has their own personal ecological niche and that:

> The personal niche thus comprises all living or non-living objects a person is in active exchange with and has influence on – family, neighbours, colleagues, home, work place, products of work etc. (Fuchs, 2007:426)

Systemic turn 4: You are part of and affect every system with which you interact

Two important breakthroughs in sub-atomic physics in the 20th century fundamentally changed, not only physics, but also Cartesian dualism and empirical method. When scientists moved from studying atoms to studying the atom's constituents, electrons, and the protons and neutrons in the atom's nucleus, they discovered that these elements were not fixed matter, but could appear as either particles or waves of energy. It was then realised that the same applied to understanding light, which can be seen as either electro-magnetic waves or particles (termed quanta by Einstein and now referred to as photons).

These discoveries ended the search for the fundamental building blocks of creation and the classical notion of solid objects. They also led to the realisation that the way that electrons showed up depended on the observer who was looking at them. If the scientist asks a particle question, they will get a particle answer; if they ask a wave question, they will get a wave answer. It is similar to the way Freudian psychotherapy clients are said to have Freudian dreams and Jungian clients, Jungian dreams! One of the great sub-atomic physicists, Nils Bohr (1934:57), wrote: 'Isolated material particles are abstractions, their properties being definable and observable only through their interaction with other systems.' Another great sub-atomic physicist, Werner Heisenberg (1958:58), wrote: 'What we observe is not nature itself, but nature exposed to our method of questioning.'

Harry Stack Sullivan (1947), the American psychoanalyst famous for his work with psychotic patients, uses the phrase 'participant-observer' to recognise that we can only know another through participating in a relationship with them; we know them through this relationship that we have co-created together.

We can never see a client objectively, for by relating to, and trying to understand, the client as an individual, organic system, we create a new system which connects the observer and the observed, a relational system in which both affect the other. The client and the psychotherapist together create two new systemic matrices; the first being the psychotherapy relationship, (see previous chapter), and the second being the psychotherapy process which goes beyond an interpersonal relationship, for it is comprised of the client, the psychotherapist, but also the life worlds each brings with them and, most importantly, the shared purpose of their work together.

You can never see the totality of a system that you are part of, for you will always see that system from the perspective of your position within it. However, supervision and other reflective processes provide the space and methods to reflect on the systemic world of the client as well as the psychotherapy or supervision systems you take part in co-creating. Supervision can help us access a greater or meta-perspective, where we can develop an awareness of, and become a witness to, the systems within which we reside (Hawkins & Shohet, 2012; Hawkins & Smith, 2013a, 2013b; Hawkins, 2011a, 2014). We will explore this further in Chapter 12.

Systemic turn 5: Embracing the systemic dance across the nested systems

Systems thinking has mainly grown out of an engineering mechanistic way of understanding the world. It focuses on closed systems and how they operate. It has been applied in both sciences and social sciences to understand how the whole of any system is more than the sum of its parts; how the whole has properties, functions and capabilities that the sum of its constituent parts does not possess. This is equally true for a bicycle, heating system, building or living organism.

Systemic thinking focuses more on the relations between nested systemic levels. It starts from the understanding that no system is an island complete unto itself (to misquote John Donne), but that every system contains systems within it and is nested within many larger systems. Nested systems do not exist as separate entities with clear and fixed boundaries, like a collection of Russian dolls, with each doll fitting within a larger doll, but rather they are open systems that permeate the systems within them and the systems they are part of.

Co-evolution is the understanding that no species, no individual, no organisation evolves as a closed system by itself. All evolution happens co-creatively and dialogically between systems and the wider eco-system of which they are part. Species do not just adapt to their ecological niche, which suggests that the ecological niche is active and the species reactive, for the species is also creating and recreating the niche it is adapting to. Co-evolution is the result of the constant dance and two-way, life-changing dialogue between any species and its ecological niche, and the dance between any system and its constituent sub-systems and the eco-systems in which it is embedded.

The holographic notion entails that the dynamic within one systemic level is mirrored in the systemic levels which are nested within it. So an individual never turns up for psychotherapy on their own, for the dynamics of their family (both of origin and current), the patterns, language constructions and mindsets of their culture, the organisational dynamics of places they might work and live in, the conflicts in the human drama, and the dynamics of the drama between the human and the more-than-human world all arrive holographically within them and are played out between them and the psychotherapist. Often the thinking about nested systems is represented in a linearly hierarchic way, so that separate systems are each nested within a bigger frame, that is nested in an even bigger one. However, nestedness also flows in the other direction, and the larger system is nesting within the sub-systems within it. The community is nested within the group and the group is nested within the individual. We are both part of our family and community, but they also are a part of us forming our beliefs and behaviours. Likewise, we are a part of our culture and our culture is the lens through which we view the world and gives us the language for making sense of the world. As will be explained in the next chapter, the ecological environment is not something that is external to the human species, it is within us, for the air of our ecological niche is in constant interchange with the air within us with every breath we take. There is a constant flow between us as a system and the world in which we live and breathe, and the boundary between the two is an artifice, a conceptual boundary necessary for our thinking, but one that is never stable or fixed in nature.

Koestler (1967) was pointing to the same concept when he described the holarchic relationship – the relationship between multiple levels of holons – as flowing in both directions, for example sub-atomic particles ↔ atoms ↔ molecules ↔ macro-molecules ↔ organelles ↔ cells ↔ tissues ↔ organs ↔ organisms ↔ communities ↔ societies, where each holon is a 'level' of organisation or system. The top can be a bottom, a bottom can be a top, and, like a fractal, the patterns evident at one level can be replicated by those at another.

This is also similar to the great contemporary Buddhist teacher Thich Nhat Hanh's notion of 'inter-being':

If you are a poet, you will see clearly that there is a cloud floating in this sheet of paper. Without a cloud, there will be no rain; without rain, the trees cannot grow: and without trees, we cannot make paper. The cloud is essential for the paper to exist. If the cloud is not here, the sheet of paper cannot be here either. So we can say that the cloud and the paper inter-are. (Hanh 1997)

Conclusion

Back in the psychotherapy consulting room, there may only be two individuals physically present, but psychologically the room is crowded. Both client and psychotherapist bring with them their current families and, if different, their family of origin; they bring identities part formed by their social groupings, their places of work, their communities, their professional identities and religious or non-religious affiliations. Their cultures frame the way they both think, the languages they speak and the lenses through which they view the world. All of these are in play in our therapeutic meeting. We cannot just attend to the internal life of our client, because that internal life contains the external interconnections within it, and for healing to happen, it has to also heal and change the connections with all those other levels of belonging.

CHAPTER 9

Embracing the Wider Ecology in Psychotherapy

No doubt about it, ecology drives people crazy, this has to be our point of departure – not with the goal of finding a cure, just so we can learn to survive without...denial, or hubris, or depression, or hope for a reasonable solution, or retreat into the desert.

Latour, 2017:13

The dire consequences of global warming are now permeating everyone's mindset.

Greenfield, 2009:1

At some point both psychologists and environmentalists need to decide what they believe our human connection is with the planet our species has so endangered... To redefine sanity within an environmental context. It contends that seeking to heal the soul without reference to the ecological system of which we are an integral part is a form of self-destructive blindness... At the heart of the coming environmental revolution is a change in values, one that derives from a growing appreciation of our dependence on nature. Without it there is no hope. In simple terms, we cannot restore our own health, our sense of well-being, unless we restore the health of the planet.

James Hillman, Founder of Archetypal Psychology (1995:xvi)

Introduction

In the last chapter, we explored how the individual is always in dynamic co-creation with the systems (groups, communities, cultures, etc.) they are nested within. In this chapter, we take that dynamic co-creation to a whole new level. Traditionally, the systemic approaches that were incorporated into psychotherapy were all focused on the human relational and social systems. Psychotherapy and its explorations, like most social sciences, were and mostly still are human-centric (Hawkins, 2017c). It was only when psychotherapy started to wake up to the ecological crisis that it started to consider what Abram (1996) refers to as 'the more-than-human world', the world of the wider ecology that we are intimately embedded within, and which is embedded within us. It provides our food, water, light and warmth and without this wider ecology we have no life.

We see this third principle of integrative psychotherapy as critical for psychotherapy in the 21st century, together with the relational and systemic principles, for several important reasons.

First, one of the key areas displaying the fragmentation of the containers within which humans create meaning and their sense of self is the ecological niche or place where they grow up and develop and where they currently reside (see Chapter 2). Today, most of us are indigenous orphans, separated from being rooted in a familiar landscape. Few of us live where we were born and spent our early years, and very few of us have an intimate relationship with the earth, trees, plants and indigenous animals, insects and micro-organisms with whom we share and co-create our local habitat.

Second, most clients who come to psychotherapy are suffering, consciously or unconsciously, from a deep split and separation from 'the more-than-human world'. Their food arrives from 'supermarkets', often chemically treated and wrapped in non-biodegradable plastic, which ends up polluting the world's oceans and fish. Wilderness is something seen on films. Other animals are mostly known in the shape of domesticated and humanised pets. Some school children think that eggs come from egg boxes and milk is created in bottles.

Third, the growing awareness of the collective human impact on our global ecology has deep conscious and unconscious psychological effects on nearly all the people we see. Gradually, human beings are waking up to the enormous number of other species that we have destroyed to the point of extinction, the forests we have cut down and burnt, and the living eco-systems such as coral reefs we have decimated. We are beginning to let into our awareness that we are part of the sixth great extinction, but the first to be created by just one species – *Homo sapiens*, and in particular the white Europeans at home and in their diaspora worldwide (Ryde, 2019). Through television programmes like Sir David Attenborough's BBC programme, *Blue Planet*, many of us realise the great harm we are doing to the oceans and the many living creatures within them. Other programmes are awakening us to the loss of bird varieties in our gardens, woods and along our coasts, and the very worrying depletion of bees, essential to pollinating not only our flowers, but also our fruit trees and vegetables. With this growing realisation comes grief and despair (Macy & Johnstone, 2012), anger at our own and others' murderous destructiveness of life, and feelings of guilt and shame for what we have done and for our wilful blindness and collusion with this process. These collective emotions increasingly emerge consciously or unconsciously within each and every human and cannot be ignored within the psychotherapy relationship.

Fourth, we believe that healing (a word that is etymologically deeply connected to the words 'whole' and 'holy') in psychotherapy, does not just come from the psychotherapist, the client and their relationships (see Chapter 7), nor just from the human engagement of the client with their lived world (see Chapter 8) but also with and through a new engagement with the more-than-human living world of our eco-systemic context.

Fifth, and most importantly, we see psychotherapy as one key practice area within a much larger and critical endeavour, which it shares with many other fields – to help the human species collectively shift consciousness so that we become healthy contributors to global sustainability, rather than its biggest threat. This is a task that psychotherapy shares with those working as psychologists, sociologists and ecologists; coaches and organisational development practitioners; artists of all mediums and genres; and those working in religion and philosophy. Indeed, this is the responsibility of all members of our environmentally dominant species.

Harari, in his book *Homo Deus* (Harari, 2015), suggests that humankind – having mostly conquered the three great challenges it has wrestled with since it first existed, namely, famine, plague and war – is now turning its attention towards new aspirations, to extend the human life span and overcome death, increase human pleasure and create super-humans through technological augmentation. He shows how humans want to become immortal and god-like. All of these aspirations can be seen as human-centric hubris and potentially destructive, not just to our own species, but the entire Gaia eco-system. Instead of hubris, we need humility, and psychotherapy has its role to play in this, helping each of us to re-discover a right relationship with the wider ecological world within which our species is dependently nested, and in which we have our life, our being and our meaning.

In writing about mental health in Chapter 4, we discussed the need for every human to face the four traditional great existential challenges of life: the freedom to choose and being aware that every 'yes' we make requires a 'no' – a relinquishing of other possibilities; that we will all face death; our aloneness as well as our connectedness; and the need to create meaning in our life (Yalom, 1980). We believe that the current and emerging ecological crisis creates a fifth central existential crisis for every human being on our shared planet.

So, in this chapter, we will look at how eco-psychotherapy helps us to understand ourselves, our work and our clients through a new lens. We will explore how psychotherapeutic practice not only includes the dialogical relationship between therapist and client (Chapter 7), which is extended to include the dialogue between the client and their lived world (Chapter 8), but is also extended even further to include the collective dialogue between *Homo sapiens* and their global ecological niche and the individual dialogue between the client and their particular ecological niche.

What is ecology and an ecological perspective or epistemology?

The word 'ecology' comes from the Greek word *oikos*, meaning household, and signifies the household of the whole planet. Capra and Luisi (2016:341–342) define ecology as: 'the scientific study of the relationships between members of the Earth Household – plants, animals and micro-organisms – and their natural environment, living and non-living'.

Ecology is not the study of plants, animals and micro-organisms per se – but the study of their multi-directional relationships to each other and their eco-system. The eco-system consists of the biotic community of all living organisms as well as the lithosphere of the ground we stand on, the hydrosphere of our oceans and seas, and the atmosphere we breath. If the dominant metaphor of the Scientific Enlightenment was the machine, the dominant metaphor of ecology is the network.

One of its first originators was the English zoologist, Charles Elton, who wrote *Animal Ecology* in 1927 (Elton, 2001), where he described the networks of food chains and food cycles that provide the interdependency of many differing species. He also introduced the concept of the ecological niche, which he described as the role an animal plays in a community in terms of what it eats and is eaten by. Since then, this term has taken on greater and more complex meanings.

It is ecology that has provided us with the notion of nested systems we briefly addressed in the last chapter, where we discussed personal niches, nested within social cultural niches, nested within local, regional and cultural niches, which in turn are nested within biomes. Biomes are the major climatic eco-systems affecting the various biological eco-systems within them. Ecologists describe eight such biomes on this planet of ours: tropical, temperate, conifer forests, tropical savanna, temperate grassland, chaparral (shrubland), tundra and desert (Capra & Luisi, 2016:344). These biomes are nested within the biosphere of all terrestrial living organisms, which Gaia theorists (Lovelock, 1979; Lovelock & Margulis, 1974) see as closely interacting with the lithosphere (the Earth's rocks), the hydrosphere (the Earth's oceans), and the atmosphere, (the Earth's air) to form Gaia – the eco-system of eco-systems in, on and around this planet. They see Gaia as a complex, evolving, living organismic system.

Ecology is a fast-growing interdisciplinary field of inquiry, and like many potent concepts and new paradigms, it has many children, not all of which get on well together or even speak to each other. To name but a few: evolutionary ecology, population ecology, community ecology, conservation ecology, human ecology, deep ecology, systems ecology and global ecology. For our purposes in grasping the role of ecology in psychotherapy, we need to understand just a few of these: sustainable ecology, eco literacy and deep ecology.

Sustainable ecology emerges from the recognition that for the first time in Earth's history, one species, *Homo sapiens*, is putting at risk the survival of all life on our planet. In this new epoch, called the Anthropocene, we are witnessing the sixth mass extinction of species (Leakey & Lewin, 1996) caused by massive human population expansion, deforestation, atmospheric pollution, plundering of Earth's biotic resources, human-caused climate change and other interconnected processes. Magurran and Dornelas (2010) in their report for the Royal Society in London wrote: 'There are strong indications that the current rate of species extinctions far exceeds anything in the fossil record... Never before has a single species driven such profound changes to the habitat composition and climate of the planet.' Sustainable ecology recognises that you cannot separate out human sustainable development from creating sustainable eco-systems, and many argue that we have, for the first time, created one interdependent global niche (Senge, 2014) and now need to discover how to enable an interdependent sustainable planet.

Deep ecology was the term coined by Arne Naess (1912–2009) (Naess, 1987) to distinguish it from 'shallow ecology' which was a study of our eco-systems as if they were separate from ourselves, displaying a human-centric concern focused on how nature can best be sustained for the benefit of *Homo sapiens*.

> Deep Ecology does not separate humans – or anything else – from the natural environment. It does see the world, not as a collection of isolated objects, but as a network of phenomena that are fundamentally interconnected and interdependent. Deep Ecology recognizes the intrinsic value of all living beings and views humans as just one particular strand in the web of life. (Capra & Luisi, 2016:12)

Deep ecology argues that the only way *Homo sapiens* can reverse the trajectory from being the destroyers of sustainable ecology to becoming positive contributors to ecological health is by embracing a fundamental shift in consciousness – from seeing nature as outside ourselves, and the environment as something that surrounds us, to realising that nature and the environment are also part of us, and we are an indivisible part of the wider eco-system. As Naess (2016) writes:

> Care flows naturally, if the 'self' is widened and deepened so that the protection of free Nature is felt and conceived as protection of ourselves... just as we need no morals to make us breathe... If your 'self' in the wide sense embraces another being, you need no moral exhortation to show care.

Eco-literacy is not just knowing more about the ecologies we are nested within and the relationship between humans and their environment – it is also about a metanoia, a fundamental change in the perspective from where we are looking. In Chapter 3, we showed how human beings naturally mature from being physically merged, to being ego-centric, to being socio-centric, to being self-authoring, to being more globally human-centric, to being eco-centric. We urgently need to help a much greater percentage of the human population to quickly develop along this path in order to reach an eco-centric ontology and epistemology – eco-centric ways of thinking and being.

Deep ecology argues for an eco-literacy that is not just conceptual, but emotional and embodied, where we overcome the dangerous splits of self and other: my tribe and the enemy; my species and others that I can exploit; humans and lesser beings; humankind and nature. 'Them' are all 'us', and self-care now needs to embrace the whole world.

Restoring the ecological container

In our work as supervisors, we have been struck by how often psychotherapists seem to become exhausted by their work. In Hawkins (2019:61), Peter shared the following story:

> In a recent supervision, my supervisee told me that she was so pleased that we were having supervision now, because she felt totally depleted and knew that when she came to supervision, she always left feeling recharged. In the past, I would have felt flattered and worked hard to best resource her. However, on this occasion I paused and then said: 'I think we might need to review how we are doing supervision together, so we can discover how supervision can stop being a petrol station where you go to be refueled and instead becomes a place that helps you create a solar panel on your heart, so you constantly tap into renewable energy in the midst of the work.' Our supervision gradually changed from being a resource she tapped into, to a place that helped her re-source herself.

Peter went on to explore how, as psychotherapists, counsellors, coaches and supervisors, we often work from a place of making an effort, rather than from source. He showed how this is based on a deep assumption that it is 'I', the psychotherapist, who is doing the psychotherapy, egoistically in denial of the fact that psychotherapy is a collaborative endeavour of the partnership between therapist and client, as we explored in Chapter 7, or a process where the most important player is life itself, as we began to explore in Chapter 8. Psychotherapy is not just a version of human relational and social life, but a place where the evolutionary forces constantly come into being – the life force of the planet and the universe in co-creation with our human explorations and endeavours.

The Ecological Awareness Model for psychotherapists and clients

As ecological denial, grief and guilt show up more and more in our psychotherapy clients, and as the world is increasingly in need of a radical shift in human consciousness, it is beholden on all of us who practise psychotherapy to work through our own ecological awareness cycle and to have the understanding and processes to also help our clients through this process.

We have developed this model of the Ecological Awareness Cycle, partly based on the many years of research Judy has carried out on white awareness, and her development of the White Awareness Cycle (Ryde, 2009;

Ryde, 2019). It has ended up having some of the same elements, but it is also very different as it is based on our own ability to make sense of the processes we witness in ourselves and our work. We and others are increasingly going through this process and, whether or not they are consciously aware of it, many of our clients will be deeply affected by the ecological crisis and be at one stage or other of the process shown in our model. It is also influenced by many writers in this field, particularly Joanna Macy, James Hillman, Sally Weintrobe and Donna Orange.

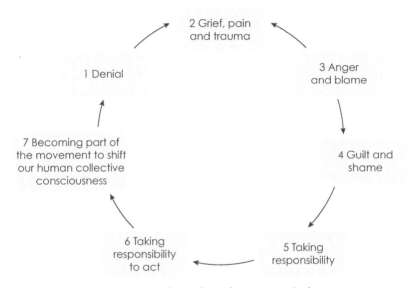

Figure 9.1: The Ecological Awareness Cycle

Stage 1: Overcoming denial

The first barrier to facing the global ecological crisis is our individual and collective wilful blindness.

Weintrobe (2012) and her co-writers very usefully distinguish between three types of denial:

1. *Denialism* –'involves campaigns of misinformation about climate change funded by commercial and ideological interests' (Weintrobe, 2012:7). It sets out to cast doubt and confusion and undermine belief in the scientific evidence and even in experts per se.

2. *Negation* – seen as similar to the first stage of Kubler-Ross's (2005) stages of grief and mourning, where there is a refusal to believe that

a person has died and to accept the loss. It is a psychological process of protection from a shock or trauma we are not yet prepared to face.

3. *Disavowal* – we paradoxically both acknowledge what is happening and at the same time split off from this knowing. 'This is seeing it but with one eye only' (Weintrobe, 2012:7). We both know and don't know simultaneously, and Weintrobe sees this as the most prevalent and dangerous form of denial: 'This is because the more reality is systematically avoided through making it insignificant or through distortion, the more anxiety builds up unconsciously and the greater is the need to defend with further disavowal' (Weintrobe, 2012:7).

As we work through our various forms of denial, including our negation and disavowal, and are less taken in by the denialism spread in parts of the media and repeated by people we know, we find ourselves having to face up to feelings of guilt and shame in what we and our species have done to the world. At this stage, it is easy to either fall into the defence of splitting, where you project all the guilt on certain industries, politicians or countries, or to take on board and introject more guilt and responsibility than is rightfully yours. The first process leaves you angry from a victim position ('it's all them'), and the second feeling overwhelmed ('it is all me'). The recognisable survival responses of 'fight' and 'freeze' regularly arise in our clients. We will explore these two opposites in Stages 3 and 4. To limit these amygdala survival-driven reactions, we all need the space and support to experience our grief and loss, to register the trauma of what is happening and address our fears of what is to come.

Stage 2: Addressing the pain, grief and trauma when we become aware of what we have done to our planetary home

Gradually, individuals are waking up to the grief that flows from the actions that we as human beings have done to our planetary home. Film makers, television producers and enlightened authors, journalists and artists are helping by developing well-designed 'alarm clocks' to wake us up from our slumbers and denial. Programmes like *Blue Planet* help us see how over-using plastic and just throwing it away causes great distress to marine life having to survive amidst great islands of plastic waste, becoming ensnared in it, digesting it. Such programmes also show how micro-plastics enter the food chain, affecting all forms of fish and amphibians, as well as the birds and humans who eat the fish.

We must emphasise here that some scientists describe our current era as the sixth extinction crisis, or as the Anthropocene – the first extinction crisis to be caused by human beings, rather than by climatic and geological causes.

To wake up to the great destruction we, as *Homo sapiens*, have caused on and to our planet, and to overcome the pervasive denial of the extent of what we have caused, involves going through the cycle of shock, anger, grief, guilt, depression, feelings of hopelessness and despair, before we can truly integrate and become congruent with the wider eco-system of our more-than-human world.

This process is increasingly becoming evident in the psychotherapy room, sometimes consciously, but more often unconsciously. Some clients will discuss how upset they have been, or are, at witnessing, directly or indirectly, the tearing down of woods, the loss of many bird species, air pollution, the waste floating in the seas. Others will share dreams of animals and plants dying, or bring free-floating grief and anxiety about the health of their children or grandchildren, or ideas of being poisoned.

When we reach the limits of our capacity to stay with the grief and pain, we either retreat back into some form of disavowal, or rush into the next stage of anger and blame.

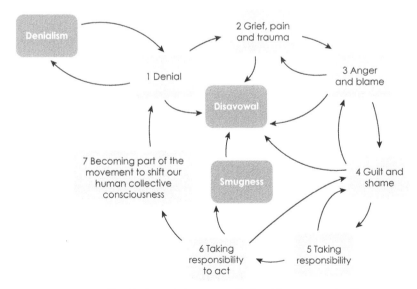

Figure 9.2: The Ecological Awareness Cycle with retrogressive flows

Stage 3: Anger and blame

Some individuals bypass the stage of grief by going back into 'disavowal' as the grief is too hard to bear, and they lack the support from others necessary to express it and be heard. We all might find ourselves in this position from time to time. Others go straight from awakening to the reality of the climatic threat and eco-destruction, to anger and fury at those they blame and see as more responsible than themselves for the growing catastrophe. For some, this will be local or international politicians, for others, the carbon fuel industry, and for some, the whole capitalist-consumerist culture. Anger can be a healthy response leading to thoughtful activism. Anger can also be an avoidant emotional mechanism, where one's own responsibility is projected on to distant others, and we enter the blame game and 'drama triangle' (Karpman, 1968), where we cast ourselves as victims to external persecutors and, consciously or unconsciously, wait to be rescued.

Stage 4: Dealing with guilt and shame

The work of psychotherapy is to increase our capacity to acknowledge our own destructiveness, and our own pursuit of our self-interest, which involves collusion with ecological destructive forces. This involves working through our appropriate feelings of shame. In her doctoral research and in her book, *Being White in the Helping Professions* (Ryde, 2009), Judy points out that guilt is something to be established – am I or am I not partly responsible and should I acknowledge my appropriate guilt? Shame is the feeling we have when we start to take responsibility for the way in which we are part of the ecological destructiveness that human beings are enacting on our local and planetary eco-systems. We start to feel shame for the effects of our consumer choices, our travel, our use of carbon-based energy and our collusion in turning a 'blind eye' to what is happening. Many psychotherapists focus more on feelings of shame which originate in childhood and the way that we tend to brand ourselves guilty of 'crimes' for which we cannot be held responsible. Shame has therefore been given a bad name by psychotherapists. We, as human beings (including psychotherapists and their clients), are capable of being very destructive, and shame is a feeling which usefully alerts us to these actions and encourages us to repair any damage we do. Feelings of shame can become hard to live with if we do not respond to their call and move on. Turning away from feelings of shame may well lead us back into disavowal, as we saw above. The Ecological Awareness Cycle (above) shows how guilt and shame fit into the process towards responding appropriately to the ecological crisis. These feelings can deepen our awareness of our own part in damaging the ecology and lead us to more thoroughly taking responsibility, which is the next stage in the process.

Stage 5: Taking responsibility

Psychotherapy can play a key role in helping us to: get beyond the way we turn a blind eye to where our consumer products come from and the ecological cost of their raw materials, production and transportation; move on from trying to rationalise away the carbon footprint of our air travel, or pollution of our car or central heating; and look our own personal responsibility squarely in the eye. Only if we look with open eyes at our part in the collective destructiveness are we able to respond, and then able to develop our response-ability. Only then can we develop an appropriate course of action that is neither taking too little or too much personal responsibility for the collective guilt.

Stage 6: Taking responsibility to act

Both insight and accepting responsibility are critical, but not sufficient by themselves. 'To know and not to act on the knowledge, is to not know' (Latour, 2017:140), for as Bateson (1972) teaches us, real learning begins, not by absorbing facts, but by a difference in the choices we make. As psychotherapists, we need to avoid the perpetual wringing of hands, the cycles of 'Isn't it awful?' and 'If only...' and ask, 'So what can I do that will make a positive difference?' Most of the steps we can each take are important, but for most of us in the privileged West, they are not nearly enough. Our awareness of what little we are able to do can drive us back into guilt and shame and grief and pain. We need to accept that these actions are just first steps on a journey, and we should be careful that they are not the personal equivalent of industries 'greenwashing' their products, to provide a false complacency that leads us back into smugness and disavowal.

Stage 7: Becoming part of the movement to shift our collective human consciousness

We cannot just take responsibility for our individual actions. The crisis is such that creating change one person at a time will not be sufficient. As we have shown in previous chapters, we are inextricably intertwined and interdependent, like the Bodhisattvas in the Buddhist tradition, who recognise that individual enlightenment is not an end in itself, but a blessing that necessitates us to return and enable others also to open their awareness, liberate their mindsets and be part of shifting human consciousness. The simple question: 'How can you use what you have learned to help others?' can be really helpful at this stage.

How can we bring eco-awareness into the psychotherapy room?

It is also important that, as psychotherapists, we are not there to judge, moralise, campaign or convert our clients to our ecological stance or beliefs. First, we need to ensure that we ourselves are neither in denial nor disavowal, or just blaming others for the ecological crisis; that we have moved beyond grief and frozen powerlessness; and that we are constantly looking at the reality of the ecological crisis with our eyes wide open. It is essential that we have worked through enough of our own ecological awareness cycle – worked through our own despair, hopelessness, anger, grief and guilt, so we can truly listen and be open to the deep ecological feelings and responses of our clients, without becoming reactive, judgemental or minimising what is present within us and outside us. We need to listen with an 'ecological ear' to the ecological within and around our client, to the emotional responses they have to both of these and to enable a constant moving around the Ecological Awareness Cycle which can enable a fuller, life-embracing response at each stage and in each cycle.

How nature can heal us

The ecology is naturally self-healing and self-evolving. We can be part of that wider healing process, if we can open ourselves to it. If we reach out to other aspects of the natural world, they reach back to us, for the ecology flows through us and enters our inner being. It can absorb all kinds of emotional distress and help us put our worries into a much larger context. In the middle of writing this chapter I (Peter) left my fretting about how to craft this chapter and how to say what I was struggling to articulate and went snorkelling among the rocks in the sea just outside where we were staying for a writing holiday. Suddenly I left the human world of land above the waters, and entered a new world of rocks and coral, with their gullies and caverns, shoals of fish of many shapes and sizes and colours. I and the fish were together rocked by the constant ebb and flow of the currents. I was immediately transported out of myself and my concerns and worries. Flowing in nature, nature flowing through me. Alan Durning captures this impact when he writes:

> When the natural world reawakens in every fibre of our being the primal knowledge of connection, and graces us with a few moments of sheer awe, it can shatter the hubris and isolation so necessary to narcissistic defences.
>
> It is these experiences that will ultimately fill the empty self and heal the existential loneliness so endemic of our times. (Durning, 1992:91)

Not everybody has the privilege of spending time by coral shores, or in tropical forests, or in so-called deserts; however, nature can heal even in the most urban of environments. In the BBC programme *Gardeners' World* on Friday 12 October 2018, they featured a London doctor who regularly prescribes gardening for patients suffering from depression, early stage dementia, anxiety, and those with long-term physical illnesses. He is involved with a community garden project in Sydenham, south London, where patients are helped by the engagement with the earth, supported by horticultural therapists and community engagement with other patients. When interviewed, the doctor said, 'The earth is a generous friend, it always gives you more than you put in.' As keen gardeners ourselves, we would also emphasise that earth and gardens are very patient, never in a hurry, are accepting and non-judgemental. Gardening slows down the anxious mind, keeps the body moving and the focus on the simple activities necessary for life. In our garden, we have had a gardening project for refugees and asylum seekers, where those banished from their roots and community because of war or imprisonment can find new connections with the one Earth we all share. We also work with WWOOF – World Wide Opportunities on Organic Farms, and welcome students and young adults from many different parts of the world to come and work with us in the gardens, fields and woodlands where we live, in return for bed, board and time to learn to speak English.

Another project to combat loneliness and depression is 'run and talk', where people join a running group in which they are encouraged to share what is happening in their world as they run. Some people report that they find it easier to open up when running alongside somebody, shoulder to shoulder, in the outdoors, than sitting opposite a counsellor or psychotherapist, disliking the spotlight being on them.

There are many other ways nature can heal us – whether through wild swimming in the sea or rivers, mountain climbing or hill walking, rambling with others, sailing the seas, or soaking up the sun.

Shifting human consciousness for humans to be healthy contributors to Gaia sustainability

It is only when we, as psychotherapists, have intellectually and emotionally worked through the Ecological Awareness Cycle sufficiently to face what is happening to the world, with eyes wide open but non-reactively, that we can truly listen to the ecological anguish as it arises through our clients. Only then can we be sensitive to when they become overwhelmed by the ecological destruction, or when they become heroic activists attempting to personally halt its tide. We can let awareness of these polarities – and how easily we swing between them – surface in our inquiry together, and search for a place where we are neither in denial, overwhelmed nor filled with human hubris. For only when we have found this aware, non-reactive presence to what is happening in the world can we truly explore how we may contribute from our unique place in the wider systems to reducing the amount of human abuse affecting our wider ecology, ready to constantly awaken ourselves and others to what is happening and to find ways to be kinder and healing to the worlds we inhabit.

To walk this path for ourselves and with our clients, we need to practise listening deeply to the human and more-than-human worlds around us. Joanna Macy encourages people to find 'listening posts', places in their garden, their local park, woodland, hillside, by the river, or sea, or on the journey to work, where they can stop, breathe and listen to the nature all around them, the birds, animals, insects; the air, the wind, the movement of the plants and trees; the rhythm and heartbeat of life unfolding around them. To practise listening eco-systemically with wide-angled empathy and compassion (Hawkins, 2019:74) for all that is unfolding in the world we are a part of. Then we can turn our attention internally, listening deeply and mindfully to what is happening inside our bodies, our feelings and thoughts – a similar process to mindfulness practices from many different spiritual and psychological disciplines, and what the neuro-psychiatrist Dan Siegel (Siegel, 2010) describes as 'time-in'. Then we can move from 'time-in' to 'time-out' or what we call eco-connecting time (see Chapter 4), listening eco-systemically once again to the world beyond our skin, beyond our family and friends and beyond our noisy species. Then we can practise 'listening-in' and 'listening-out' at the same time, sensing the harmony and the discordance between the inside and outside. Then we may gradually allow the two to come into attunement with each other, sensing how the eco-system is flowing through us, not just outside us, how we are flowing in and through the eco-system, not just confined within our skin. We can attend to how the air around us enters through our mouth and nostrils, becoming part of us and then the way that changed air leaves through our airways and becomes part of the atmosphere that surrounds us; how the sunlight enters through our pores, changing the feelings of warmth and the chemistry inside.

Healing the split between the human and more-than-human world

John Seed, the Australian ecology writer and campaigner, writes about healing the split in our thinking between ourselves and the world we inhabit, the split between the human and more-than-human world:

> When humans investigate and see through their layers of anthropocentric self-cherishing, a most profound change in consciousness begins to take place. Alienation subsides. The human is no longer a stranger, apart. Your humaness is then recognized as merely the most recent stage of your existence, and as you stop identifying exclusively with this chapter, you start to get in touch with yourself as mammal, as vertebrate, as a species only recently emerged from the rainforest. As the fog of amnesia disperses, there is a transformation in your relationship to other species, and in your commitment to them. (Seed *et al.*, 1988:35)

Seed confronts the hubris of ecological campaigners trying to save the planet:

> 'I am protecting the rainforest' develops to 'I am part of the rain-forest protecting myself. I am that part of the rainforest recently emerged into thinking.' What a relief then! The thousands of years of imagined separation are over, and we begin to recall our true nature. That is, the change is a spiritual one, sometimes referred to as deep ecology. (Seed *et al.*, 1988:36)

To develop beyond being human-centric is not to become ethereal or 'other worldly', removed from this physical evolving planet, but to be fully in contact with all the stages of evolution and development that are both within us, and also surround us.

Peter's book co-written with Eve Turner (Hawkins & Turner, 2019) describes five ways or dimensions in which coaches can open up their work to awareness of the ecological. We think that the same can be said of psychotherapists.

1. Inviting the ecological in to the room.

2. Looking out through the window.

3. Opening the window, both externally and internally.

4. Working out of doors.

5. Nature-assisted therapy.

Thinking about the work in this way helps to uncover the fact that the ecological is always with us. It is not that it is something separate that we should invoke but is more a matter of whether or not we pay attention to something that is present but often ignored.

This reminds us of a notice that is on one of the roads leading to Bath which says, 'We live within the sky, not under it'. In other words, we don't have to look up at the sky as it is inextricably part of our existence. This shift in viewpoint is hard to make so these five dimensions can be helpful.

The first, inviting it in, is simply to notice it and invite it in. We notice, for instance, that we live within the sky. We also might notice whether we are 'friendly' to the Earth in our work, so we care for plants, recycle or avoid using plastic. Do we notice clients' references to the ecological or do they pass us by?

The second, looking through the window, is about remembering to look out for the ecology to speak to us. Judy mentioned in Chapter 7 the impact that seeing a fox playing with her cubs through the window of her psychotherapist's consulting room had on her, so that it became one of the most significant occurrences within the work. It was a reminder of the natural world, the love of mothers and babies and the importance of play that came came 'by grace', irrespective of her narrow concerns.

The third is opening the window. Jung, in writing about synchronicity, described opening the window to wonderful effect:

> My example concerns a young woman patient who, in spite of efforts made on both sides, proved to be psychologically inaccessible. The difficulty lay in the fact that she always knew better about everything. Her excellent education had provided her with a weapon ideally suited to this purpose, namely a highly polished Cartesian rationalism with an impeccably 'geometrical' idea of reality. After several fruitless attempts to sweeten her rationalism with a somewhat more human understanding, I had to confine myself to the hope that something unexpected and irrational would turn up, something that would burst the intellectual retort into which she had sealed herself. Well, I was sitting opposite her one day, with my back to the window, listening to her flow of rhetoric. She had an impressive dream the night before, in which someone had given her a golden scarab – a costly piece of jewellery.

While she was still telling me this dream, I heard something behind me gently tapping on the window. I turned round and saw that it was a fairly large flying insect that was knocking against the window-pane from outside in the obvious effort to get into the dark room. This seemed to me very strange. I opened the window immediately and caught the insect in the air as it flew in. It was a scarabaeid beetle, or common rose-chafer (*Cetonia aurata*), whose gold-green colour most nearly resembles that of a golden scarab. I handed the beetle to my patient with the words, 'Here is your scarab.' This experience punctured the desired hole in her rationalism and broke the ice of her intellectual resistance. The treatment could now be continued with satisfactory results. (Jung, 1969:109)

Here Jung has faith that, if he is open to it, life will bring to them what he and his patient needed in that moment.

The fourth, working out of doors, is more obviously and directly 'in nature'. Without forgetting that we are always 'in nature' it is easier to remember this when so much of life can be seen, felt, smelt and heard. This advantage, and that of being side-by-side, is more common recently, as we saw above.

The fifth dimension is 'nature-assisted therapy' or 'animal-assisted therapy' (Hall, 2018). Here, animals become a third partner in the work. Because the animals have well-developed limbic resonance, the psychotherapist can help the client leave their verbal left-hemisphere neo-cortex forms of communicating and relating, and discover more about their own embodied forms of communicating, relating, building trust, giving clear signals and so on. We have some examples of this in Chapter 11.

The presence of ecology in our work is not something we need to strive for. It is there if we are open to it.

Eco-spirituality

'Let us imagine the *anima mundi* (the world soul),' the imaginal Jungian psychotherapist James Hillman tells us, 'as that particular soul spark, that seminal image, which offers itself through each thing in its visible form' (Hillman, 1982:77). The French philosopher Henri Bergson (1907, 2016) pointed in a similar direction when he wrote about '*élan vital*', the life force that flows through every aspect of our world, every living organism, but is also active in all the connections between them, and through the ways they are all evolving in dynamic relationship to each other. Seeing the world as a whole was a door of perception that was unlocked for many of us when we saw the first pictures taken from space. We saw the Earth as a beautiful blue planet. The scientist James Lovelock (Lovelock, 1979; Lovelock & Margulis, 1974) went further in re-animating our sense of the Earth, in his ground-breaking metaphor of the Gaia hypothesis, which studies the whole planet, the biosphere that includes the atmosphere of the air, the lithosphere of the rocks, and the hydrosphere of the seas and oceans, as one interconnected living system, balancing itself and constantly evolving.

In this book, we have explored that in order to be truly healthy, we need to develop integration. This integration happens individually in our brain, as well as between our experiencing self and the narrative self of the stories we tell ourselves, between our brain and our body, in which the brain is distributed and embodied. Integration is also relational, for the self is always in dynamic relationship with others, in both the physical and imaginal worlds. The self in turn exists within the systemic contexts of communities and cultures which frame our thinking and shape our behaviours. Now we can see that we need to expand our self and our integration further, and see that our self is not just formed by ourselves, our relationship, our communities and cultures, but that we are an indivisible part of the ecological Gaia system and need to find integration between our self and the more-than-human world. We need to be able to experience our 'eco-self' and live and breathe as a whole, integrated individual, who is just one small part of the one ever-changing human family, and an even smaller part of Gaia.

Spirit can be understood as the life process, in the same way that Bateson understands the mind as the mental process (see Chapters 4 and 8). It can be seen as the evolutionary force that is constantly evolving in and between every species, and in and between every organism. Rather than privileging spirit or soul, spending hours in philosophical and theological debate about where they are to be found and what they consist of, we can awaken to the experience of soul and spirit as a living process in which we partake. Rather than owning a soul, we can experience being ensouled, feel ourselves swimming in the spirit of life.

As we connect more broadly and deeply with the wider eco-systemic levels, we open up deeper inner levels of consciousness. In the same way that relational psychotherapy helps us develop an internal witness on our patterns of behaviour, our emotional states and reactions and even our ways of thinking and being, the systemic perspective helps us see the cultures we are embedded within and that are embedded in us. At the same time, the eco-systemic lens helps us see our human-centricity and our humanness and how to go beyond the personal internal witness, to a deeper level of pure awareness.

Pure awareness is described by our good friend and teacher Elias Amidon as being present with all that shows up without judgement, being able to do what is necessary, what is required, without the distraction of 'extra' – thoughts, reactions, plans, regrets and so on. That, when we can just be in pure awareness, we know that we have enough, that there is no striving, no lack, no neediness. We can find the freedom from the culture of 'more' (see Chapter 2), the narcissistic focus on self, our entanglement in our social and culture contexts, and just rest in pure awareness.

Eventually we might be blessed and able to go further and discover even greater depths of this pure awareness, where the duality of subject and object dissolves, and find that in non-duality, there is no one being aware and no object of awareness – 'the still point in the turning world' (Eliot, 2002: *Four Quartets*). But this comes by grace. It is not a realisation acquired through individual development, nor by psychotherapy, nor by just listening or reading spiritual teaching, for as Bateson (1972) said of this level of learning, it begins when experience is no longer punctuated by 'I'.

Conclusion

We now live in the sixth great extinction of life forms, and the first to be driven by one species of animal – *Homo sapiens* – and have created a new geological age, the Anthropocene, where even the geology and atmosphere of our climate are being fundamentally transformed by uncontained human activity. We have an urgent task to transform how our own species thinks, feels and behaves. Gregory Bateson said back in the 1970s:

> I believe that this massive aggregation of threats, to humanity and its ecological systems, arises out of errors in our habits of thought at deep and partly unconscious levels... As (change agents) clearly we have a duty. First to achieve clarity in ourselves, and then look for every sign of clarity in others and to implement them and reinforce them in whatever is sane in them. (Bateson, 1972:487)

What more important task can psychotherapy possibly have? But we can only step up to this challenge if we also understand how inextricably intertwined the human and the more-than-human world are.

In earlier chapters, we explored how a baby is formed not just by their DNA and their genes, but by the relational world of attachments they are born into. And then we showed how our minds and mental health are co-created with and by the family, communities and cultures we inhabit, all of which simultaneously inhabit us. In this chapter, we have gone further and showed how our self is formed by the larger eco-system and how in small ways our self is constantly impacting and changing the eco-system around us. We can begin to grasp how our development and the development of the human and more-than-human systems in which we reside are dialogically and dynamically intertwined. Evolution, learning and development are always in the dance between systems, between us and our ecological niche. We are neither just adapting to our ecological niche, fitting in, nor able to make the ecological niche fit us. All evolution is co-evolution, between species and between systemic and eco-systemic levels.

Part 4

The Fruits and Flowers: Integration in Practice

Introduction

We have now explored a great deal of theory, and we are sure readers have many questions. If you have never been in therapy, you might well be asking: 'Yes, but what do you actually do when you are doing psychotherapy, rather than writing about it, or talking about it?' 'If I was a fly on the wall in one of your sessions, what would I see and hear happening?' Alternatively, if you are an experienced psychotherapist, you might be curious to know how we apply these important perspectives to our own work, and what difference it makes, not only to what we do, but how this benefits the client.

Having explored the three epistemological stems or strands, we will begin to show how these three strands can be woven together in and through practice and produce both the flowering in the integrative psychotherapy work and its fruition. First, in Chapters 10 and 11, we will explore how they inform and shape integrative psychotherapy practice, both in how we create the frame and container for the work and how the work unfolds. Then, in Chapter 12, you will see how they shape ways of supervising, not just for psychotherapists but any people professions that use a psychotherapeutic understanding or approach. This includes all of the professions parallel to psychotherapy (counselling, coaching, spiritual guidance) and all the helping professions we mentioned in the Preface, as well as parents and teachers and those who work with people who may be vulnerable and have overwhelming needs. Being a professional, or indeed a parent, brings with it a power imbalance, and we all need to be ethically sensitive and aware of the way in which we manage our power and influence. This is addressed in Chapter 13. In Chapter 14, we will look at the implications of this approach for designing and delivering the training of psychotherapists (and other professionals), not only in ways that enable people's ethical maturity to grow, but also their capacity to work relationally, systemically and ecologically, even under extreme psychological and interpersonal pressure. We have argued throughout that all human beings in our current age need to increase their relational, systemic and ecological capacities, but this is particularly critical for those working therapeutically with other people.

When we weave the three strands of relational, systemic and ecological into an integrative ever-changing tapestry, psychotherapy can be seen as a mosaic – a dialogue of dialogues. The dialogues that need to be attended to in particular include:

- The client's internal dialogue – how they integrate their many sub-personalities, including their various narratives connecting aspects of their life (Chapter 11).

- The intersubjective relationship between the client and the psychotherapist (Chapter 7).

- The dialogues between the client and their current 'life world' – the many systems and cultures they inhabit (Chapter 8).

- The dialogues between their current life world and their past and hoped-for future; how the current patterns of interaction and sense-making are coloured by the past and drawn forward by the future.

- The intercultural dialogue between the client and psychotherapist and the shared and differing cultures they both bring into the room through their ways of seeing and narrating the world.

- The dialogue between *Homo sapiens* and the more-than-human world of our living planetary eco-system, and how we discover a new relationship between the two.

Finally, in Chapter 15, we will reflect on all the themes of this book and attempt to integrate them, as best we can, in a way that does not create artificial closure, but is a springboard for further dialogue and development, with and by others. We will also return to the challenges of our times and lean into the future to explore how psychotherapy can make a positive difference in facing the crisis that confronts our whole world.

CHAPTER 10

The Practice of Integrative Psychotherapy: Part 1, Setting the Frame

Introduction

As we saw in Part 3, *relational, systemic* and *eco-systemic* psychotherapy are the three strands we weave together to form our model of integrative psychotherapy. In Part 4, we bring these together into one thread, which runs throughout the practice, be it in psychotherapy, supervision or training.

In this chapter, we will explore what actually happens in practice, so that theory is not divided from practice, but both are brought together in integrative praxis. Having said that, part of this praxis is not to be dogmatic about the way that 'things are done'. Rather than have traditional rules, we bring an understanding of key principles and approaches to the areas that need to be carefully thought about, as well as the way they affect the relational and systemic fields in which the therapy sits.

In many ways, the relational and the systemic ways of seeing are not separate and should naturally include the wider, more-than-human world. As we saw in Chapter 9, our planet is under threat in many ways. This is becoming more and more obvious and concerning to clients who come to us for psychotherapy. The ecological has been largely, though not entirely, ignored by psychotherapists, but we have separated it out to give it special attention. We also need to learn how to bring this aspect of the experiencing world of the client and therapist into the therapeutic space. Here we bring all three together so that some of the examples which illustrate these chapters more explicitly include the wider systemic levels that the client is nested within and are nested in us, including the more-than-human eco-system.

It is sometimes easier to write about the theories behind our work than to be explicit about the way this shows up in our practice. In this chapter, we attempt to demonstrate as clearly as we can what integrative, relational, systemic and eco-systemic psychotherapy actually looks like in practice, and how this differs from, and is similar to, other approaches.

Most 'schools' of psychotherapy are recognisable by the distinctive way in which they practise. Seating arrangements, to take one example, tend to be a mark of the school. Such arrangements are taught and demonstrated when the students are in psychotherapy themselves. Traditional Freudian and Kleinian psychoanalysts have patients lying on a couch while their analyst sits behind their head. This is thought to encourage unconscious material to arise. Many other psychotherapists sit on chairs facing their client; some sit an at angle so the client can more easily look away from the psychotherapist, if they want to. Certain humanistic therapies have both client and psychotherapist sitting on the floor. This gives both a feeling of being grounded and therefore more in touch with their bodies and the feelings, sensations and emotions which arise in them. The sense of being in touch with the earth, the ground of our being, leads some eco-therapists to carry out the psychotherapy walking together outdoors, if possible, in more rural and less humanised settings, in order simultaneously to be more in touch with themselves and their ecological environment.

Integrative psychotherapists tend not to have a standard way of doing such things. That does not mean that 'anything goes'. It is important for integrative psychotherapists to think carefully about how they carry out their work with clients, to ensure that the work is effective and safe (Finlay, 2016:60). Integrative psychotherapists do not think that there is only one valid way of conducting a psychotherapy process, but there may be certain ways which suit the relational, systemic and eco-systemic context of each therapist and each client. Some therapists will unilaterally come to some decisions about how the therapy is set up, such as where the work will take place, but some will be negotiated with the client, as we will see below.

The contract and the 'frame'

The first thing to consider is the contract, or agreement, which sets up the working arrangements for each psychotherapy (Scott, 2004). The practical arrangements for this may seem relatively superficial but can be extremely important for providing a good sense of holding in which the client and psychotherapist can open up to the emotional connection that will allow the healing of psychotherapy to occur. The exact arrangement is not as important as the consistency and rationale for creating the arrangements in the way they are set up (Gray, 2014).

Whether or not to make the contract, or agreement, in writing has to be considered. When a client first visits a psychotherapist, they are usually full of distress and concerned about what has led them to seek psychotherapy. Spending a long time going through a contract can seem insensitive and unimportant to the client, even though it exists to protect them. Providing a written contract or agreement is often good practice, and it does not have to be spoken about in the first session. A written contract ensures that later in the psychotherapy there will not be disagreements about what was negotiated. If it is in writing and given to the client, they can be asked to read it and questions can be brought back at the next session. The relational and eco-systemic nature of the work may well be alluded to in the contract, but usually not in so many words. For instance, the contract may include something like, 'How our work together turns out will very much depend on what emerges between us and the many and various influences from the worlds we live in. Both of our lives will inevitably come into that and be present for us in the background of the work.' This may be a message we give verbally at the start of the therapy rather than fixing it in the written contract.

Rather than having a set way of making the contract, it is good to think of the areas that need to be taken into consideration. Below are some of the most important areas which need to be thought about.

The venue of the psychotherapy

If the psychotherapist is working within an organisational context, there may not be much choice about the room in which the work occurs. We have known many organisations, particularly medical ones, which do not have specially dedicated rooms for therapy, and this could be a red line that the psychotherapist does not want to cross. They may wish to insist on consistency of place for the therapy. However, there are other things that will need to be considered, such as the likelihood of interruptions to the work, whether the place is available each week at the same time, whether or not they can be overheard and whether it is clean and warm. It is incumbent on each psychotherapist to consider the needs of their clients for the consistent holding of a specially arranged and furnished room – as well as the needs of an organisation that may have few resources. The setting of the psychotherapy will influence the work and needs to be thought about by the therapist, if not actually discussed with the client in so many words. A room with a view of a garden with paintings and plants will enable a very different experience to a doctor's consulting room, for instance.

If the psychotherapist is working privately, they will have more control over these factors. The therapist will need to consider whether to work from home or not. If they do, they need to think about whether other people living in the house will be able to hear the client and whether the client will overhear the family. Family life could be unacceptably disrupted by the presence of a client. The question of personal effects in the room also needs to be considered. Freudians, for instance, think that the therapist should be, as far as possible, a 'blank screen' so that the client can project unconscious thoughts and feelings on to them. The ability (and willingness!) to be a blank screen is hard, if not impossible, to achieve, but the presence of photos and other personal items in the room will always have an effect on the client's experience of the psychotherapy, as will reminders of the natural world such as plants. The window this gives into the therapist's life could put too much emphasis on the therapist and thus be a distraction or have some other effect. Alternatively, it could help the client to feel safe within the relationship. What is important for the therapist to consider is whether or not they want to address such possible effects with the client when they arise, and whether they think this will adversely affect the therapy or be helpful.

The therapist may prefer to rent or buy a room away from home to make some of these matters easier though this is, of course, a more expensive option. Whether or not the room is in their own house, the therapist needs to consider what they want the room to look and feel like. The seating arrangements can be important. If the room is rented, there may not be a lot of choice, though this consideration could affect the choice of room that is rented. If the therapist has sole use of the room, they may decide to have a range of seats – maybe cushions and chairs and/or a couch, for example. Whatever is decided on, the important consideration is that the therapist needs to feel comfortable working there, so that they can be relaxed, grounded and present for the client. A relational, integrative psychotherapist knows from experience that a sense of ease within the situation is something they ultimately find with the client, but it starts with the therapist setting up a situation in which they feel comfortable.

This could be outdoors in certain circumstances, and some psycho-therapists do sometimes work outside 'in the wild' (Hasbach, 2016). Though this is little done at present, it may become more popular as the ecology becomes more threatened and awareness of this increases. Kelvin Hall, who does work outdoors, particularly with animal-assisted therapy, reports that people often feel safer outside. In his paper 'Coming home to Eden: Animal-assisted therapy and the present moment', he gives this as an example of a woman who reported how she felt when outside:

> I recall sensing, during such sessions, that the dyad feels less of a 'weight'. When incidents arising out of the environment – the fall of a leaf, the gusting of wind, the approach of a horse – are treated as interventions, it feels as if the living world, as well as the therapist, is supporting the process. Simultaneously, however, the therapist is called on to be fully aware of these events on the periphery of the dyad, and this requires a different kind of awareness to that required indoors, as described in McMullan's comments on peripheral vision to which I refer later. (Hall, 2014:59)

Whether or not the room is accessible for disabled people also needs to be given consideration. This can be quite challenging as, for instance, someone who uses a wheelchair will need, not only level entry, but to be able to access toilets. Of course, not all disabled people use wheelchairs, so thought can be given to the extent to which the room is accessible to a diverse range of people. If it is not possible to offer disabled access of any sort, it is good practice to make this clear in the therapist's publicity.

Examples

One psychotherapist worked in a GP surgery in a room normally used for podiatry. This was not a very satisfactory arrangement but was good enough for the therapy to continue without ill-effects until the therapist was asked to move her work from time to time to various other rooms, including a small internal room with no windows and a doctor's office. This had a disturbing and disruptive effect on the therapy of several clients and the psychotherapist decided to move her practice away from the surgery.

One student psychotherapist went for an initial session with a psychotherapist who had what looked like medieval torture aids hanging on his wall – chains and armour and so on. He did not return!

Another psychotherapist rented a room once a week in which to see clients. In the room was a plant, which the therapist was not in the habit of noticing or thinking about. As the room was used by many therapists, she did not feel much ownership of the surroundings. A new client, however, became focused on this plant, particularly as it sometimes looked healthy and sometimes had wilted from lack of water. For the client, this plant represented her own sense of well-being or lack thereof, and a connection with nature was important to her. The plant also represented what she felt to be the waxing and waning of her therapist's care of her. The psychotherapist tended to focus on the symbolic meaning of the plant to her. Her supervisor, however, pointed out that this plant represented the natural world within this room, which was otherwise rather stark and lacking in beauty. It also demonstrated how the therapist was seen to take responsibility or not for nature.

The frequency and duration of the sessions

Most integrative psychotherapists work once weekly, though some work twice or three times when they feel it would be helpful. As a general principle, we think it is best only to give the number of sessions that the therapist has experienced themselves as a client. If that is the case, they will know from experience how the intensity of the therapy increases with the number of sessions per week. Some therapists will see people once a fortnight if a less intense therapy is called for. Others may never do this.

It is usual for certain humanistic therapists to give sessions which last for one hour. Psychoanalytic psychotherapists more often have 50-minute sessions. Integrative psychotherapists may do either, depending on their preference. When the time boundary is set, it is probably best to stick to the pattern, as the rhythm of that time span becomes habituated and it is easier for both parties to have a feel for what can be worked with during that time. Nevertheless, as integrative psychotherapists are not doctrinaire about practice, it is possible that they may give longer timeframes to the session such as one-and-a-half hours, particularly if they use active techniques such as drama or bodywork, or if the client has come from a distance and it makes sense for them to work for two hours fortnightly. The important factor is to consider the likely effect of the chosen timeframe and duration and to discuss this with a supervisor to determine whether or not it works for the client and is not disturbing or ineffective.

Some psychotherapists, particularly those with psychoanalytic origins, are very strict about finishing times of sessions. Others might be more flexible and let people continue, particularly if they are in the middle of a crucial shift in the work. For an integrative psychotherapist, these factors need to be taken into account:

- It is important that clients do not encounter other clients as they arrive and leave, which could happen if the the gap between sessions is brief and the previous session ends late. Although this meeting of clients may be 'grist to the mill', it can feel that the therapist is not taking good enough care. It may be necessary, therefore, to finish on time to allow enough time for the first client to leave before the next one arrives. It also gives the therapist a breathing space between the two. Freud had two doors – one for clients to enter and one to leave. Not everyone has that luxury!

- The client is more likely to arrive late if their therapist does not keep good time boundaries. The therapist will not be able to rely on their working schedule, particularly if bad time keeping becomes the rule and the client becomes erratic in their attendance.

- If time is kept to very strictly, the client may be interrupted in the middle of a sentence because time is up. This can feel as if the therapist is not really interested in what they have to say and thus there is a huge breach of empathy. Winnicott says that psychotherapists show their love by being present for their clients and their hate by providing boundaries to the session (Winnicott, 1947). If this is sensed to be true, and hate is felt too keenly, the client may well feel uncared for and leave.

- Another issue to consider is whether or not to warn a client that the end of a session is imminent. This may sometimes be helpful, particularly if a new and difficult subject is broached near the end. Whether or not the therapist warns the client about the impending end of the session, it may be more important to reflect on the effect of any intervention and possibly do this reflecting with the client.

Examples

A psychotherapist was not very good at keeping time boundaries. She often did not finish on time, so clients got used to this state of affairs. Nevertheless, she seemed to 'get away' with it, in that she maintained a good practice. However, one day one of her clients left as another was arriving. The clients happened to know each other and all three were very embarrassed at this meeting. One of these clients was very angry when she returned the following week. They talked it through, and it was agreed that better time boundaries would be put in place and kept to. The psychotherapist took full responsibility for the event, saying it was her fault for not finishing on time. The other client did not return at all.

A supervisor had a supervisee who normally saw her clients two or three times a week. She did not experience any resistance to this in her clients and they made good progress and worked at depth. Another of her supervisees was in the habit of seeing her clients weekly. They also made progress and she made good therapeutic relationships with them and the work was good and productive. When, with the agreement of the client, this supervisee moved to see one of her clients twice weekly, the client soon became erratic in his attendance, effectively making the session weekly. Maybe, although she had experienced twice weekly therapy herself, this was not extensive, and she did not often offer this to clients. One explanation for this was that the disturbance in this field was picked up by the client and voted for by his feet!

Total length of the psychotherapy

Whether to work short term or long term is one of the basics of psychotherapy practice and part of the contract made with the client (Scott, 2004). This could be something decided on unilaterally by the therapist or in negotiation with the client. There are several possibilities:

- The psychotherapist always works short term. Within public sector and not-for-profit organisations this is frequently the case, but it could apply to private practice too. Short-term work is often called counselling but could be psychotherapy (see Preface) (Elton Wilson, 1996).

- The psychotherapist always works in an open-ended way and this is said to the client as a 'given' at the start of the work.

- The work could be either short term or open ended and this is decided on in the contracting phase with the client.

- The psychotherapist sees the client for a definite number of sessions, after which time they decide whether to continue or not.

- This continued term could be for another definite number of sessions or it could be open ended.

All these ways are valid, but it is good to be clear about it when making an initial contract with a client. It is also good to be aware on what basis this decision is made.

Examples

One therapist became ill with a chronic disorder and was unsure about how long she would be able to continue to work. She made a decision at that time to see people for no longer than 12 sessions and made this known to everybody who approached her for therapy. Although she was tempted to break this rule from time to time, particularly as she was able to continue for several years, she followed her rule steadfastly. It provided her, and therefore her clients, with a safe container that she knew she was able to follow through on.

Judy has found that when students offer clients six sessions before taking them on for further work, both they and their clients tend to think the other will reject them when they come to discuss it, usually in week five. Unconsciously for the client, it is as if the therapist is saying, 'I am not sure I could bear to work with you. I'll give it six sessions and see.' The therapist has a similar fantasy about what the client thinks. In fact, this arrangement is made to ensure that they do not take on someone who would be too difficult for them to work with and acts as a safeguard against this, thus protecting both. It is best to consider the potential implications when making this kind of contract, particularly therapists who are not students and do not need this safeguard. Rejection can seem to be 'in the field' and likely affect the therapy.

Psychotherapist's presentation

How the psychotherapist dresses and holds themselves more generally will have an effect on the client and may well determine whether or not they choose a particular therapist to work with. While it is important to feel comfortable in your own skin and clothes, it can be useful to give this some consideration. Here are some of the things to think about:

- Is your style of dress likely to cause a strong reaction – is it too formal or informal, for instance?

- If you have tattoos, would it be best if they were not visible? Tattoos may cause a strong reaction and while this is this something that can be worked with, consider if you need to have them on show.

- How tidy or untidy is your room? Is it too cluttered and therefore could cause a distraction for the client?

- Are the spaces that lead to your room tidy or untidy?

- What do the books on your shelves, and other artefacts in the room, say about you?

Examples

A student supervisee habitually wore dirty jeans and a T-shirt. He had great difficulty keeping clients for more than a few sessions. He was not happy with the supervisor saying in supervision that they may be reacting to his clothes. How we dress is very personal and this is not always an easy conversation to have. However, when he dressed a little more smartly, he had less difficulty keeping his clients.

Another student saw her clients at home. She was so keen to be thought suitable for each individual that she would change her clothes before each one arrived in order to appear to be well matched. In supervision, we speculated that her difficulty with keeping clients was connected with her anxiety to be acceptable enough for them. Frequently changing and matching her clothes was a symptom of this anxiety. As she became more relaxed, she dressed in her normal way and her clients did not habitually leave prematurely.

Level of fees

If the psychotherapist is working privately, they will need to make a decision about the fees to charge, and how to approach this with clients is often a big issue. The therapist may think that, as they are a student, they may be unworthy to take the money from the client, or it could be the reverse. They may feel that training is expensive and money to fund it has to be earned as soon as possible. Some integrative schools may have rules about how much students can charge or only assign to students the clients attending their own clinic. Sometimes the client pays the clinic rather than the student.

Our view is that it is important to practise psychotherapy as a student in the way that they will continue, including mastering the challenging issues around payment. Such issues can be explored as part of the training to ensure good practice. This area often needs significant support to be handled well. Some trainings, particularly in counselling rather than psychotherapy, do not allow students to work privately. While this could be seen as good practice as students are not experienced enough to work independently, it does mean that the issues concerning private practice are usually not taught in the training, nor practised while the training institution monitors the student's work. This is less of an issue in more extended psychotherapy trainings, so students have a longer period to gain relevant experience. Qualified psychotherapists, particularly newly qualified ones, may still feel uncomfortable with the issue of money, and supervision can help them to explore their issues.

While there is no rule stipulating particular fees, psychotherapy operates in a 'market' and psychotherapists need to be aware of how much other colleagues with a similar level of experience charge, and make decisions based on that information, while taking their own needs for a good enough income and their expenses into account. They must also be aware that charging too much may lead to fewer clients, as will charging too little – advertising at a very low rate may give the impression that the therapy itself is not worth much.

Many psychotherapists, however, are concerned that a lot of people cannot afford their fee and they do not want to work only with affluent people. However, if the psychotherapist only sees low-paying clients, their work may become unsustainable over time. If they practise a mixed economy of people who pay the full fee, then they will be able to offer some low-paying places to those who cannot afford the full fee. This can mean that, if the client's financial circumstances change, they may start paying more as the therapist's full fee is known to them.

If the client is seen long term, it will be necessary to put the fee up from time to time and to revise the normal fee charged to new clients. Psychotherapists are becoming more experienced over time and can therefore charge a higher fee. It is also important that the fee should go up with inflation, or their income will be decreasing in real terms.

Although our belief is that psychotherapists should be free to set their own fees, it is possible to have anomalies in an unregulated environment. We have had the situation where inexperienced students were charging more than experienced psychotherapists who found it hard to charge a good fee. Some rules were put in place to ensure this did not happen as a high fee can give the misleading impression to the public that a student therapist is better than a qualified one.

Payment for missed sessions

This is a very thorny issue, particularly for students, who find it difficult to charge for sessions which did not actually take place. Our feeling is that the most important thing is to be clear about the policy. It is possible to:

- always charge for missed sessions, whatever the reason

217

- charge only for missed sessions if no notice was given

- charge only for missed sessions if a certain number of weeks' or days' notice is not given

- charge only for missed sessions if a good enough reason is not given

- never charge for missed sessions.

Always charging for missed sessions may feel harsh but, to have a sustainable professional practice, a reliable enough income needs to be made. Here are some other considerations which may aid decision making:

- The client is not actually paying for each minute of therapy given, but for the time and thought being given to that person over time.

- We find that colleagues who always charge for missed sessions find that their clients rarely do not arrive, not just because they have to pay for the session, but because the frame feels secure. It is rarely a reason for leaving the work prematurely, particularly if it is clear from the start that this is the arrangement.

Not charging or only charging on certain conditions may feel more compassionate, particularly if the person does not come because they are ill, or in hospital, or other unavoidable circumstance but, as indicated above, the container may feel less safe or the therapist seems to take care of themselves less well. The money paid to the therapist ensures that there is a fair exchange of energy.

An integrative psychotherapist 'never says never', however, and there may be circumstances, such as long-term illness or having a baby, which could make it realistic to revisit the contract and take a break in the therapy.

Example

A supervisee normally worked with a contract that said that clients missing sessions would always incur a fee. However, he had one client to whom this did not apply because the client was sometimes obliged to go to work during session times. The therapist began to realise that it was not always for work-related reasons that this client did not attend. After reflecting on this with his supervisor, he decided to charge for all missed sessions. The client was angry at first but quite soon managed to negotiate with his employer not to come in to work at session times. The sessions became more settled and productive as a result.

Confidentiality

It is an article of faith within psychotherapy that the client can be sure that what they tell their psychotherapist is held confidentially. This intent is part of the holding that is offered within the secure frame (Gray, 2014). Most psychotherapists will say, and write in their contracts, that they hold clients' information in confidence and then they will specify exceptions to this rule. Most ethical guidelines in professional bodies such as the UK Council for Psychotherapy spell out the exceptions (Scott, 2004). Unlike priests, psychotherapists do not have the protection of law when it comes to not divulging what they have been told by clients. It is therefore important to be clear with clients about all of these exceptions. A lack of clarity and a subsequent breaking of confidentiality is more likely to derail the psychotherapy than being clear in the first place (Bond, 2015a).

There are some exceptions to confidentiality:

- Anything said to a psychotherapist must be available to tell a supervisor or supervision group. They, in turn, must keep the information confidential. A psychotherapist agreeing or deciding not to tell a supervisor about something that arose in the psychotherapy probably means that the psychotherapist is colluding with the client. It is important that the client knows that anything they say may be told in supervision, so that any disclosure is made in that light. They should also know that what is revealed in supervision is part of appropriate confidentiality that makes the work safe, thus providing a stronger, rather than weaker, container for the work.

- It is generally agreed in psychotherapists' codes of ethics that, if the client is a danger to themselves or to others, then confidentiality can be broken. Under these circumstances, we consider it to be good practice for the client to be told beforehand that confidentiality will be broken and given a chance to take action themselves. Of course, this may not always be possible or appropriate but is more empowering to the client when it is. For instance, a psychotherapist may want to let a doctor know that a client has suicidal intentions but allow the client to alert the doctor first. If the danger of self-harm is thought to be imminent, it may be better for the psychotherapist to take action as it might otherwise be too late.

- Where the danger of harm to others is very serious, the law may specify that there is a duty to tell the police or social services. This is particularly true in matters of safeguarding the vulnerable (such as children and vulnerable adults). It also applies to dangers to the public such as acts of terrorism.

- If something that is thought to have arisen in psychotherapy is possibly relevant to a court hearing, then the lawyer or judge can subpoena case notes to shed light on the matter in hand.

- Sometimes lawyers ask for case notes to be sent to them and clients may waive their right to confidentiality. In this case it is, if possible, best practice to talk this through with the client before handing over their notes. They may not have considered the consequences, such as how the breaking of the psychotherapeutic container may affect the psychotherapy.

As with any matter of ethics, there are rules of confidentiality, but the *intention* of the psychotherapist is the most important factor. Clients often reveal sensitive matters from their lives, including their deepest thoughts, feelings and inner agonies. They do so while trusting that this will be held seriously by the psychotherapist and not 'spread around' as gossip. They expect all that they say to be respected and taken seriously. Whatever the psychotherapist does with the information they receive from clients, it should be received in that spirit so that, even in a supervision group, they do not gossip but respectfully explore what they have been told in order for the work to deepen and be supported.

Keeping notes

Keeping notes about our client work is part of the therapeutic holding as it:

- helps us to digest our thoughts and feelings about our sessions with clients

- helps us to remember what took place

- provides a record of what happened over time so that the psycho-therapy can be looked back on to see patterns that emerge

- provides a record for the purposes of bringing the work to supervision.

It is important that these notes are kept safely so that they cannot be read by unauthorised people, including by those who might hack into the computer (Bond, 2015a). Some people write by hand for this reason and keep notes in a locked cupboard, or write them on the computer, print them out and delete them. Others might password-protect their notes and keep them on a computer.

Psychotherapists who work for agencies may have other protocols in relation to client notes which might be quite brief. In that case, they may take separate notes of their own that help them to understand the therapeutic processes that the client is going through.

European data protection laws are now very clear that client notes should be made available to clients at any point if they so wish. It is good practice to make this clear in drawing up a contract. It is important to be mindful that the client's data, including their names and contact details, are not made available to unauthorised people and that clients are told what procedures are put in place to protect their data.

As we saw above, client notes can be requested or subpoenaed by the courts and it is important that they are kept in a form that can be handed over if necessary. Sometimes lawyers are happy with a report rather than the notes. In either case, it is important that clients give their permission for a report to be written unless they are subpoenaed, in which case neither client nor psychotherapist has a choice. If a report is written it is important that it is shown to the client before it is sent. It may be appropriate for it to be written in collaboration with the client, which can increase a feeling of safety and respect and even strengthen the working alliance. A report should never be written and sent without the client's knowledge.

There are many forms that notes can take. Each psychotherapist can choose one that helps them most. Here are a few examples:

- a straightforward narrative of the session

- a list of significant events within the session

- some significant verbatim exchanges

- columns with what took place on the left-hand side and thoughts/feeling on the right-hand side (or some variant of this)

- a mind map (Buzan, 2009) or other diagram showing different events in the session with connecting lines

- a drawing of the session using images, shapes and/or colours.

Although the taking and keeping of notes has a somewhat legalistic feel now that data laws have been strengthened, we should not lose sight of the way that note-taking can help the therapeutic process.

Working virtually

As technology exponentially develops, the possibility of its facilitating psychotherapy and/or supervision increases, as does the assumption that it is a viable option. No doubt as time goes on, this will become increasingly the case, particularly as technology becomes more sophisticated and a greater part of everyday life (Weitz, 2018). As this is the case, it is as well for us to think carefully about the issues involved in successful psychotherapy online, just as psychotherapists in the past have considered the appropriate frame for face-to-face working.

There are various platforms that can be used for virtual psychotherapy. Some are more used in the present day and others may well become commonly used in the future (Stone, 2019). Those that are often used today are:

- telephone

- email (e-therapy or e-supervision) (Hawkins & Shohet, 2012:72)

- video conferencing.

Those that may well be common in the future include:

- online instant messaging or 'chat' communications on the internet

- instant messaging, such as WhatsApp

- use of virtual reality.

The convenience of all these methods is clear in that neither party has to leave home, which has obvious advantages from an ecological point of view as there is very little carbon usage. It also means that the whole world opens up for a choice of psychotherapist or supervisor. For instance, one of us (Judy) has two supervisors, one in Reading in the UK (Judy lives in Bath) and one in California. Some people find it hard to see a psychotherapist in their vicinity as they know so many people who live nearby.

Despite these considerable advantages, there are many traps for the unwary which can lead to serious problems. Before going on to describe these, we address a more general difficulty when not being physically present with a client or supervisee. We now know that there is an exchange that happens between people when they meet physically, which is a particularly important consideration when working relationally. This may include hormonal exchange, communication by smell and by subtle cues that may not be picked up, even by online communication that has a visual element. When seeing someone through a webcam, we tend to see their face and shoulders and not the rest of their body, which may well be communicating through subtle movement. This applies, of course, to both the client and the psychotherapist. This issue can be mitigated to some extent by asking the client to more their screen so that more of their body can be seen.

However, mirror neurons and other methods of attunement are likely to be weaker when we are not physically present. This lack means that an important ingredient in the psychotherapy is lost or reduced when there is no embodied meeting. It means that the therapeutic alliance needs special attention so that trust is developed between client and psychotherapist (Dunn, 2018). Many psychotherapists think that it is beneficial to meet in person initially, and from time to time, to maintain an embodied relational engagement.

Here are some other considerations that need to be thought about:

- The security and privacy of the platform. Some are more secure than others; others, like email, can be encrypted.

- Checking that the person is who you think they are (particularly when using text methods).

- Protocols, such as who initiates the contact, how payment is made, what procedure you use if the internet fails, ensuring privacy – no one else should be in the room and the door should be shut. The conversation should be in an appropriate place (not on the bus!).

- Messaging and email may not be instant and in 'real time'. Thought needs to be given to when initial contact is made and when a reply is expected. Most people have an agreement about when the client writes and when the therapist replies.

- Some platforms can easily be recorded, so agreement needs to be made about when this is appropriate and that it is never carried out without the other's knowledge.

- If the work is with people resident in other countries, consideration needs to be given to their privacy laws when setting up the contract, as these may differ.

There is clearly much to be gained as well as to be lost in working virtually, but this way of working will no doubt become increasingly common (Stone, 2019). We need now to discover the best and safest way of setting up virtual work that mitigates some of the difficulties, makes the most of its advantages and ensures that good therapeutic work can be undertaken.

Holding the ending process

It is important to make clear in the original contract how the work will end. As the contract is not only made at the beginning, it is possible to revisit it, as is the case with all other aspects of the contract, such as in the example above of the psychotherapist who first did not charge the client for missed sessions because of his working pattern and then changed the contract when he realised that this was not the only reason for his changing session times. That is not to say that the time or manner of the ending needs to be spelled out. Here are some considerations:

- A certain number of sessions can be specified to begin with. If this is the case, it needs to be constantly held in mind and the client reminded of the number of sessions left. It can be agreed that the last session is to review the work.

- The number of sessions can be specified, but it could be agreed at the beginning that this will be reviewed towards the end of the contract and the ending time revisited in light of how the work is going.

- It can be agreed that the therapy is open ended, but client and therapist could decide together how an ending is decided on. The therapist can indicate when they think the client is ready to finish or, more likely, the two of them can agree and either can say that they think the process has reached the closing phase.

- In a long-term therapy, it is best to spend some time in an ending phase when the end date becomes known. This gives a good enough amount of time to review what has gone well, what was disappointing and to mourn the imminent loss. As a rule of thumb, an ending phase of one month of sessions per year of therapy seems right, so that a three-year therapy is in an ending phase for three months. This gives time for the sessions to be integrated. Psychotherapy that ends badly is hard for the client to integrate into their life and hard to draw the most benefit from it.

- Alternatively, the client may suddenly decide to leave. While a client can be challenged for seeming to avoid the ending phase, they may have their own good reasons for doing so.

- In many cases, it is important for therapy processes not to 'peter out'. However, we find, in the case of very traumatised refugees, that fortnightly and even intermittent returns are good for them, as their lives often lack important others with whom they share a strong attachment. The end of therapy can become more like 'leaving home' with intermittent returns – and this can work well.

Examples

Judy had a client who left quite suddenly after three years. He only had one finishing session. He felt that the time to leave was just right and it was important for him to leave when he wanted to and not feel constrained by Judy's needs as he had with his mother, when he struggled to leave home. Judy did not try to persuade him otherwise.

Judy has a refugee client who comes back to see her from time to time and has brought her small child to meet her. She has no parents in this country to take her child 'home' to and it is an important contact for her.

Conclusion

This chapter has provided some ways of thinking about aspects of the therapeutic frame which holds and contains the therapeutic process. As integrative psychotherapists we need to develop thoughtful ways of working which are strong and reliable whilst being flexible and responsive (Finlay, 2016:62). Having read this chapter you may like to consider ways in which you devise and maintain the frame you set for your own work and those you have experienced as a client. Your own preferences are likely to influence your choices but it is good for the boundaries and choices you make with each client to be one that will arise out of the intersubjective relationship and within the systemic and eco-systemic nature of your work together.

CHAPTER 11

The Practice of Integrative Psychotherapy: Part 2, Working with the Relational, Systemic and Eco-Systemic Approach

Introduction

In the last chapter, we set the framework in which good integrative work can be held in a way consistent with relational, systemic and ecological principles. These boundaries are not separate from the main business of the work, since the way the work is 'set up' will have a direct effect on the client–therapist experience and the outcome of their work together. It also provides the context in which ways of working together can occur, and that is why we have given it a separate chapter.

At the core of psychotherapy is 'life-making' – not just living but making sense of one's life and developing coherent meaning – that both deepens and integrates our experience (Yalom, 2011). In this, we are following the Socratic dictum that 'An unexamined life is not worth living.' This chapter is about how psychotherapist and client join in the business of life-making. This life-making is not something that is done in a vacuum but is deeply embedded within the nested systems and eco-systems we wrote of in earlier chapters. We do not do special work that is systemic or eco-systemic but these are lenses and contexts for all our work, as we will see below.

As we saw in Chapter 7, the therapeutic relationship is of the greatest importance in this work (Erskine, 2015; Finlay, 2016; Gilbert & Orlans, 2011), and we will show different ways of working with the relational field, as well as the systemic and ecological levels embedded within it, with a number of illustrative case examples.

We start with the working alliance which, maybe, straddles the frame that we described in the previous chapter and what happens within the frame. It both sets a context for the therapeutic relating and is also deeply part of the work itself, and needs to be attended to with care throughout the process of the psychotherapy.

The working alliance

A working alliance is the bedrock underpinning relational work, so that the client feels able to trust the integrity of the therapist to undertake the work with care and certainty and without any danger of abuse (Gilbert & Orlans, 2011; Scott, 2004). This is particularly important in psychotherapy: the client comes to us in an emotionally vulnerable state and expects to be able to open up about sensitive areas on the basis of a safe enough relationship. There are factors that can encourage a good working alliance:

- Good quality listening skills (see below).

- Showing that the intention is to understand at depth what the client has said, taking into account their systemic and eco-systemic context.

- Being clear about the contract without making it seem more important than the person and their concerns.

- Re-attending to the working alliance if there has been a rupture in the relationship.

Example

A psychotherapist changed the time of their sessions at the request of the client. The time it was changed to was not very convenient for the therapist, but she agreed as it would otherwise have meant the therapy would have to end prematurely. The client had found full-time employment and the therapist felt that this landmark event had great importance. On the second occasion after the change in session time the therapist forgot to attend. This was an unusual time for the therapist to be working and that, no doubt, contributed to her forgetting. On exploration with her supervisor, it became clear that she resented having to work at this time and they thought that this would have contributed to her forgetting. Forgetting to arrive put a strain on the working alliance as it felt to the client that her therapist's care of her was dependent on her being 'convenient'. It took some time for a good working alliance to be re-established, and the therapist's consistency and lack of defensiveness importantly contributed to this restoration.

A working alliance is built on the small but important attention to the agreement between the therapist and the client which is adhered to consistently enough to be considered reliable. Being human, we cannot be 100% reliable but being open and non-defensive about that unreliability is important in maintaining a healthy working alliance. If the client has experienced unreliable and defensive attachment figures in the past and within their systemic context, then new ways of experiencing the holding environment of the therapeutic relationship can play a key role in generating good therapeutic outcomes (see below).

Working with the wider relational systems

If we are to work intersubjectively, systemically and eco-systemically with the relational system, we are aware that when a client enters the room, they do not enter alone. They bring in their wake all the people within their family – both present and past – all the people within their community and culture, all those who have influenced and affected them throughout their lives, and all in the more-than-human world that has accompanied them thus far. This can even include ancestors whose influence comes down the years transgenerationally. We discussed in Chapter 7 the way this influence may be very powerful: it is brought about, not just psychologically, but can be transmitted epigenetically as well (Gerhardt, 2015). In other words, although the genes cannot themselves be altered, their expression may well be affected by transgenerational experience. Of course, we psychotherapists also bring our past and our significant relationships with us into the room, both personal and professional. This includes all the theorists and practitioners who have influenced our work as therapists. They are present with us to a greater or lesser degree at any particular time within the meeting with our client.

Of course, this would be a very crowded space indeed if we had these relationships at the front of our mind all the time. Mostly these others are there 'at our elbow', guiding and shaping our responses to each other. It is important, however, for us as therapists to be aware of the richness of the systems and significant relationships present in the room. The meaningful events encountered with others both enhance the experiencing self and contribute to our narrative self (see below). For the therapist, awareness of these worlds enriches our ability to see an arc of possibility that stretches into the future. It is our job to help shape the client's experience within the therapeutic space, so that the beneficial process of relating within the therapy may contribute to a healthier future for our clients. As Siegel sees it:

> Part of the art of being a therapist is to learn to see across time, including looking into the potential future possibilities so that we can intentionally support the movement of those we are helping forward to a more integrated way of living. (Siegel, 2012)

Working in a relational and systemic way rests on an underlying understanding that the world is relational, systemic and eco-systemic in nature. It is a way of looking to understand what is happening in the therapeutic process, not a choice or 'technique'. If techniques are used (a role play, for instance) or anything else that emerges in the therapy, it will be seen through the lens of working relationally, and understood not only as having an impact on the relationship between client and psychotherapist, but also as assuming that the way of being together at this particular time arises out of the relational, systemic and eco-systemic context of the present meeting.

If we 'lean into' (Shama, 2009) the future in the present day, it looks very uncertain. With much of the world undergoing political upheavals, large-scale migration, withdrawal into nation states and the ecological crisis becoming ever more serious, this is going to increasingly affect our clients. Winnicott famously implied that we do not attend to the socio-political world in psychotherapy, but we might know that 'the king is dead'! Andrew Samuels has been particularly influential in encouraging psychotherapists to engage in the socio-political world, both by being active in these worlds with a psychotherapist's eye, and also allowing material about the outer world to be explored in psychotherapy without insisting that the material is symbolic and an internal preoccupation (Samuels, 1993). For us, this polarity is not helpful. A dream about nuclear war or the ice caps melting would speak to both internal representations and realistic fears for the world.

Example

Judy worked with a refugee client who had lost her father when she fled her country. In the chaos, her father had disappeared and was probably killed. Tearfully, she said how important he had been to her in helping her to navigate life, and how hard it was to be without him. It felt as if her father had powerfully entered the therapy space and Judy suggested that, although he was not present in person, he was still a compelling presence. The client agreed that she often felt his presence, particularly in her dreams.

Judy suggested she imaginatively put him on the chair next to her and ask him what he would say to her now. Speaking to him in her imagination helped her to make a difficult decision in relation to her children and to discover that, not only was her father's wisdom still available to her, but so was that of her ancestors. The context of the relationship became part of the wider context of the client's world. It also met with Judy's own context of having a wise father who had died and her previous training in psychodrama which gave her the confidence to intervene in this way. The meeting included their wider systems and led to an important, embodied learning for the client and for Judy – 'embodied' because, through the role play, the client didn't just have an intellectual understanding that her father was available to her, she had an experience of it which became a resource she could return to. Judy's own embodied sense of her father was an important aspect of it being embedded in their work together.

This example shows not only how a 'technique' can be understood and used in a relational and systemic context, but also how the 'organising principles' of therapist and client are both present within the client–psychotherapist system. The term 'organising principles' was first used by the intersubjective systems theorists (Stolorow & Atwood, 1992) and described in Chapter 7. Briefly, organising principles are the unconscious principles behind a person's subjective awareness of the world and are built up through the myriad of relationships, systemic contexts and cultures that each of us have been part of. They provide a structure of interpretation through which the person understands the world. Our organising principles are based on the shape of our experiencing self and we hang the stories we tell about ourselves, our narrative self, on them.

The example also shows how Judy's ability to understand in an embodied way led to her client feeling understood. Judy's embodied understanding informed her decision to make a somewhat risky intervention. We now know that 'mirror neurons' in the brain allow us to know what others feel as we recognise their feeling state in ourselves in a deeply embodied, not just cognitive, way. As Siegel says:

> Mirror neurons enable us to soak in the internal state of another person, providing a neural mechanism with which we both simulate another's internal state and imitate that person's behavior. Mirror neurons link what

we see from others with what we feel and what we do. In other words, they serve as a kind of antenna enabling us to pick up the sometimes subtle signals from others, shift our bodily state, and then sense these changes in our own body to then imagine what another person might be feeling. (Siegel, 2012)

Here is an example of Judy's work in which the mirror neurons enabling deep recognition, not only between the therapist and client, but between therapist and interpreter, were aligned:

I wrote in my book *Being White in the Helping Professions* about an African client I saw with the help of an interpreter. I felt it was important to speak of the painful bodily experience of my client as I sensed it so strongly in my own body. A difficulty arose because my interpreter said she felt concerned about having to interpret my words as it was not considered correct for a younger woman to mention the body of an older one. We discussed this together and I could feel the fearful reluctance in my interpreter as well as the need to be understood in my client. I asked the interpreter to make an exception as a leap of faith at this time as I felt it was important. I would not have insisted if she was too uncomfortable, but I experienced our working alliance as strong enough to allow her to make this culturally inappropriate response. I therefore turned to my client and acknowledged that the murder of her daughter gave her an intense pain in 'every cell of her body'. It was interpreted in a way that matched the intensity of my concern. This intervention created a breakthrough in the therapy and the interpreter knew she had made the right decision. All three of us sat in a shared and deeply felt silence.

Example

A client, John, was normally seen for therapy at 6pm but arrived on this particular day at 6.30pm, just as the therapist was about to go home, thinking he was not coming. It was the first session back after a break. The therapist, Sally, expressed surprise when she opened the door to the client but ushered him into the consulting room saying they only had half an hour left for the session. Sally knew that it was a well-known phenomenon that clients often miss a session after a break or come late. She had experienced this herself several times and, indeed, had done this when she was in therapy. Because of this, she held in mind that this was a way of communicating distress and anger. When she gently told him that he had arrived late, John looked alarmed and said, 'Oh, I am so sorry, I thought we had agreed a new time!' It was only then that Sally remembered that she had agreed to this time as the client had moved office and could not manage to see her before 6.30pm without leaving work early. She had agreed to this reluctantly as it made her later getting home. She apologised and owned that this was her own mistake. She found it hard to feel really present during the session, partly because she was conscious that she had let John down by forgetting an important change in his life and to their work together and partly because her husband would be expecting her home earlier and she had family coming to dinner.

Later, in supervision, Sally and her supervisor reflected that certain things might have been in play for her. She herself had felt reluctant about going back to work after the summer break. Her thoughts were more with a new grandchild than her clients. She resented having to arrive home late on Thursdays, although she wanted to support John to continue therapy in spite of him moving office. John's own commitment to the therapy did not seem to be in question but she and the supervisor wondered if she was 'hanging on' to this client and could start to think with him about his readiness to finish. They decided to leave this possibility for a few weeks to see what emerged in the therapy, particularly after her mistaking the time. They also decided to explore whether she herself really wanted to retire. She had not relished going back to work after the break in the way she used to.

In the next few sessions, John expressed his anger at Sally's mistake and said he felt 'dropped' by her. They managed to work this through, but it was agreed that they would work towards an ending by Christmas.

This example demonstrates several aspects of the relational and systemic nature of the work. John was immediately apologetic and assumed it was his mistake, as did the therapist. This reveals an expectation that is held by both – that mistakes are made by John, not by Sally. Sally held the idea that, as a professional, she should not make mistakes and, more fundamentally, that as an oldest child she should always be the responsible one. John made an assumption that professionals do not make mistakes. He was usually deferential to, and even afraid of, authority. This had been a factor in his being under-achieving at work, something that the therapy had helped him with. This event of Sally mistaking the time of the session helped John to assert his own authority and it helped Sally to realise that she was both hanging on to him and, at the same time, that she was unconsciously expressing her reluctance to see him.

We can see in this example how both the therapist's and client's systems were interrelating, leading to difficult feelings on both sides. However, the psychotherapy system, a third system in play, allowed for an open and non-defensive exploration of the dynamic that had arisen between them. This resulted in a fruitful dialogue and both were able to learn from it. The psychotherapy system provided the context for this exploration and their relationship and working alliance were strong enough to 'take' the rupture and 'hold' their difficulties to allow the learning to take place.

Integrating the narrative self and the experiencing self

We have come to realise, through our reading about how the brain works and through considerations of different theories about the 'self', including Stern (1985), Mollon (1993), Wilber, who writes of distal and proximal selves (Wilber, 2000) and Kahneman, who writes of the 'experiencing' and 'remembering' (Kahneman, 2012), that it is helpful to make a distinction between the narrative self and experiencing self. The narrative self is discussed by various authors, including Stern in the latest edition of his book, *The Interpersonal World of the Infant* (Stern, 2018).

We have identified six different aspects of the narrative self:

1. *Our internal self-narrative* – the stories we tell our self about our self.

2. *Our presentational self-narratives* – the stories we tell others about our self, which may be varied and diverse.

3. *Collective narratives about our self* – the stories others have about us, that they tell us or others.

4. *Our various social self-narratives* – myself in my family of origin, or as a member of the local football team or as a manager at work.

5. *Historic narratives* – stories have a life of their own, and some stories live on beyond the time when they are useful or relevant.

6. *Emergent lived narrative* – a narrative that can be discovered from the pattern of actions, behaviours, habits and events of the person's current life.

As we discussed earlier, our consciousness resides in both the narrating self, which has language, reflection and sense-making, and the experiencing self, which is embodied and resides in the continuous present. It is important that the psychotherapist engages not only with the narrating self, which is the various stories that are related in the therapy sessions, but also with their own and the client's experiencing selves.

Psychotherapy importantly engages the experiencing self of both parties to the dialogue. The psychotherapist attends to their direct experience as they listen carefully to the client – what am I sensing in my body as I sit and listen to this client, or to the silences between the narration. The therapist may also invite the client to pause and notice what they are experiencing while recounting this tale, or even invite the client to express their direct experience in non-verbal ways that bypass the linguistic narrating mind, for example by drawing their experience, making sounds or adopting a posture.

It is essential to engage and connect these two selves, as often in psycho-therapy we may reframe and rework our self-narratives, but this may have little impact on our reflex reactions, when we are once more triggered by life's many stimuli. As psychotherapists, we may over-rely on insight and attempts at changing the nature of these self-stories, and the client's good intentions to create change. New understanding and good intentions are rarely enough to create fundamental sustainable change in our lives. Insight is located in the cognitive neo-cortex, which gives rise to the narrative self or selves, but lived change is always embodied and requires a change in the experiencing self. In this way, the various self-narratives we have, for there may be several of them, can be integrated. We may, for instance, see ourselves as both 'a good listener' and 'a lover of freedom'. We might find these two in conflict but they can only be truly integrated, rather than held as separate stories, if we allow ourselves to bring both into our experiencing self.

The rupture mentioned in the example above, when the client was forgotten, goes further and deeper than the working alliance. Ruptures that are well attended to are a fundamental part of the therapy which will affect the experiential self and the narrative self. One of the dilemmas experienced by psychotherapists over the decades has been how to bring the *experience* of the client directly into the room so that it can be present, seen, understood and, if necessary, changed. Often the client will talk *about* his experience rather than live it in the present, and in many therapies this is not challenged. Another way of putting this is that the clients often bring their narrative selves to the therapy and stand outside their experiencing self.

As we saw in Chapter 7, it is not easy to 'stay with' or 'abide in' our experiencing self. It is more like a flowing stream that we cannot catch as it passes, as future turns into the past. The present is elusive as it becomes the past constantly and the new present is then with us, also disappearing into the past instantaneously. It simply does not stay or abide. It flows and we have to flow with it. Nevertheless, it is within our experiential self that we are alive, where our feelings and emotions live. Our narrative self tries to explain our experience – tells a story about it. Sometimes this telling is congruent with our experiencing self and beautifully describes what is real for us.

It is with our experiencing self and that of our client that we are most likely to contact the ecological self. We may not yet have allowed ourselves to have a narrative which includes a deep participation with the more-than-human world but our experiencing self may well have a sense of this. This is explored by Kelvin Hall when working with a woman psychotherapeutically outside with the help of a horse.

The immediacy of the contact with the horse provided a way of being in the flow of the experiencing self. He reported that she was able to experience being 'met' in the moment by the horse:

> We were discussing my client's desire to be 'seen' in relationship, and the way this had often been disappointed. She then went into the ring with the horse and stood by him as he grazed. She said that this induced a pleasant and agreeable sense of being accepted, but that what she really wanted was for the horse to lift up his head and look at her. I said to her, 'Maybe just let yourself want that.' Very soon after, he lifted up his head and looked at her. He then gently rubbed her front – her heart space – with his nose. We were both filled with the wonder of this moment. The horse then resumed grazing, and they then went through the exact sequence again. It is my perception, supported by subsequent discussions, that this offered the client a profound experience of being seen. (Hall, 2018:25)

This example reminds us of an incident told by the philosopher, Martin Buber, who was so influential with many psychotherapists, including Fritz and Laura Perls. In his book, *I and Thou*, he recalls this incident as an example of an I/thou meeting which was with a horse:

> When I was eleven years of age, spending the summer on my grandparents' estate, I used, as often as I could do it unobserved, to steal into the stable and gently stroke the neck of my darling, a broad dapple gray horse. It was not a casual delight but a great, certainly friendly, but also deeply stirring happening. If I am to explain it now, beginning from the still very fresh memory of my hand, I must say that what I experienced in touch with the animal was the Other, the immense otherness of the Other, which however

did not remain strange like the otherness of the ox and the ram, but rather, let me draw near and touch it. (Buber, 2004:11)

In this example, Buber is describing what he called 'I and Thou' relating which was an embodied experience of the other in connection with the self. The other is known as other but also as deeply connected. He contrasted this with the 'I/it' relating where the other is not known or experienced as in embodied connection with the self.

I think my granddaughter experienced something similar in this example:

When she was four years old she said, 'when I see that flower, I am in love'. She did not say 'I love that flower'. Her narrative (in this case her internal self-narrative and emergent self-narrative) told of the feeling of love that arises in her experiencing self when she sees the flower. It is much harder for adults and older children to narrate their experience so directly. She was never happier than when crouching down in the countryside, being with the plants and creatures she found there.

These examples show how we can be in contact with our experiencing self. Addressing the dilemma of how to align our experiencing and narrative selves is central to meditation and mindfulness. Many psychotherapists encourage their clients to take up mindfulness and practise it in their sessions, to encourage more contact with their present awareness and experience. In using such practices, we can encourage our clients to loosen attachment to their fixed narrative self, simply watching it and letting it go, rather than over-identifying with it. The experiencing self is naturally connected with the greater system of the world, including the more-than-human world, and feels the distress when this connection is broken.

Particularly in the fast-moving world of today, our narrative self is often not congruent with our experience. This can be a source of unhappiness, and it can be important to notice and address it in therapy.

Examples

A client was born and lived most of her life in Africa, with her family and community, working as a subsistence farmer. Until she came to Britain, she had never tasted sugar except in fruit. When she arrived in Britain she lived in a town with few green spaces. She said she found it hard to feel 'alive' here. She put on a lot of weight by an addiction to sugary food which, she said, numbed the pain of her losses. Her presentational, historic and collective narratives were confused. She did not know how to make sense of any narrative of her life in the new setting. She lost touch with her experiencing self, which had been embedded in the land around her where her self-narratives were based. One day, she went to stay in the countryside with her church and, in the evening, went outside. To her surprise, she saw there were stars. She had thought that there were no stars in Bristol and that this applied to England more generally. It was an important moment for her that the stars she saw in Africa could also exist here. Her narrative of losing stars was challenged and helped to put her back in touch with her experiencing self and led her and her therapist to find an emergent lived narrative for these times. It was one in which she had felt more in harmony with the natural world and she was now able to articulate a deep sense of loss. The urban landscape in Bristol with its pollution and light pollution cut her off from a deep connection which had previously been part of her experience and narrative. This new experience created a new connection for her, linking her past and present and her narrative and experiencing selves.

Another client was a very good pianist, but only played when she was on her own. She mentioned her piano playing in passing, because someone had asked her to accompany her singing at an awkward time. The therapist stopped the flow of her narrative to ask her about this. It emerged that her personal and presentational narrative of her piano playing was not good in her estimation – 'others would not want to hear it'. Although the therapist had seen this client for some time, she had not been aware of her piano playing, or that the client played well enough to provide accompaniment. The client demurred, saying that she didn't play well. As the friend who wanted her to accompany her singing persisted in asking her, and the client felt harassed by this, it became something that was brought to therapy each week for some time. The client's narrative about her playing was that she 'messed about' on the piano because she enjoyed it, but it was not something others would enjoy. When this was explored more closely, it emerged that the client would have liked to play to others but her narrative about herself was that she could not play well enough and would be laughed at if she tried. This had antecedents in her childhood as her parents mocked her efforts in various endeavours, including her piano playing. Her enjoyment of her own playing was very intense and became a private joy she did not want to share for fear of spoiling her own pleasure. She stayed with this self-narrative that piano playing was a private joy, while her presentational narrative self told the story of her incompetence in this and other areas where her experiencing self found enjoyment in her skill and creativity. Through challenging these assumptions, the therapist was able to help her to risk experimenting with playing in public, safely at first with her friend, and then more widely. A new emergent self-narrative was being brought into being.

This story also demonstrates 'four levels of engagement' that Peter, along with his colleague Nick Smith, first developed in working with executive coaches (Hawkins & Smith, 2013a). These four levels help us to navigate around the often chaotically narrated material brought to therapy by a client, and to respond in ways that take a client to a place that is transformational. The four levels are as follows:

1. Data or narrated story.

2. Patterns of behaviour and relating.

3. Emotional patterns/reactions/triggers.

4. Beliefs, assumptions, stories we tell ourselves, our organising principles.

   - Applying these for levels to the above example: The data is the raw material brought by the client. We have the data that the client plays the piano: She enjoys it but does not want to play for others.

   - The pattern of behaviour found in her relationships has various aspects, including that she withdraws from contact when approached and tends to be triggered by the advances of others, which she feels to be intrusive.

   - Her emotional reaction is anger, though fear is clearly in the background – she might be sneered at and made a fool of.

   - The story she tells herself is that she is not very good at anything and that anything she does is not of a good enough standard. This is a holding belief or structure on which her experiences are hung.

By challenging these underlying assumptions, we can then climb the levels in the other direction and change the narrative. In so doing, the client was able to find a new emotional response as well as new, healthier and more satisfying relationships, not only with her friend but with her experience of the wider world.

Working with the observing and observed self

Similar to the narrative and experiential self is the 'observing' and 'observed' self, or what, as we wrote in Chapter 3, Wilber (2000:33–35) usefully describes as the difference between the *proximate self* (what we experience as our 'I', our subjective being, through which we see the world), and the *distal self* (what we experience as our 'me', a self we can objectify and see). He shows how the 'I' at one level of development, becomes the 'me' at the next level, as deeper levels of reflection and self-witnessing open up:

> what you are identified with (or embedded in) at one stage of development and therefore what you experience very intimately as 'I' tends to become transcended, or disidentified with, or de-embedded at the next, so you can see it more objectively, with some distance and detachment. (Wilber, 2000:34)

By bringing to the surface the deeper, normally hidden, levels of engagement in psychotherapy, the client can observe their patterns of behaviour and how these are created by deeper patterns of emotional triggers and their 'organising principles' built on past experience. The client is able to see them for what they are, part of 'me', rather than being part of 'I' and the lens through which the client views the world.

In the example of the piano player, her proximate 'I' would see reality as, 'I am no good at the piano but love playing it to myself'. Following the work in psychotherapy, she could say, 'I can see that I was afraid of being criticised, the way I was when I was young, if I play the piano in public, but now I realise that I am good enough to play for others and accompany them in their music – that is me, a piano player.'

Self-disclosure

The story above of the therapist who forgot her client's session, having changed its time, reveals another aspect of integrative psychotherapy, and that is the extent to which a therapist should reveal themselves to clients. Before coming back to the example, here are some of the issues connected to being self-disclosing as a therapist. We will set out why it can be useful and why it is often discouraged.

It is good to be self-disclosing because:

- the client feels more comfortable and trusting if they are seeing a 'real' human being rather than just a professional (Jourard, 1971; Yalom, 1980, 2011)

- the therapist's experiences may relate to those of the client's and it can helpful to disclose them (Yalom, 2011)

- it is defensive of therapists to hide their ordinary humanity

- research shows that self-disclosure by the therapist increases the amount the client is willing to disclose (Jourard, 1971).

It is not good to be self-disclosing because:

- it may serve the therapist's narcissistic need to have their concerns aired as well as those of the client's

- the client has come to therapy to explore their own issues, not the therapist's

- it interferes with the client's ability to project their unconscious processes on to the therapist, thus rendering them unavailable to exploration (i.e. the transference)

- it is an intrusion into the private life of the therapist.

These considerations look different from the perspective of a relational and systemic departure point, because the system that the client and therapist meet within is constructed as a complex interrelating of their organising principles. The dualism created by considering whether or not to be self-disclosing falls away. In the example above, we have:

- a meeting of two human beings who have discovered a mutual respect and warmth

- a woman who has had children and grandchildren and is reaching the end of her career

- a man who is near the beginning of his career and possibly might in the future make a life partnership and have children

- a psychotherapy system where there is a tradition of exploration and openness and value given to reflecting on what occurs when the two meet.

In this situation, any self-disclosure on the part of the therapist happens within the context and holding milieu of the therapy. She does not need to speak in detail about her family but can reflect with the client on the meaning of her forgetting and on his response to it. It does not leave him with the mistaken feeling that he is 'at fault'. He experiences the honesty and integrity of the therapist and her fallibility as a human being. He also experiences that someone he sees as being in authority can make mistakes and own them without feeling shamed; and he can express his anger without being rejected or the therapist being weakened.

These experiences help the client to make changes to his 'organising principles' so that his self-structure, which had previously been 'authority should be obeyed and feared and is always right', was changed in a nuanced way. It did not become 'authority is often wrong and can harm you' but 'those in authority are human beings, who can also make mistakes'. As the therapy continued, there were further changes to this particular organising principle that now said, 'it is okay to challenge authority and it is okay for me to take authority myself.' As a result, it helped the client to find a stronger sense of self and more confidence in his own place in the world.

There was also learning within this systemic context for the therapist without it being merely narcissistic gratification. She saw the way that hanging on to her work in general, and this client in particular, led her unconsciously to make mistakes, or that her experiencing self was communicating to her narrative self and this gave her an opportunity to reflect on the nature of her commitment to the work. She was an experienced therapist, whose own professional organising principles included that it was okay to own her mistake, to hear the anger of the client and, importantly, to survive it. It also shows that she thought that she should always keep going, so her wanting to 'let go' was unconsciously acted out, before she was able to fully recognise it. There was learning within the system for all involved and its functioning could be strengthened.

As Yalom points out, self-disclosure can be important, given the right timing and degree, and judging this well comes with experience. He says:

> Keep in mind, the purpose of disclosure is always to facilitate the work of the therapy. Self-disclosure too early in the course of the therapy runs the risk of dismaying or frightening a client who needs more time to ascertain whether the therapy situation is safe. But careful therapist disclosure can serve as an effective model for clients. Therapist disclosure begets patient disclosure. (Yalom, 1980:262)

Here is an example of self-disclosure leading to a greater and deeper disclosure from a client, in a way that brought in the community, cultural and ecological systems nested in the story.

Example

A client who was a Hindu immigrant mentioned that he was going to Wales. As this was something unusual, the therapist asked why he was going. He said that he was visiting a Hindu temple, on which the therapist expressed a warm interest and said she had been to many temples herself. This allowed the client to speak of his sadness at the loss of temples from his childhood homeland, and recall his memories of playing in the countryside with his friends. The Welsh temple reminded him of these times, but he also needed to mourn the loss of those carefree days in a rural landscape which has now become urban and so normally only lives on in his memory. We could then mourn together the creeping urbanisation of India and Britain and the loss of ecological wild spaces.

Working with collaborative inquiry dialogue

We can see from most of the examples above that relational, systemic and eco-systemic psychotherapy is a dialogic process. Psychotherapy is not a series of questions. Direct questions have a tendency to appeal to the left-hemisphere neo-cortex so that the issue is 'thought about', rather than inviting an emergent and embodied response. While it is sometimes good to work specifically with the rational brain, it is not there that underlying and intransigent patterns of behaviour are found and potentially amenable to change. We therefore favour an inquiry where we discover life together. We 'never know first and never know best' (Hawkins, 2017a).

If questions are to be asked, one that is half finished in a musing way, inviting the other to finish it, is sometimes useful, such as 'If you did play the piano then you might...' If we did ask this to the client who played the piano, the subsequent conversation could go something like this:

Psychotherapist: If you did play the piano you might...

Client: Fall flat on my face!

Psychotherapist: Really?

Client: Well, I couldn't risk it in case I did.

Psychotherapist: Let's imagine you coming into a room and sitting at the piano. To make it easier there is only one other person in the room. Okay, can you see yourself sitting there?

Client: Yes, yes, I think so.

Psychotherapist: Are you there now?

Client: Yes okay, I can imagine it.

Psychotherapist: What happens now?

Client: I start to play.

Psychotherapist: Okay, follow that in your imagination. [There are a few moments of quiet]

Psychotherapist: What is happening now?

Client: I am just playing the piano.

Psychotherapist: What is that like?

Client: Well, okay, it's not too bad.

Psychotherapist: Is that an English understatement?

Client: Yes, I guess it is. [They both laugh]

Psychotherapist: What does the person listening do or say?

Client: She claps!

This dialogue and invitation to explore gives the client an experience of something different, something that challenges her underlying assumptions and organising principles. It will need more work though.

Conclusion

Integrative psychotherapy often does not look very different to psychotherapy with other names within psychoanalytic, humanistic and behavioural schools, but does have different ways of understanding and holding theory which overcomes some of the dilemmas and contradictions often found in other psychotherapies. This psychotherapy is integrative, because it draws on the insights and methods of several approaches (Erskine, 2015). Much wisdom has been built up over the years in all these approaches, and our model of integration recognises and takes on board many of their insights and practices. If we understand that the system provides a holding container for all those who contribute to its make-up, it allows a full and nuanced grasp of the complex dynamics occurring when people meet, as well as a way of understanding how to intervene that takes this complexity into account.

We feel that it is important that our practice is congruent with our theory. This way, theory provides a real holding frame for the practice and truly reflects the way that the therapy is undertaken. That is not to say that the theory is prescriptive about how the therapy should be conducted. What is described in theory is a way of understanding the relevant and emerging relationships, how they can best be nurtured and worked with therapeutically and how they are nested within systemic and ecological contexts in which all parties to the therapy partake. This allows for many different ways of acting and being within the therapy, which can then be reflected on so that new ways of being can emerge and new choices become available.

CHAPTER 12

Integrative, Relational, Systemic and Eco-Systemic Supervision

Introduction

In this chapter, we will focus particularly on how supervision can be relational, systemic and eco-systemic in the way it is practised and and how it can support integrative psychotherapy practice. We will show how it is important not to ignore the eco-systemic in supervision and how this aspect can be encouraged in the practice of the supervisee. We have written extensively elsewhere about relational and systemic supervision and, in particular, how this is supported by the Seven-Eyed Model which was devised by Peter in 1985 and developed with colleagues over the subsequent years (Hawkins & Shohet, 2012; Hawkins & Smith, 2013a). We suggest that those particularly interested in supervision read the book, *Supervision in the Helping Professions* (Hawkins & McMahan, in press; Hawkins & Shohet, 2012), where much more detail is laid out.

Many of you who read this book will have received supervision and we would like you to join with us in considering what has been, and you hope to be, important in the experience of supervision. Some of you will have given supervision to others and we invite you to step back and think about how you approach the work to help others to reflect and preflect (Hawkins & Shohet, 2012:18) on their work with clients. For those of you who have not received supervision, we hope this chapter will help you to consider what you would like from supervision when and if you receive it. We hope it will encourage you to engage with these questions with us and spark new questions for yourselves.

To this end, we invite you to consider with us the following core questions:

- Why is supervision essential?

- Who or what does the supervision serve?

- What particular value can relational, systemic and eco-systemic supervision add? We use the Seven-Eyed Model of Supervision to explore this.

- How can supervision serve the needs of all stakeholders?

What is supervision and why is it essential?

Over the years, we have written extensively about supervision and our own definition continues to mature. Our current definition is:

> Supervision is a collaborative process between a supervisor and one or more supervisees, that focuses on the challenges and learning emerging from the work with clients, in order to deepen the understanding, improve the quality of the work, develop the cognitive, emotional and ethical capacities of all parties, and deepen the resource from which the supervisees do their work.

Supervision is an integral and necessary part of integrative psychotherapy. Continual reflection on our practice, both within our own selves and with our clients, as the work unfolds, is the *sine qua non* of our work. With the best will in the world, we have our blind and deaf spots (as well as dumb spots) and need to reflect with others to help us understand what the work is revealing to us as we proceed. Regular supervision is important as it is the place where this reflection occurs, beyond our own individual confines.

We have shown, and will show further below, that we understand that the systemic nature of life plays out in the therapeutic encounter so that, within any therapeutic meeting, space is crowded with actual and potential stakeholders. The supervisor of the work is a vital part of this system as they have a special place of influence, based on having more distance from the therapeutic encounter and often a wider and longer range of experience. Even ex-supervisors can also be present, particularly where they also have had an influence on our practice and when there are undigested feelings about the way in which the supervision ended.

It is important to recognise that it is not only those close to clients and supervisees in their daily lives who are present but also those in the wider culture, such as the various communities to which the client, supervisee and supervisor belong, their extended family, including ancestors and, in fact, the world at large as well as the more-than-human world of the shared ecology.

In work with asylum seekers and refugees, for instance, where family members are far away, lost or have died or even been killed, our recognition of the systemic nature of life can be all-important as we can bring others consciously into the room where they can be 'spoken to' and their wisdom imparted. It is important to help the supervisee to understand that these unseen-but-present family members and ancestors are vital to the healing of these clients, where they understand that the wisdom of those who have come before them, as well as the needs of those who come after them, are an important part of learning to live life well, and give a sense of continuity and 'home'. The more-than-human is often more consciously acknowledged as important to those who come from non-western cultures, and the supervisor needs to be alive to this to help the supervisee be sensitive to this need.

One supervisee realised that bringing in a small vase of flowers to put on the coffee table between herself and the client held meaning for him as a remembrance of the natural world of which he saw little in Bristol.

The presence of significant others is also true, of course, of the supervision space itself, where the current and future clients become an unseen but third presence in the room. This means that the supervisor has access to this client as they will experience him or her through their experiencing self, sometimes called the countertransference, as we explore below.

We can see then that supervision is an important feature of reflective practice and one that is often recognised and valued as such by supervisees. We also suggest that it is indirectly valued by the supervisee's clients, even if they are consciously unaware of it happening, through a felt sense of their psychotherapist being themselves held and supported and bringing fresh awareness to the relationship.

Supervision is also essential in the action learning cycle of linking the theory and understanding learned in training sessions with what happens in the more complex world of the therapeutic relationship, in ways that change and digest the theory and make it more useable and supportive in the critical moments of the work.

In our own careers, we have experienced many critical moments in our practice, where we sensed that what we did next, how we responded, really mattered and we were at the edge of our unknowing, unprepared for this moment by our previous experience or training. What made the difference in our capacity to respond was our 'internalised supervisor', who metaphorically held us and provided an internal dialogical space, where we could reflect on and discover what was needed. We would argue that only through many years of receiving supervision do we develop a strong internal supervisor, which is essential at these critical moments.

Who does the supervision serve?

The supervision encounter takes place between the supervisor and the supervisee(s). Maybe because of this, there is a tendency in the practice and theory of supervision to focus on the needs of the supervisee as they are the one present in the room in person.

Most supervisors of psychotherapists are themselves psychotherapists and the supervision set-up of coming and sitting with the supervisor in their consulting room is reminiscent of therapy with which both supervisor and supervisee are very familiar. It is tempting therefore to ask the supervisee, 'How can I help you today?' or some such opening question which invites them to focus on their individual needs. Of course, the concerns of the supervisees are important. They need to be well resourced for the work, as we will see below, and they need support in undertaking what is often tricky and difficult work. However, in our view, supervision is primarily there to serve the work of the psychotherapy and, only insofar as it does this, is the support of the supervisee important and truly served.

When the psychotherapist and client meet, we say that they are undertaking 'work' together. We tend to say this automatically, but it is an interesting turn of phrase. We might use the word 'help' or 'healing' or various other words, but we tend to use the word 'work'. In our view, the 'work' is to understand more fully the internal world of the client and how they relate to others, both human and more-than-human, within their systemic and eco-systemic context. This work is carried out within the systemic context of the therapy itself and this is the work that is brought to the supervision.

We suggest that, rather than ask, 'What would you like to bring to super-vision today?', which tends to focus the supervisee on their personal internal world, we ask, 'What does the work you are undertaking with your clients need from us today?' This question focuses both supervisor and supervisee on the work of the therapy and invites it into the supervision space.

We find on supervision courses that therapists are often perplexed about the difference between psychotherapy and supervision as they are frequently faced with a disturbed, distressed and emotionally entangled supervisee where their own internal worlds are implicated in the work they are undertaking with clients. Sometimes, the supervisor will have to raise with the supervisee their need to go back to see a psychotherapist themselves to address the disturbance that has been revealed by the work with the client. However, the way in which the supervisee has been impacted by the material of the client will be valuable information about the work they are undertaking and can be addressed with that in mind. The disturbance has entered both the therapeutic and the supervision space so that the supervisor may also feel the energy of this distress in their own body.

Example

One supervisee came to supervision feeling ill and tired. She was seeing a client twice a week and felt she could no longer cope with their incessant demands. On further inquiry, it became clear that her own demanding and needy mother was evoked within the work. Exploring this further facilitated a release from the grip of this and helped the work to continue.

It was clear with another supervisee of the same supervisor that her need to 'be helpful', and the distress she felt when she was not 'being helpful', was not so easily resolved through reflection in supervision and she needed further work in psychotherapy to understand this in herself.

As we have seen elsewhere, through our ability to attune to others by sensing their internal experience in our own bodies, we can understand and meet others' internal worlds. This goes for the supervisor as well, as they attune to the clients presented in supervision, via the supervisee's narration of the story, but also via the supervisee's embodied experience. As Siegel (2012) shows, from a neurobiological point of view, this way of attuning to others leads to the important ability to integrate, both internally and within relationships. He says, 'These forms of attunement are examples of integration – beginning within ourselves and then linking our own inner world of primary experience to that of others. This is truly joining from the inside out' (Siegel, 2012: loc 2680).

The relational, systemic and eco-systemic supervision found in the Seven-Eyed Model of Supervision

The Seven-Eyed Model of Supervision was originally designed as a relational and systemic understanding of supervision, though this is not always appreciated.

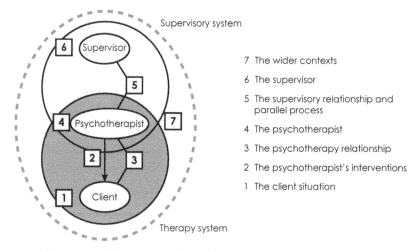

Figure 12.1: The Seven-Eyed Model of Supervision (Hawkins, 1985)

In this model, there are three systems: the supervisory relational system comprising the supervisor and supervisee; the client–psychotherapist relational system; and the wider systemic levels that surround both, represented by the outer circle. The supervisory system and the client–supervisee system overlap and are connected through the psychotherapist–supervisee who is found within them both.

It is through this interconnection that the relational linking is made so that the supervisor has access systemically to the client. Both are mutually influencing within the systemic work of the therapy. The wider systemic levels include the immediate contexts in which the relating takes place, the organisational context, the social, community and culture contexts of all parties and the more-than-human ecological context they all share. These connect all three so that both the other systems are held within them and provide the systemic connection with the other two. Each of the seven modes addresses specifically a relational or systemic aspect of the whole. In holistic terms (Koestler, 1967; Polanyi, 1969) these are holons, whole in themselves but also parts of a greater whole (see Chapter 8).

A larger discussion of all these modes, and research on them, can be found in Hawkins and McMahan (in press) but here we will focus on the way that the modes are relationally, systemically and eco-systemically held in dynamic connection.

Before doing this, we will lay out a brief definition of the seven modes as a guide. These are not 'things' but viewpoints from which to see the work, which is why they have been given the name 'eye'.

- *Mode 1* concerns the client and their world and how they show up in the consulting room.

- In *Mode 2*, we are interested in the interventions that the psychotherapist considers and makes in their work with the client.

- In *Mode 3*, we reflect on the relationship between the client and the psychotherapist.

- In *Mode 4*, we are concerned with the reactions and responses that the psychotherapist has in relation to the client (including their countertransference) and their responses to the work.

- In *Mode 5*, we reflect on the relationship between the supervisee and supervisor and how this might contain a parallel process to that in the psychotherapy presented.

- *Mode 6* concerns the experiential responses of the supervisor.

- In *Mode 7*, we focus on the systemic and eco-systemic levels which provide the many layered contexts in which the therapy and supervision takes place and the influences that flow through the work.

We would like to invite the reader to think of a possible or potential client and join us in engaging with the ways in which the relational, systemic and eco-systemic are present within these various supervision modes.

Mode 1

Mode 1 describes the phenomenological presence of the client. The client is the focus of the work and is therefore in relationship with all of the rest. In this model the client is also in direct relationship with the supervisee, physically within the room. How does the client typically enter the room? Describe their appearance, their ways of moving, sitting. What is their typical facial gesture? What is the harmonic of their voice, the pitch, timbre, volume, rhythm? How do they connect or not connect with you?

The supervisor can encourage the supervisee to notice in detail how the phenomenon of the client shows up in the psychotherapy room and discourages them from making assumptions that are not examined.

Example

A supervisee reported that, following a session where there had been a 'misunderstanding', her client came into the room looking grumpy and she made an assumption that this was because he was angry with her. Various assumptions had been made here: that the client was angry with her, that his coming into the room displayed his anger because she thought he looked 'grumpy'. She felt that his grumpiness was a denial of his anger with her. The supervisor encouraged the supervisee to describe the actual phenomena they saw and heard. 'He came into the room with slouched shoulders and unsmiling, his gaze was lowered and his voice slower than usual.' The supervisor then invited the supervisee to consider other possible reasons the client may have entered this way, which led to a realisation that he had come straight from work and had later mentioned an argument with a colleague.

In *Mode 1*, the supervision is guided by the phenomena rather than assumptions and we are metaphorically bringing the client into the room. Sitting in another chair and 'speaking as the client' can also be useful in this mode.

Mode 2

Mode 2 opens up the way in which the supervisee considers and makes interventions within the client–therapist system. As we have explained above, the supervisee will be informed in their response to the client, not just by what they have said or done, but in response to the memories, genetic inheritance, gifts and attributes of all those who have influenced them over their lifetime, including the theoretical and practical help of other psychotherapists and supervisors. The interventions made by the supervisee will be guided by mirror neurons (Siegel, 2010:59–63, 223–225) which allow the supervisee to recognise and attune to the subjective inner world of the client and respond in an appropriate way.

The supervisor will encourage the supervisee to understand why and how they made any particular intervention and look at alternatives. An integrative supervisor will help the supervisee to have a wider perspective than just the immediate relationship in the room.

Example

One supervisee had a client who was originally from a Middle Eastern country where food had a greater meaning than satisfying hunger. The client brought some food to the session to share with her therapist. While it is unusual in therapy to eat a meal with a client, the therapist decided to forgo this usual boundary and accept this offering with grace. She came to supervision worried that the supervisor might be critical of her intervention of accepting food from the client and eating together in the session. Following exploration in supervision and in further inquiry with the client, it became clear that this act had multiple and complex meanings for the client. It connected her, in an act of remembrance, with her mother, grandmother and other female relatives and ancestors; it brought these into the therapeutic space so that the therapist was incorporated into the important female rite of nourishing the family and holding people together within a meaningful ritual; it brought these important family members into the room to be remembered; it honoured the therapist who had provided a space for the client to re-connect with her culture in an alien land; and it allowed the client to give something back to the therapist who was being paid through a charity. The intervention of accepting and appreciating this food was an important turning point in the client's recovery from the trauma she had suffered.

Mode 3

Mode 3 concerns the relational system of the psychotherapist and the client. This relational system will be shaped by the connection they have been able to make as they encounter each other and the ways they are able to respond to each other. Importantly, when a rupture in their relationship occurs and the two are not in good contact, the manner in which this rupture can be healed, if it is by non-defensive owning on the part of the psychotherapist, can strengthen the tie between them.

The supervisor will notice the relationship dynamic, often more than the psychotherapist who is part of co-creating it, and then can encourage a focus on it, particularly when there is a blockage in relating or a relational rupture. On our supervision training, we often use a 'desert island' exercise where the therapist imagines themselves on a desert island with the client they are exploring. This reveals hidden aspects of their relational dynamic, with the metaphorical reframing allowing implicit sensations and memories that are in the relational field to surface imaginatively.

Example

One psychotherapist who imagined he was on an island with a particular client discovered an antipathy which sent them to opposite ends of the island! In exploring this it became clear that the psychotherapist's brother, who had severe mental health problems, seemed to have entered the relational dynamic with the client, and the psychotherapist's anxiety to 'cure' his client was connected with an urgent desire to cure his brother. The resistance of the client to the psychotherapist's attempts to 'cure' him as if he were his brother led to angry feelings on both sides which were hard to own as the psychotherapist was apparently well intentioned. The client tended to feel that he was not understood by his parents and hated it when others thought they knew best for him and he interpreted the psychotherapist's attempts to help him through that lens.

The reader might like to consider what they imagine would happen if they were left alone with one of their clients on a desert island, and what this says about the relationship with this client.

Mode 4

Mode 4 is a window to the felt responses of the psychotherapist. Here the supervisee will take what Rock and colleagues (2012) call 'time-in' (see Chapter 4) to contemplate their own internal responses to the client. The psychotherapist should take these seriously as these responses could be called 'the royal road' to the understanding of the client, just as Freud saw dreams as the royal road to the unconscious. In order to make use of this deep reflection, we need to de-centre from our own preoccupations and 'feel out' what our internal experience is telling us about the client and our response to them. These deeply felt and intuitive responses are often different from unprocessed reactions to clients such as the ones we saw above in the example of the 'grumpy' client. At the same time, it is important to stay tentative and open and not to become attached to anything we regard as an insight or interpretation, as further exploration, both in supervision and with the client, may point to something different.

The supervisor will help the psychotherapist to take the time to focus on their responses and see them as possible clues to what is happening, both for the client and in the relationship. As the American existential psychotherapist and writer, Irvin Yalom, says, 'Your most valuable tool as a therapist is your own reactions to the patient' Yalom (2011:230).

Example

It became clear for one psychotherapist that her sister, who self-harmed, was colouring her perception of the client in the psychotherapy session, and the psychotherapist's anxiety led her to see her client as having identical issues to those of her sister. However, after further exploration, it become clear that the triggering of this connection was a clue to a hidden disturbance in the client, which then became available for exploration in later sessions.

Mode 5

Mode 5 concerns the relationship of the supervisor and the supervisee. Their relationship and working alliance are an important part of the healthy holding of the supervisee's work with clients, particularly as their emotional well-being is entrusted to those within the supervisory system. The reader could reflect on relationships with supervisors/supervisees that you have experienced. Often these become very important to us and a rupture in this relationship can be very disturbing.

A disruption in the relationship between supervisee and supervisor can be a reflection of something similar happening within the client–psychotherapist relationship. The two systems overlap and affect each other. This is known as 'parallel process' (Hawkins & Shohet, 2012:101; Searles, 1955). We find that most of our supervision trainees recognise parallel process as a phenomenon that occurs in supervision. Have you noticed it in yours when giving or receiving supervision?

The supervisor makes it clear that reflection on their relationship is a legitimate part of the work of supervision as it provides important holding and offers information.

Example

A supervisor had a good enough working alliance with a psychotherapist whom she was supervising to own that she found herself strangely uninterested in the work she was doing with one of her clients and could well have colluded with the supervisee in finishing the work early. They explored a parallel process with the supervisee who also was bored with this work and related it to aspects of the client's life where girls were held to be uninteresting and not worth putting energy into. This fresh insight re-invigorated the therapy and allowed it to move on. It would have been easy for her not to notice this feeling and collude with the client in finishing, particularly as all parties – the supervisor, the supervisee and client – would have been relieved. As it was, it deepened and expanded the work.

Mode 6

Mode 6 provides us with an eye to the felt responses of the supervisor. As the systems are connected, the responses felt by the supervisor are relevant to the work, and the 'time-in' work of the supervisor is also valuable.

The supervisor takes time to focus on and access their own responses. They make a decision as to whether or not to speak of this or just to allow it to tentatively inform their work. It is important that a response to a feeling in relation to the work is not dogmatically believed but held lightly as possible information. If the working alliance with the supervisee is strong, the supervisor is more likely to discuss their felt response than if it is not yet well formed, particularly if the supervisee does not well understand the role of the supervisor's felt responses in informing the work. Often the supervisor, noticing their felt responses, in Mode 6, provides the entry to understanding what is happening in Mode 5 and in the parallel process.

If you are a supervisor, do you value your own responses and how do you use them? As a supervisee, are you interested in the felt responses of your supervisor? Are they helpful in considering the work with your client?

Examples

A supervisor felt uneasy in the presence of one of her supervisees, despite liking him as a person. Rather than dismiss these feelings she explored them on her own and in supervision and realised that she suspected that there were unethical aspects of his work, such as being less than honest about his credentials, which she had not wanted to notice. The supervisor recognising and taking note of this feeling was important in enabling the supervisee to face up to his unethical behaviour.

In another example, a supervisor was rather startled when he said to his supervisee that he had an image of the client with an albatross sitting on his shoulders. The supervisee looked astonished and said that the client had used this exact same image.

We have an exercise in our supervision training in which a trainee becomes a client (and has a short counselling session) and is then a 'fly on the wall' in a supervision session between the counsellor who has just met with them and a supervisor who was not present in their session. The supervisor is asked to focus on Mode 6, sharing their own responses. We find that they most often experience the supervisor as more in touch with them than the psychotherapist! This can be understood by the supervisor having more free-floating attention and being less concerned with the next intervention.

Mode 7

Mode 7 concerns the wider world and the larger systemic levels in which both the psychotherapy and supervision relational systems are embedded. Every one of the first six modes has its Mode 7 aspect.

- *Mode 7.1* is the wider contexts of the client's life world, what is happening in their family, work, community and so on.

- *Mode 7.2* is the professional context and training of the psychotherapist, their orientation and approach.

- *Mode 7.3* includes the similarities and differences in background, family, community and culture that play out in the psychotherapy intersubjective relationship.

- *Mode 7.4* is the wider contexts of the psychotherapist – what is happening in their life world, including their training, family, work, income, community, organisation and so on, that is affecting how they are in their work.

- *Mode 7.5* includes the similarities and differences in role, stage in career, background, family, community and cultures that play out in the supervisory intersubjective relationship.

- *Mode 7.6* is the wider contexts of the supervisor – what is happening in their life world, including their family, work, income and work organisation and so on, that is affecting how they are in their work.

- *Mode 7.7* includes all the elements of shared context that affect all parties in both the psychotherapy and supervisory systems.

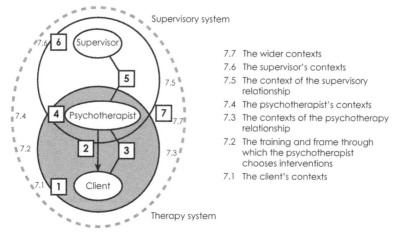

Figure 12.2: The various elements of mode 7

In Figure 12.2, we have all the various elements of the immediate contexts of all parties and relationships. However, as described in Chapters 8 and 9 and above in this chapter, there are wider worlds that are very present in the work and should not be forgotten. Many of those in the larger systemic and eco-systemic levels are direct stakeholders who impact and are impacted by the therapy and supervision. These can be understood to be in concentric circles, some close to the supervision and therapy and broadening out from there.

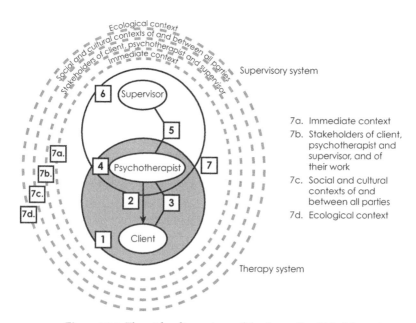

Figure 12.3: The wider dimensions of the Seven-Eyed Model

In the first ring (7a) is the immediate context of both the psychotherapy and supervision settings, the settings where they take place, the organisational context in which they happen.

In the second ring (7b) are the various stakeholders who impact and are impacted by the work: the client's family, colleagues and community; the psychotherapist/supervisee's other clients, their family, colleagues, training, community of practice, the profession and their future clients. It is the same for the supervisor.

In the third ring (7c) would be the social and cultural contexts of all three parties, and the cultural and social differences between them that form the intercultural relationships (Hawkins & Shohet, 2012: Chapter 8).

In the fourth ring (7d) lies the ecology of the more-than-human world, which is shared by all parties (see Chapter 9). The need for a healthy awareness of the eco-system is becoming increasingly important and is likely to grow in importance over the next few years, as is the mourning for what we are losing as the environment around us becomes more degraded.

The supervision needs to listen and attend to how these wider systemic levels are present, consciously or unconsciously, in the work and are attended to, and not drowned out, by the immediate issues that are more obviously present in the room.

Example

In the supervision of the psychotherapy of a woman of Iraqi origin, a supervisor discovered that the client suspected that her step-father was physically abusing her elderly mother who had Alzheimer's disease. The psychotherapist had focused on the anger that her client felt for her step-father, both in the present day and when he first entered the family soon after her father's death. The supervisor explored with her the present-day needs of her client's mother and encouraged her to seek help for such a vulnerable person. In doing so, the psychotherapist invoked the presence of various others beyond the therapy room. These included the Iraqi Muslim community to which they belonged, the Muslim beliefs and how such issues might be dealt with in their own culture, the role of social services, doctors and police, as well as the impact of their poor housing conditions and of the inner-city environment.

How can supervision serve the needs of all stakeholders?

To ensure that supervision considers the immediate needs of the psychotherapist's practice as well as their longer-term development and the wider systems that supervision serves, we hold in mind the model of three 'legs' of supervision process. The three legs are qualitative, developmental and resourcing (Hawkins & Smith, 2013a). So, who are the stakeholders that supervision serves, beyond the immediate supervisee, supervisor and client being focused on in supervision? We consider that there is a wide range of people who are directly or indirectly affected by the supervision that psychotherapists receive. These include supervisees themselves, their current and future clients, the client's family and community, the psychotherapy profession and any organisations that are concerned with the client or the psychotherapist and need to protect their reputation and good standing, public services such as the NHS and the police, and indeed society at large.

The three 'legs' of supervision ensure that the needs of all stakeholders are considered, as we will see below.

Qualitative

All stakeholders will want to ensure that the quality of the work with clients is as good as possible, not least the supervisee who will hope that the in-depth reflection that occurs in supervision will constantly improve their practice. They will be particularly keen to reflect on and develop their relationship with the client so that their capacity to provide the necessary insight and healing the client needs is constantly improved. This will include developing a greater and greater sensitivity to ethical considerations (see Chapter 13).

When the psychotherapist works for an agency, the supervisor has a formal role in regard to this and could also have the role of line manager. When the supervision is of private work, the supervisor does not have a legal or formal responsibility in the same way but has an ethical responsibility to ensure that the psychotherapist is fit to practise. Registering and accrediting bodies such as the UK Council for Psychotherapy and the British Association for Counselling and Psychotherapy hold psychotherapists responsible to ensure that they are in suitable supervision and so it is beholden on the supervisor to hold the psychotherapist to quality and ethical practice.

As we have seen elsewhere in this book, we are all interconnected systemically and eco-systemically. Any psychotherapist, well trained and supervised or not, is likely to develop blind spots, deaf spots and dumb spots (Hawkins, 2011b) and become collusive with their clients, drawn in to their world in unhelpful ways. While it is useful for therapists to have close, empathic, experiential contact with clients, they also need to be able to step back and see with a greater perspective. Supervision helps with this ability to reflect on the work and ensure that it is of good quality. Supervision also provides an opportunity to talk through alternative approaches to the work, carry it out and then reflect back with the supervisor to understand and adjust interventions made in the work.

An understanding of the systemic nature of the work (mode 7) helps to make sure that splitting (Hinchelwood, 1991) does not occur when attending to an employing organisation's need for qualitative supervision to be uppermost. An employer is an important stakeholder. They may be employing and paying the wages of both the psychotherapist and the supervisor and need the psychotherapist to work to a particular standard and the supervisor to help them to provide this. There may be differences of opinion about the needs of clients and it is tempting for supervisors to ignore a splitting process and collude with the supervisee against the employer (Hawkins, 2011b).

Example

One supervisor who was new to the work noticed that staff of a particular agency were very stressed and frequently needed to take time off work. She felt that her job was to focus on this as she was worried about their health and well-being. She felt critical of the organisation in its lack of care for its employees. While this was a legitimate concern, she lost her supervisees as they felt that they needed more support in actually carrying out the work well. She was attending to one part of the system – the health of the staff – while ignoring the need of the organisation and the need of the staff to improve their work. A more system-aware response might have been to have taken her concerns to the management or encouraged her supervisees to do so.

Developmental

As psychotherapists we need to constantly develop our work, including our cognitive, emotional and ethical capacity (Hawkins & Shohet, 2012:131), both to keep our work fresh and creative, and to keep abreast of new developments. Supervision has a big role to play in this as that is where our work is seen by someone else and our need for development can be discussed and reflected on. Furthermore, it is important that this development does not just attend to cognitive knowledge but also continuously develops our emotional and ethical capacities as well, as these are vital to the ability of psychotherapists and supervisors to carry out their work well and safely (Hawkins, 2011a). A trusting and open relationship between supervisor and supervisee allows for the vulnerability necessary to be open about difficulties as they arise and for development needs to be identified and worked with.

This is true at all stages of our career, but supervision has a particular place in the development of students. As students, we learn that psychotherapy and supervision come together in both theory and practice and find their necessary integration. It is important, therefore, with students that the supervisor understands and is aligned to the approach of the training that the student is undertaking. How the theory is being played out in practice and how the practice is deepening and informing the learned theory is an important part of the supervision work. Some supervisors set aside time for this to be reflected on and some do so whenever it seems apposite, or they do a mixture of the two. For supervisors of students, it is essential to hold the developmental needs of the student in mind.

While it is good for student psychotherapists and supervisors to have a similar approach, it can sometimes be helpful for experienced therapists to have a supervisor with a different approach as they may be better placed to challenge received ideas and limiting frames and help the therapist to reflect on how they could widen their approach.

The bringing together of theory and practice is not the only developmental need of psychotherapists, whether or not they are students. As many supervisees do not have an understanding of the systemic and eco-systemic nature of the work, supervision provides an important place to understand this or deepen this understanding. It can be learned, not just by explaining it, but by experiencing it first-hand within the supervision. It is a place where a systemic understanding can be brought to bear both on the work of the supervisee with their clients and on the systemic nature of the supervision process itself.

When working in mode 6 (see above), for example, the supervisor is demonstrating that their responses are relevant because they are part of the system.

Example

If the supervisor mentioned above, who was worried about the well-being of staff, had reflected on her overwhelming desire to help them with this, she could have encouraged her supervisees to see that they were caught in a systemic drama triangle (Karpman, 1968) where clients are seen as victims, people in their world are seen as persecutors and the staff see themselves as rescuers. As often happens in the drama triangle, this triangle turns and the staff experience themselves as having become the victims, with the management and clients as the persecutors, and they then invite a supervisor to become the rescuer. Stepping back and reflecting on this may have helped all parties to think about their needs in a less reactive way.

Resourcing

Through our systemic interconnectedness, we are inevitably affected by the pain, depression and anxiety expressed by our clients (as well as more joyful feelings!). We need time to process these, because they are important clues to understanding the client and the work needed, and also to avoid them creeping into our lives and leading us to be over-stressed and burnt out by our work. When working with badly traumatised clients this can lead to 'vicarious trauma' (Quitangon, 2015) and this can have a serious effect on the mental and physical health of the psychotherapist, creating issues with anxiety, depression, sleep disturbance and intrusive thoughts. Simply ignoring these feelings or trying to 'leave them behind at work' is not very effective and can lead to the shutting down of our own human responses and will blunt our effectiveness as therapists. Talking through our experience and expressing the feelings keeps us alive and vital in the work without burdening our bodies and minds with unprocessed stress. In this regard, it is legitimate for the supervisor to inquire into the way that the supervisee attends to their own life and their own 'Health Platter' (Rock *et al.* 2012 and see Chapter 4 in this book) with sufficient rest and, in particular, breaks from the work at holiday times.

Developing a healthy work–life balance is important but not as important as developing an ability to work in the moment in a less taxing way. Peter has written elsewhere (Hawkins, 2019) about the importance of working from 'source' in our work – literally we need to re-source ourselves – to find the source within and beyond ourselves from which to approach the work with sufficient awareness and strength and to recognise when we have been triggered into reactivity by our clients. In this way, the supervision does not only discourage us from taking on more work than we should, but, more importantly, can ensure that we find a place of spiritual connectedness from which to approach it. The supervisor can help the supervisee to catch their reactivity, not only to their client, but also to other people and systems in the client's narrative, and help them to respond to the client and everyone in their story with compassion, as well as being compassionate to their own reactivity. This 'wide-angled empathy' (Hawkins, 2019) and ability to be compassionate to oneself is an important part of coming from source. Developing this in ourselves as supervisors, and helping supervisees to develop in this way, is an important aspect of the resourcing 'leg' of supervision as it ensures that the work does not just drain us but can itself be a 'source' of nourishment.

The supervisor who was worried about the stress of her supervisees above was right in understanding that carrying this amount of stress is counterproductive and ultimately unhelpful to the people they are trying to help. If there is stress, and distress in the system, it is not helpful merely to join in with it.

Example

Judy is the Director of Trauma Foundation South West, which provides psychotherapy for asylum seekers and refugees. The clients that are seen are highly traumatised, often having been tortured, threatened with death and their families threatened and killed – sometimes in front of them. They have suffered loss of all that is familiar, including loved ones, culture and country. Their traumatic experiences do not end there. The journey to reach the UK is often traumatic, as is the asylum process that they have to go through. Working within a system which has such trauma in it is inevitably distressing for staff. Supervision is an important part of working through and processing this trauma, allowing staff to 'stay with' the pain and not turn away from their clients. At the same time, supervision helps to ensure that staff do not take on more work of this nature than they can manage, take good breaks and have a balanced life in which healthy activities also play a part.

Integrating the 'three legs'

All three legs are important in all supervision but one or two of them might have greater emphasis in certain circumstances or at certain stages of a supervisee's career. For instance, a student psychotherapist will need all three but the developmental will have particular prominence. Those who work in public services may find that qualitative is given prominence, though the other two must not be forgotten. Anxieties or preconceptions of employers or from the supervisee or supervisor can over-balance the supervision in one direction or another. It can be important for supervisors to talk with either or both employers and therapists about the potential of supervision to give value to all three functions. The three areas are not watertight compartments and one area may serve two or three of the functions. For instance, a student supervisee might find it difficult to end with her clients on time. Working with her to improve this would have a *qualitative* function in that an inability to keep firm boundaries could undermine the quality of her work, a *developmental* function in that she might need to develop this ability, and a *resourcing* function in that she could become burnt out if she doesn't know how to create necessary boundaries for herself.

Conclusion

Supervision is well placed to be a space where the relational, systemic and eco-systemic can be brought to mind and reflected on. It is not, of course, outside this system which, in any case, would be epistemologically impossible! We are inevitably part of any system we touch on. By supervisors recognising this systemic inclusion in the work they explore with supervisees, they simultaneously provide an insider's and outsider's perspective.

As supervisors we bring the *humility* to know that we do not know and that any potential insights are partial and contingent, an *ability to reflect* on our experience in a non-reactive and unattached way and 'wide-angled' empathy, *care and compassion* for those in every part of the system (Hawkins, 2019). Wide-angled empathy and compassion are particularly necessary in supervision where we need to be empathetic, not just for our supervisee but also for their clients; not just for their clients; but also for others within the narrative of their lives; not just for these people but for the wider communities in which we all live; and not just for the wider human family but for all of life in the more-than-human world. If supervision can bring this perspective then it makes a contribution to a more peaceful world, starting with the particular client engagement and then fanning out from there.

CHAPTER 13

Integrative
Psychotherapy Ethics

Introduction

One of Peter's doctoral supervisees, Elizabeth Dartnall, carried out research on psychotherapy supervision (Dartnall, 2012). She interviewed a number of experienced and mostly trained supervisors. One of her questions that was most illuminative was: 'What ethical dilemmas have you had to face in supervision and how have you addressed them?' Two of the respondents replied that they had not faced ethical dilemmas and one explained that this was because none of their supervisees had been involved in unethical behaviour. In the analysis of the transcripts of the interviews it became clear that many supervisors equated ethical issues with the emergence of unethical behaviour.

In this chapter, we will argue that all issues that are brought to supervision have an ethical component and that the work of the supervision is not to legislate on what is ethical and non-ethical, but rather to use every ethical issue and ethical dilemma as an opportunity to develop the ethical sensitivity and ethical maturity of the psychotherapist, the supervisor and the wider system (Gilbert & Orlans, 2011).

Integrative psychotherapy, as we emphasise throughout this book, is at heart relational, systemic and ecological and eco-systemic. Not only does it view the psychotherapy practice as relational and systemic, but also as based in a dialogical, systemic and ecological epistemology – that is, how we know about the world – and sees theory as emerging dialogically between practice and reflection (often mediated by supervision as in Chapter 12), and in the dialogical co-creation between writers. Theory is not created in the individual mind of the great psychotherapist or philosopher but emerges from relational learning processes which themselves are embedded in a cultural context and social history. Ethics, like theory, is based on and emerges from practice and serves practical purposes. It is not fixed, but constantly evolving along with our understanding of human beings, human interaction and the human connection with the worlds beyond our species.

Taylor (1991) points out that morality has fundamentally changed in the western world from the 18th century onwards. For millennia, morality was hierarchic. It came from on high, either from history and nature, via the tribal elder or shaman, or later from God, mediated by the priest, imam or guru, or from the state and government and mediated by the judge. With the growth of romanticism and individualistic humanism, there has grown a reversal, and now morality comes from within. The individual is encouraged to look inside themselves, listen to their inner conscience and consult their own feelings. Every individual is the arbiter of what is right and wrong; they need to decide for themselves. Morality from above posited a universal objectivity of a God-given truth or a government-legislated right and wrong. Morality from within creates a subjective relativism, where everybody's sense of what is moral may be different and equally valid.

We can see this moral polarity played out in the governance of psychotherapy, with some calling for regulation and absolute standards for psychotherapists, set by government or by a recognised expert authority. They would argue that you cannot be a proper profession unless you have objective standards to which all practitioners can be held to account. If they transgress, they can be disciplined, including, in serious cases, being struck off the professional register. While others, fighting against any authority control, argue that the individual is the ultimate arbiter of whether they are 'fit to practise', and at best will accept some peer challenge and review of their own practice.

We have argued for many years for a third position that transcends what we see as an outdated polarity, one based on critical eco-systemic intersubjectivity. This has several components.

First, most psychotherapy ethics fall into what Charles Taylor (1991) called the 'monological fallacy' of seeing isolated systems, rather than the way that these systems are dialogically and systemically co-created. They focus on the perceived competence and moral behaviour of an individual psychotherapist, removed from the relationships and systemic contexts in which the events happen.

This dialogical, systemic and ecological approach does not remove individual accountability. On the contrary, it expands our understanding of it. To reach accountable moral judgements, ethics cannot be conceptualised as an individual enterprise, but has to be seen as a practical endeavour embedded in social interactions, within a systemic and ecological context, within which moral and ethical understandings are being negotiated and discovered.

The individual needs to accept that although their subjectivity is the starting point for any ethical reflection or decision making, they, like every other person, form perceptions from their limited position within the system, and can be systemically blind to other parts of the system's needs and the unintended consequences of any action they may take. They can suffer from 'illusion, delusion and collusion' (Peter Reason: personal communication 1981) and 'wilful blindness' (Heffernan, 2011) or 'disavowal' (Weintrobe, 2012:38–40).

There needs to be a recognition that in psychotherapy, as in all relationships involving a professional and a client, there is a power imbalance between those coming for help and those offering it, based on their wider experience and expertise. With greater power comes greater ethical responsibility and accountability.

This is why we believe that all integrative psychotherapists need not only to be in regular supervision (see Chapter 12), but also to be part of an active community of practice. However, we also recognise that schools of psychotherapy and communities of practice can suffer from collusive groupthink (Janis, 1982) and community collusion, illusion and delusion (Heron, 1981). They can become sectarian and doctrinaire, insisting on the rules of the founder, or on 'methodological fidelity'. They may believe that they have the one true approach and all other approaches are wrong or even dangerous. This can develop to a state where all new thinking becomes heresy, and the social dynamic becomes authoritarian. Other schools can slip into subjective relativism, where everyone finds their own integration and no one's approach can be challenged from any jointly held standards or principles. We believe there also needs to be a community of communities, of which every school and accrediting body is a member and can be challenged and reviewed on what is happening within their community. This approach is based on a radical eco-systemic intersubjectivity, which sees an individual actively holding their community of practice to account and, in turn, being accountable to the community. The individual is nested within the community of practice and the community of practice is nested within a wider community of communities, which once again it is actively contributing to and emergently forming and reforming, and in turn is accountable to. This exists, and is nested within, the country, regional and international laws that currently apply. These need to be formed by humans learning from, and responding to, the teachings and needs of the wider ecology. This is not a hierarchy, as existed in the old objective morality, but an intersubjective holarchy of mutually co-creating and responding nested systems. A holarchy is the pattern of connections between holons, where a holon is both a part and a whole. It is also a holarchy where the large holons are accountable to the holons nested within them as well as the other way round – a circularity of accountability. The term was coined by Arthur Koestler in his 1967 book, *The Ghost in the Machine* (Koestler, 1967).

We need an ethics not of fixed rules, but one based on values, principles and dialogical inquiry. But above all, we need an ethics that is based on an expanded notion of the self, where the self is not bounded within an individual's skin but is experienced as intimately connected with the human and ecological worlds in which it is embedded.

Arne Naess (2016), the founder of deep ecology, writes:

> If reality is experienced by the ecological Self, our behaviour naturally and beautifully follows norms of strict environmental ethics. We certainly need to hear about our ethical shortcomings from time to time, but we change more easily through encouragement and a deepened perception of reality and our own self, that is, through a deepened realism. How that is to be brought about is too large a question for me to deal with here. But it will clearly be more a question of community therapy than community science: we must find and develop therapies which heal our relations with the widest community, that of all living beings.

Again, we would like to engage your thinking before you go deeper into this chapter, and invite you to complete the following sentences:

1. The work of a psychotherapist (or my work) is in the service of…

2. I am accountable to them for…

3. I exercise my accountability to them by…

4. Ethical behaviour in my profession is characterised by…

5. Unethical behaviour in my profession is characterised by…

6. A complex ethical dilemma I have been engaged in was when…

Alternatively, you might like to write your own 'statement of ethical intentions', standards you commit to holding yourself accountable to, while recognising that we will continue to need to compassionately learn from our failure to live up to them. At the end of the chapter we share one written by Peter.

The ethical process

Our colleague Michael Carroll has made one of the biggest contributions to our understanding of ethical practice right across the helping and people professions, with a particular focus on psychotherapy, counselling psychology and coaching. With Elizabeth Shaw, his last book (Carroll & Shaw, 2013) shows how acting ethically is full of complexity and ambiguity. It then goes on to outline an excellent process framework for thinking about the various stages of ethical activity, which provides a strong ethical scaffolding for thinking about ethics generally and ethical difficulties specifically. We believe this needs to be taught on all integrative psychotherapy programmes. We will now outline these six stages, adding our own understanding from our integrative psychotherapy stance.

1 Creating ethical mindfulness and ethical sensitivity

Tim Bond, who has contributed a great deal to the exploration of ethics within counselling and psychotherapy, defined ethical mindfulness as, 'A commitment to professional integrity in ways that are informed by ethical sensitivity and thoughtfulness' (Bond, 2015b:302). We need to start our exploration of ethics by understanding 'ethical sensitivity'. Kathryn Weaver gives us a good starting point when she writes:

> Ethical sensitivity was introduced to caring science to describe the first component of decision making in professional practice; that is, recognizing and interpreting the ethical dimension of a care situation. It has since been conceptualized in various ways by scholars of professional disciplines. While all have agreed that ethical sensitivity is vital to practice, there has been no consensus regarding its definition, its characteristics, the conditions needed for it to occur, or the outcomes to professionals and society. (Weaver, 2007:141)

It is increasingly recognised that ethical sensitivity needs to be taught to school children as they now need, more than ever, to make ethical choices in responding to internet communication from a younger and younger age. One school training manual provides a very simple but useful definition:

> Ethical sensitivity is the empathic interpretation of a situation in determining who is involved, what actions to take, and what possible reactions and outcomes might ensue. This component is influenced by Ethical Motivation and Ethical Judgment. (Endicott, 2001)

This helps us realise that ethics starts with 'wide-angled empathy' (Hawkins, 2019), stepping into the shoes, feelings and perceptions of all parties and stakeholders in an ethical situation. Only after this can we engage in the discernment of ethical motivation and in ethical judgement.

Thus, in this first stage, we need to foster ethical sensitivity and watchfulness in ourselves and those we work with, creating ethical antennae that keep us alert when ethical issues or dilemmas are present and enable us to avoid premature judgement.

2 Formulating a moral course of action

In this stage, we need to explore the interplay between the phenomena of the situation, garnered both from our experiencing self and our narrating self (see Chapters 3 and 11), and create a further dialogue between these and any ethical guidelines taken from professional systems we may be part of and our own ethical principles, with the intention of forming the best possible moral course of action. This involves being able to make an ethical decision informed by the light of ethical principles and differing needs of all those we are accountable to, including our self, our clients, the organisations we work for, the wider society and professional communities to which we belong.

3 Ethical conversations

It has been shown that if we discuss our ethical dilemmas with others, whether colleagues or supervisors, the resulting actions are nearly always more moral than if we act alone. The exception to this is when we deliberately choose people whom we know will collude with us and justify our pre-formed conclusions, rather than take an open-ended question and dilemma to someone we know will bring us a different perspective, support and challenge. In Peter's research on 'tomorrow's leadership' (Hawkins, 2017c), one chief executive officer of an organisation commented on how the world was changing so fast that legal advice and ethical guidelines were often lagging several years behind the newly emerging ethical dilemmas. He added, 'Furthermore we all live in a transparent bubble surrounded by social media that can ruin reputations in minutes.' He reported that now, rather than ask his legal counsel for advice on an ethical dilemma, he asked his executive team, 'How would this look if it got into the social media or press, a year from now?' Another reported asking his colleagues, 'How would we explain this to our grandchildren?' It is important to have the ability to consider your ethical choices from an outside-in and future-back perspective (Hawkins, 2017c).

4 Implementing an ethical decision

This refers to the need to follow through and implement the ethical decisions you have made, while coping with the resistances both inside and outside, such as politics, self-interest, protection of a colleague or fear of making a mistake.

It is important to be able to articulate and justify to yourself, your supervisor, your organisation and any other possible stakeholders the reasons for your ethical decisions and how you implemented them.

5 Living with the ambiguities of an ethical decision

The capacity to cope with doubt and uncertainty about your ethical choice and actions is a vital capability for embracing and containing a moral dilemma.

Achieving closure on the event and being at peace with it, even when there were other possible decisions or better decisions that you could have made, is also an important step.

6 Integrating the learning into our moral character and future actions

Every ethical dilemma or challenge is an opportunity, not only for learning, but also for maturational development. Time needs to be spent in supervision incorporating and integrating the learning from an ethical challenge and one's response to it, in order to consider how it will deepen future practice.

Like Carroll and Shaw (2013), our 'relational, systemic and ecological ethics' rejects impartiality as a prerequisite for ethical decision making. Individuals can never be isolated agents, devoid of emotions, biases and prejudices. Therefore, requiring or expecting individuals to make ethical decisions alone based on rationality and logic is impractical, unrealistic and impossible. Carroll and Shaw (2013:72) argue that relational ethics, combined with a healthy dose of self-knowledge and awareness, gives us a 'more viable and richer place to start a moral debate'.

Ethical maturity

Based on their six-stage process, Carroll and Shaw (2013:137) define ethical maturity as:

> having the reflective, rational, emotional and intuitive capacity to decide actions are right and wrong or good and better, having the resilience and courage to implement those decisions, being accountable for ethical decisions made, being able to live with the decisions made and integrating the learning into our moral character and future actions.

In previous writings on ethics, Peter defined ethical maturity as: 'The increasing capacity to embrace ethical complexity and deal with appropriate respect and fairness to all parties involved in a situation' (Hawkins & Smith, 2013a:288). Now we would, in the light of our three key strands of integrative psychotherapy expand this to read:

> The increasing capacity to embrace ethical complexity and deal with complex ethical issues with appropriate respect, fairness and accountability to all parties (personal, collective and ecological) involved directly or indirectly in a situation.

We would see all six stages of the Carroll and Shaw framework as essential. However, based on the work of Loevinger (1976), Kohlberg (1981), Kegan (1982) and Torbert (2004), we see ethical maturity, not as a fixed state at which one arrives, but as a developmental process that continues throughout one's life. Ethical maturation requires continual learning from the many ethical dilemmas that one's work throws up and one's life provides. Indeed, one can regress from a state of maturity towards a state of ethical immaturity.

It is possible to see various stages in the ethical maturational journey. First is what Torbert (2004) terms the stage of *the opportunist*, where the individual is focused on survival and is self-centred, doing what is necessary to get by. The second stage is termed *diplomat* by Torbert. When faced with an ethical dilemma, the diplomat will be most concerned about not offending either their client or their profession and will be anxious to discover what is expected of them. *The expert*, at stage three, will focus on what is recognised as good practice by their profession. If in doubt, they will consult the ethical guidelines and rules of their professional body, and/or seek advice from their supervisor or colleagues. At stage four, *the achiever* is outcome focused. They will ask, 'What is needed to achieve the best possible outcome for the client and the work?' Their approach will be less rule-bound and more pragmatic, based on the specific needs of the situation.

Torbert (2004), then goes on to explore three further stages, which he describes as post-conventional, indicating they are rarer in our current society. These stages are borne out by the research he and others have carried out in Europe and North America (Rooke & Torbert, 2005). Our view is that the integrative psychotherapy approach we have outlined in this book requires these later stages of ethical maturity. Too often, to seek answers to ethical dilemmas or quandaries, psychotherapists either base their ethical decision making on their own judgement of what will create the best outcome (going inside), or on codes of practice or regulatory guidelines (going outside). We contend that instead there needs to be an internal and external inquiry that embraces the complex multiple perspective and systemic levels in play at all levels. This requires ethical maturity at the following post-conventional stages of development:

At stage five, *the individualist* is more deeply relational in their approach and will be more interested in what is happening in the relationship between themselves and their client, their client and the client's self and the client and their 'lived world'. They will be interested in the interconnecting pattern between this triad of relational systems – the client's internal relational system, the pattern of the client's external relationships and the psychotherapy relational system of which they are part. They will also see things less through the lens of a linear, cause and effect understanding, but be self-reflexive about how they are co-creating every system they are perceiving (see Chapters 8 and 9).

At stage six, *the strategist* has the awareness of the individualist described above but will go on to focus on how to intervene in ways that will serve the maturation of all the relational systems and be beneficial to all systemic levels.

The alchemist of stage seven has an increasing capacity to embrace ethical complexity and deal with appropriate respect and fairness to all parties involved in a situation. They combine the capacities of the individualist and strategist but are less focused on working it out cognitively or getting it right as an individual; rather, they see they are just doing what is necessary and required by aligning with the evolutionary and healing flow of ecological life.

Applying integrative psychotherapy ethics

When exploring ethically complex situations, either in our own practice or in supervision with other practitioners, we apply the above ethical frameworks using a variety of methods, which we will now briefly outline.

1. Listen to how the individual is creating and framing the narrative of the situation. The frame in which the situation is presented may be one where the individual sees themselves as a victim, blaming others for the problem, or one where they are taking on too much responsibility. One can also listen for which of the Torbert frames mentioned above the person is using as their action logic. They may have also framed the ethical situation as an either/or dilemma with only two opposing solutions.

2. Invite a 'multi-perspectival' viewing of the situation from all those directly involved. Ask the other to explore different ways of perceiving the situation: 'How else might you view this situation?' and 'Besides the two either/or solutions you have presented, what might be some other options?'

3. Take an 'outside-in' perspective, viewing the situation from the perspective of other interested parties and levels of systemic involvement. 'How might your organisation view this response? What would your manager say? How would other involved agencies view this? How would the client's family respond?'

4. Take a 'future-back' perspective. 'How might this situation appear if people read about it in a year's time? How might our future children or grandchildren view this situation?'

5. Create a dialogue between the multiple perspectives. Invite the different perspectives to speak to each other, so that a new perspective can emerge from the dialogue, or find the pattern that connects them.

6. Choose a possible course of action and possibly rehearse it. It is easier to decide what to do in theory than to put that intention into practice. As the old saying informs us, 'The road to hell is paved with good intentions'. For a wise choice of action, based on embodied learning, the individual (client or supervisor) often needs space to do a 'fast-forward rehearsal' of their planned action.

7. Review what emerged from your course of action, amending what you do next, and harvesting the learning. It is important, whether in therapy or supervision, later to ask how the intended ethical action went, to reflect on it and ask, 'So what is the learning you take from all the stages of this episode?'

Here are three psychotherapy ethical dilemmas, which, although complex, are very typical of the dilemmas that show up in our psychotherapy and supervision practices. As you read them, we invite you to make notes of your emerging answers to the following questions:

1. What are the ethical issues that are evident in each of these cases?

2. Who are the parties that need to be thought about in each of these situations?

3. How might you view this situation from each of their perspectives?

4. What are their significant needs that should be borne in mind?

5. What actions, if any, need to be taken in each situation?

Ethical dilemma 1

Your supervisee works for a counselling agency where six sessions of counselling are normally provided. A further six can be negotiated with the agency if it is felt that there is a need. In the contract with counsellors who work with the agencies, it says that clients may be referred on to other counsellors after the allotted sessions have been completed but that the counsellor who has seen the client in the agency cannot take them on for private counselling themselves. The supervisee felt that a further six sessions were needed for this client, but the agency did not agree that this was necessary. Normally, only people 'at risk' are allowed the extra sessions. It had already been agreed in the supervision that further sessions were indicated as the client had revealed in the last two sessions that he had been sexually abused in childhood. The client had told the counsellor that she was the only person he had felt safe enough with, to tell. At the next supervision session, the supervisee admitted to the supervisor that she had offered to see the client privately and, to show that she was not trying to gain financially from this arrangement, was seeing him free of charge.

Ethical dilemma 2

A psychotherapist told her supervisor that a complaint had been taken out against her by an ex-client. She had been in dispute with the client because he had left without paying a bill of £600, which represented the cost for 12 sessions. As the client had left without informing her, the psychotherapist had included two payments for missed sessions. After those two missed sessions, the client told the psychotherapist that he did not want to return. In the contract with her clients, the psychotherapist stated that four weeks' notice must be given. Four of the twelve session were thus for the four weeks' notice that should have been given. Since the ending, every week for ten weeks, the psychotherapist had sent a bill to the client, and no payment had been received. On the eleventh week, she had said that, if the bill was not paid, she would take him to the Small Claims Court. On hearing this, the client took out a complaint against her with a registering body. The psychotherapist had not discussed taking the client to the Small Claims Court with the supervisor before taking this action.

Ethical dilemma 3

A supervisor had a psychotherapy supervisee who worked in a practice setting where several others worked. The practice had a waiting room in which there was a water cooler with plastic cups. One day these cups disappeared and were replaced with pottery mugs. The manager of the practice rooms asked if anyone knew who had taken the cups as they were the property of the water cooler company and there was no proper facility to wash up the mugs. The psychotherapist suspected that this action had been carried out by one of his clients. The client was a climate activist and had mentioned that she disapproved of the water cooler and the plastic cups. The psychotherapist felt that he could not mention this to the manager because of confidentiality. He also wondered if he should bring this up with the client if she did not raise it herself.

Conclusion

At the beginning of this chapter, we wrote about the importance of each psychotherapist creating their own 'statement of ethical intentions', and regularly updating this. We invited you to create your own. If you have done this, you might want to now go back and update and develop that statement in the light of reading this chapter. If you have not written one at the beginning you might want to do so now.

We have benefitted from reading famous psychotherapists who have not just written about their theories but have been generous enough to share their ethical intentions, such as Jung, Sheldon Kopp, Carl Rogers, Irvin Yalom and others, and want also to be generous, without in any way suggesting that these intentions are ones to be followed by others, or better than yours.

Here is Peter's statement:

I will be fully present for my clients, listening with my whole being, to receive and accept their experience, without judgement.

I will work collaboratively with my clients, dialogically making sense and meaning of their experience together. I will 'not know better or know first', but work towards new 'knowing' emerging from our joint explorations.

I will approach each session with what Otto Scharmer (2009) describes as an 'open heart, open mind and open will' – curious to discover how the client will show up and what narratives and feelings they will bring.

I will attempt to have empathy and compassion for my client and also wide-angled empathy and compassion for every person, group and system in their stories.

I will focus on the work that life is showing needs to be addressed and bring into the room more fully the wider systemic levels that are asking to be heard.

I will continue to explore my own white maleness and how that impacts on every relationship.

I will continue to explore my own ecological awareness and be alert to how I can enable my supervisees and clients to work through the Ecological Awareness Cycle (see Chapter 9)

I will actively reflect on what is happening 'here and now' in the relationship between us, including seeing myself as part of this relational co-creation.

I will not impose my beliefs or issues on the client but be open and self-revealing, when this is requested by the client and in service of the work. I will seek to neither hide nor impose myself.

I will continue to learn from my clients, through ongoing development of my practice, through having regular reflection and supervision on my work, and through focusing on my own ongoing maturity and development of myself.

I will inform the client if I think they are in a state of danger to themselves or others, and work with them on how they and others can be protected. In extremis, if they are unable to take responsibility for the danger to self and others, I will contact the appropriate agencies.

I will only share information about what is discussed in the psychotherapy with the expressed agreement of the client, and in supervision, which I will inform them about.

I will abide by the laws of the country where I work, in terms of reporting issues such as child abuse, terrorism, money-laundering and so on, but only after I have made it clear to my client that I will do so.

I will abide by the laws on data protection.

Mahon (2002:76) wrote:

Each time we invest ourselves in dissimulation, we do so with a degree of dis-ease. We hear a bell ring. We may not think we hear it, or we may hear and misinterpret it. Nevertheless, the bell rings.

We hope this chapter has helped you more clearly and regularly hear the bell and continue to grow your capacity to be both ethically sensitive and ethically mature in how you respond.

CHAPTER 14

Training Integrative Psychotherapists

Introduction

In this chapter, we will engage with the questions: what is needed for the development of integrative psychotherapists, and how should training be designed? How can training help students to understand the world in a way that is intersubjective, systemic and eco-systemic? In what ways does integrative training differ from psychotherapy training that does not consider itself to be integrative? Are there particular principles behind the choices made in deciding on the content and the process of the teaching? In other words, do we consider the what, how and why behind these choices?

To those outside the profession of psychotherapy, the training of psychotherapists seems inordinately long. For instance, in the UK, the UK Council of Psychotherapy has stipulated that training must comprise at least four years and include at least 600 hours of supervised practice. Many psychotherapy training courses are longer than this, particularly taking into account the, often lengthy, final written work. Why should this training be so long? The necessity for this will be explored in this chapter.

Training methodology for integrative courses

Most psychotherapy training courses, particularly those that are integrative, use a range of methods for teaching theory and practice to ensure that their graduates emerge from the process able to work effectively and ethically with their clients. Although there is a complex and extensive literature on psychotherapy theories (see Chapters 5 and 6), psychotherapy is, above all, a practice, so students need to deeply engage, both with a body of knowledge and practical experience – intellectually, emotionally and spiritually.

It has long been our contention that practice should come before learning the relevant theory. The practical ability and skill to undertake the work takes precedence over understanding theory. Of course, theory is highly important for good work, helping us to shape and hold our thinking, but as it is absorbed through reflecting on practice, it becomes embodied and integrative. Many training courses start the other way around – putting theory first. We think that it is essential to know both, but strongly advise that theory should always be based in practice, not just an intellectual endeavour. Practice well integrated with theory is a core assumption of our integrative approach. It is for that reason that we start here with training methodology and not theory when discussing training for psychotherapists.

When we started providing psychotherapy training, most courses in the UK were run by private institutions, often not-for-profit organisations. In the late 1980s, there was a move to have these courses validated by universities, both by the training organisations pushing for academic recognition, and by universities approaching the trainings. Some universities also started their own courses in psychotherapy. This became quite controversial, as practitioners feared that universities would be intent on making training too much about theory and academic research. Some argue that this has indeed become the case, but in our experience, this has, on the whole, been a positive development: many universities have taken on board the central importance of practice and allowed for that, while encouraging a more rigorous approach to theory and research. The main disadvantage, in our view, has been the increased cost for training which puts it further out of reach for people on average and low incomes, who cannot afford to pay university fees. In other European countries and in the USA, psychotherapy training is, and has been, more university based and open mostly to those who are already psychologists or psychiatrists. In the UK, psychotherapy can be a stand-alone training at master's level.

So, what are the methodological factors that need to be in place for a good integrative psychotherapy training? In our view, training should contain the following elements:

- The student's own psychotherapy with a therapist recognised by the training. This therapist should be sufficiently in tune with the course the student is undertaking so that the teaching on the course seems consistent enough with their experience of psychotherapy.

- An intentional learning community where students reflect on their experience, with group time explicitly dedicated to such exploration.

In the training 'day', trainees learn within the trusting atmosphere created over years of training together to broach difficult feelings and dynamics with each other. They can challenge each other and the trainers in a setting that feels safe because it has created and agreed its own 'group norms'.

- Individual tutorials with a member of staff where individual feedback can be given in both directions and special learning needs can be addressed, including difficulties such as dyslexia.

- Practice of psychotherapeutic skills such as the ability to listen, question, paraphrase, empathise, challenge, support and give and receive feedback. This can be most usefully carried out in twos, with a third person present to provide feedback. Each of the three gets a turn at all the positions of client, therapist and observer. Training staff can visit these groups to provide their feedback too.

- Presentation of theory, including human development, with time to engage with the theory experientially, reflect and relate it to one's own experience to ask questions and explore the issues dialogically. Engaging with theory experientially ensures that it has become embodied and therefore will come to mind when working with clients. Theory is only relevant insofar as it is alive in us today, in our everyday relating.

- Written assignments which help students to digest, internalise and fully understand the practical and theoretical work they have been undertaking.

- A mental health placement where students will meet patients suffering from severe mental illness so that they can recognise these disorders and know how and when to refer to a psychiatrist or doctor if and when necessary.

- After a sufficient period of training, taking on clients for therapy. Often this is after a minimum of one year's training alongside work in an agency and at least two years' training prior to private practice. Students usually take on one client at first and then see more people as they develop their abilities, with not more than three clients at any one time in the first year.

- Groups to discuss issues of practice, using case material for illustration and reflection.

- One-to-one and group supervision of work with clients.

- Individual and group time to support the writing process for final submissions.

This list clearly demonstrates that there are many aspects to the training beyond understanding theory and practice cognitively, or even gaining technical skills. It is not just a profession or a craft, but, in our view, a calling – to understand and to meet the emotional pain and barriers to spiritual and emotional development clients bring into therapy. It requires being prepared to meet the deep pain that is often experienced on life's path, and help their clients to find a good sense of their life's purpose, perhaps lost under the weight of relational and existential distress. The capacity to meet the complexity of this path requires training of a good length, to ensure that the student is ready to engage with themselves and their clients at this level of depth and to undertake the emotional, spiritual and intellectual journey essential for developing the necessary resources. This is not a journey that ends with the end of the training, but continues throughout the therapist's career.

One of the important ways psychotherapy trainings attend to these needs, particularly the integrative, humanistic or psychoanalytic/psychodynamic schools, is to require students to undertake psychotherapy themselves. Yalom (Yalom, 2011:232) writes about how 'personal psychotherapy is (or should be) at the core of every psychotherapy training'. In the early days of psychoanalysis, the main method of training was through being in psychoanalysis oneself. It was thought that a doctor had all the other necessary qualities and abilities for this work and that being analysed would ensure that they were sufficiently free of their own psychopathology not to become entangled in the patient's material. Freud thought that it was possible to be so completely and thoroughly analysed that one's self-knowledge left no stone unturned, thus rendering one free of neurosis. Since those days, we regard self-knowledge and good mental health as a 'work in progress' (see Chapters 3 and 4), rather than something that is ever finished. Modern theories of development show that we are constantly developing and finding new challenges as we progress through different life stages (see Chapter 3).

So, what are the advantages to psychotherapists in training engaging in personal therapy? The reader may think of other benefits, but we offer the following:

- It provides emotional support during the rigours of the training which can face students with uncomfortable insights about themselves that were previously hidden.

- It encourages emotional and cognitive insight into our own psyche and life world.

- It encourages a habit of reflection on one's own experience.

- It gives the student an experience of the process that the client goes through when receiving therapy.

- It develops our emotional, cognitive and ethical capacities to be open to greater systemic complexity in our relating to others and our life world.

For many students, the experience of their own therapy is the most profound and useful aspect of the training.

An approach to the teaching of skills

Some of the skills needed for working with people are the same as many of the skills needed for the people professions besides psychotherapists, such as counsellors, psychologists, social workers, religious leaders and teachers. All these encourage a special kind of conversation with their clients, different from conversations we have with our friends. In a social conversation, both parties are present in the same capacity, whereas in professional encounters, one person has a special role. Thus, the following abilities and capacities need to be developed:

- Listen well at all levels, cognitive, emotional and spiritual (see Hawkins and Smith 2013:252–254).

- Show the client that you have heard at all these levels and check you have heard correctly.

- Reflect on what has been heard in conversation with the client.

- Facilitate further exploration.

- Reflect on what is happening live in the relationship between you.

These are important skills which are relevant to all these professions, though psychotherapists may need to take the conversation to greater depths. It is particularly important that psychotherapists and counsellors develop these skills, and in the UK, psychotherapy training is often based on completing a counselling training first so that these skills are already in place. Whether or not this is the case, basic skills need to be attended to. They could be said to be the 'base camp' for scaling the heights of psychotherapy training. These skills can be returned to for re-orientation when we are seemingly lost or need to re-group.

At this early stage of the training, students may not be aware of the intersubjective, systemic and eco-systemic way of understanding the world, but students will also be encouraged to understand other approaches and thus be embedded in their culture and communities. This includes an understanding that the relationship with the therapist, even if it is practised in a small conversation with a fellow student, constitutes the context in which this particular conversation has arisen. They will learn that we are embedded within relationships and culture but also within a world that is wider than just its human components, including all elements of the more-than-human world (see Chapter 9).

Many integrative training courses consider that it is most effective to teach skills in group settings, offering experiential exercises to illustrate and deepen understanding. It is common in these courses for students to practise in pairs with a third observing and giving feedback and staff visiting the three from time to time, as described above. Because work with another human being – rather than knowing it theoretically – is all-important in the training of psychotherapists, work in pairs and threes is highly beneficial. It means that the student can begin to practise their craft in a small way with peers before doing so with people specifically coming for help. Students build their confidence without staff present all the time, while also having staff feedback when the need arises.

Insofar that theory *is* taught at this stage of the students' training, it is theory about *practice* – the theory necessary for knowing which skills promote good work and why these skills, and the theory behind them, matter. Carl Rogers asserted that the 'core conditions' of counselling and psychotherapy are 'congruence, empathy and unconditional positive regard', and the basic skills are set in the context of these core conditions (Rogers, 1959). It is often considered in integrative training that this can form a basis on which to build further work. As mentioned above, in the UK this is achieved either by providing counselling training before embarking on a psychotherapy course or by teaching these skills at the beginning of the psychotherapy training. Even if they have been taught before on a counselling course, it may be good practice to revisit them to deepen the learning.

Giving useful feedback

Particularly as work in threes is so important for psychotherapy training, it is necessary to ensure that students are able to give good quality feedback to each other. We developed a useful mnemonic for giving quality feedback which is CORBS: clear, owned, regular, balanced and specific (Hawkins & Shohet, 2012).

Clear: It is important to be as precise and unambiguous as possible when giving feedback. The person receiving it is often anxious about what might be said, so the more lucidly feedback is conveyed, the more likely it will be understood as intended.

Owned: It is important to realise that the feedback you give, however good the quality, will say as much about the giver as the receiver. It is therefore good to qualify what is said with something like the phrase, 'In my view...' or 'It seems to me...'. This reminds both parties that others may have a different view.

Regular: If feedback is only given at the end of a process, then the recipient has no time to adjust how they work as they go along. A large amount of negative feedback at the end of a process can be devastating, but if it is given in smaller amounts as you progress it helps the person to learn from mistakes and build on strengths.

Balanced: It is tempting, when giving feedback, only to mention what was amiss with the tacit understanding that 'everything else was okay'. Being told when something went well helps us learn from our successes as well as our failures and to build confidence and the optimism to know that we can be successful. However, only hearing about our success can lead to complacency. We need to be shown where there is a 'learning need' and where we are developing excellence in our practice. Although these do not have to be slavishly covered with every piece of feedback we give, overall it is important to keep our feedback balanced.

Specific: Most importantly, feedback is best if it is specific, whether it be positive or negative. It is hard to make use of feedback that says something like, 'That was great!' What about it was great? What about it can I build on? We all find it hard to hear that something we did was not good enough. What about it was not good enough? Was it actually harmful or just ineffective, maybe? If you cannot give specific feedback, maybe because it is hard to formulate a response, it is probably better not to give feedback at all.

Learning to give good feedback provides students with a useful skill, and, at the same time, improves the quality of the training process – it means that staff are not the only people giving feedback, and feedback loops become a constant part of the learning process.

This importantly also applies to feedback to staff who must be open to feedback at any time, and we provide a special place for this, both in the group and in one-to-one tutorials with a student. This leads to good communication and non-defensive dialogue useful to the staff in working with the students, but this practice also demonstrates how to receive feedback non-defensively, whether it be positive or negative. Positive feedback is sometimes harder to receive gracefully, particularly for British people whose culture teaches them to demur under these circumstances!

The learning cycle and learning styles

Kolb noticed that learning happens through experience, supporting and underlining our approach of primarily learning from experience. He said, 'Learning is the process whereby knowledge is created through the transformation of experience' (Kolb, 1984:38). He showed that we go through a four-stage 'cycle of learning'. We have built on his learning cycle with our own experience (Hawkins & Smith, 2013a:153) and describe four stages:

1. Thinking and understanding.

2. Planning (or preflection).

3. Doing.

4. Reflection and reviewing.

Action Learning Cycle

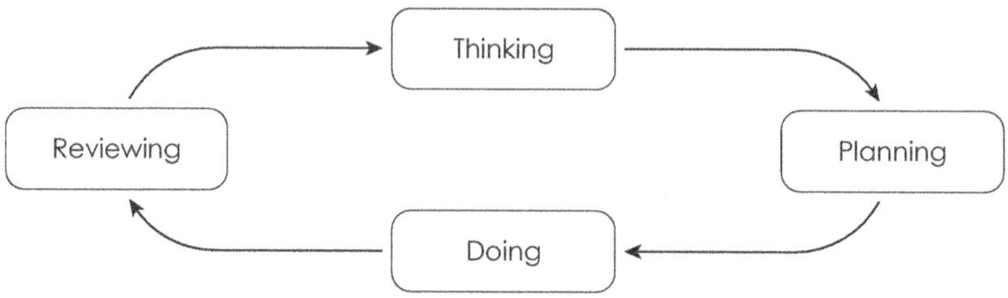

Figure 14.1: The Action Learning Cycle

Psychotherapy students in training can be encouraged and guided to reflect on any new experience, consider what it means to them and to others who share the experience, including the emotional and bodily effect it has on them, and then find ways to allow this experience to deepen their practice, which in turn may lead to new experience and the cycle begins again. In this way, the learning is not 'introjected' (Perls, 1992, first published 1969) and swallowed whole but really chewed and digested and integrated into the student's knowledge and understanding of the work.

Kolb also showed how different people have different learning styles which may affect the varying ways they approach the learning cycle:

- *Divergent* – feeling and watching. Divergent thinkers tend to be sensitive and like to watch and wait before acting. They need to be given time to assimilate new learning.

- *Assimilate* – watching and thinking. Assimilative learners prefer abstract ideas to relationships and would prefer to learn theory before trying something in practice.

- *Converge* – doing and thinking. As convergent learners are most at home with technical skills, psychotherapy may not be the best profession for them, but if they can learn by doing, then they are more likely to learn what is needed.

- *Accommodate* – doing and feeling. Those who have an accommodating learning style prefer to do something immediately without having analysed it, and rely on intuition rather than logic.

Each of these learning styles above may create a limitation to a person fully using the complete learning cycle and becoming stuck in just one segment.

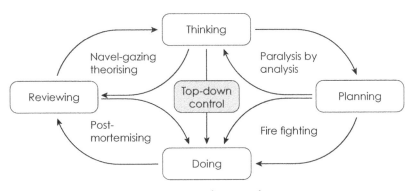

Figure 14.2: Action learning shortcuts

Most people have a tendency towards one style or another, but it is important for students and staff of integrative training to understand that people do have different learning styles and to allow for that, starting by building on the student's dominant style, but helping them to extend it and avoid getting stuck in a shortcut learning loop. Psychotherapy training is maybe best suited to divergent learners, if and when other learning styles are understood and taken into account so that all students' needs can be met.

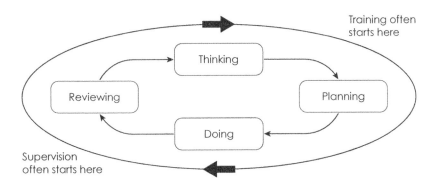

Figure 14.3: Traditional starting points for training and supervision

An approach to the teaching of theory

If psychotherapy training is provided by a particular 'school', then the theory to be taught is obvious, even when new theory and new approaches to the theory are added. In integrative training, decisions need to be made about what approaches to include and what pathways to follow. It can be tricky to create a body of theory that is both coherent and comprehensive without overwhelming the student. As we said in Chapter 1, integration can mean various things, but one of them is the integration of multiple theoretical approaches. So, besides teaching theory itself, the criteria for choosing these theories need to be clarified, based on a coherent philosophy of human development, pathology and therapeutic method (see Chapters 3, 4 and 11). The training institute may also want to encourage students to read more widely than the theories presented on the course, so they can form their own fuller integration by following a path based on their own principles, as long as they are sufficiently in tune with the course they are undertaking. The skills to follow such extensions could also be taught.

At the end of the training, students usually write a dissertation and/or an extended case study. This document needs to show:

- why the student chose this particular research question

- how psychotherapy theory and practice have contributed to the research and that the student has an ability to critically evaluate and integrate theory

- how theory and practice have been understood and integrated by the student

- how this research project has helped the student to develop their own epistemology (ways of knowing about the world), and their ontology (sense of being as a person as well as a therapist)

- how their research has had a positive impact on their work with clients

- how their particular research has added to the general sum of knowledge available to the profession of psychotherapy.

Action research theory says that the research must be 'for me, for us and for them' (Reason & Marshal, 2001:413). These are all-important aspects of research and none should be left out in our view. Writing just for oneself can tend towards narcissism, and writing only for others can be purely cognitive and intellectual with no real, embodied incorporation of the learning that comes with learning from our own experience. Contributing to the body of knowledge in one's own 'school' is important, but so is knowledge that is disseminated more widely.

In a written-up case study, the student is discovering and demonstrating how they have applied and developed theoretical understanding and meaning-making in their work with a specific client. They can explain how the theory has both supported their work and been changed by it, showing all four stages of the learning cycle in action. They are showing how the work has changed both the client, themselves and their practice.

Teaching integrative theory and teaching theory integratively

Those who devise integrative training courses tend to follow an integrative approach to theory. They usually have a philosophy that guides their choice of theories based on ones that are helpful to integrative work with clients. Theory helps us to organise and formulate our thinking about our clients and how their suffering can be approached (see Chapters 3 and 4). Training in a single approach has its advantages, as we show in Chapter 15, but how can we think about the teaching of integration when the clarity of what is to be taught is not immediately evident as it is in schools that teach a single approach? How can bringing together different theories make sense in the training of psychotherapists?

The inspiration for making an integration often comes from thinking that bringing two or more theories together might enhance each of them. Those, like us, who came to the conclusion that humanistic work, which we valued for its direct and powerful effect on the emotional and relational difficulties we faced in life, does not sufficiently address the origins of our own and our clients' suffering and neuroses. The integration may thus include psychoanalytic theory and practice as it has a clearer theory of human development, particularly that of object relations in England (Gomez, 1997) and self psychology in America (Kohut, 1971). These are often felt to be in tune with humanistic theory and practice, as they encourage emotional understanding and engagement in their approach to therapeutic work and bring empathic understanding to their theories of human development.

Another common type of integration puts together cognitive and behavioural therapies (CBT). Cognitive theory has also been combined with psychoanalytic theory to make the integration called cognitive analytic therapy (CAT). These also make sense as integrations based on sound principles. CAT (Ryle, 2002) is an integration which brings together cognitive understanding, empathic relationship building and psychoanalytic insights to help people to make necessary changes in their lives (Corbridge, Brummer & Coid, 2018).

Integrative training courses may want to incorporate further theories as time goes by. It is important that these develop and expand thinking within a basic philosophy rather than adding on a fashionable theory to appear 'up to date'. For instance, we have integrated intersubjectivist approaches from the school of 'intersubjective systems theory' (Orange, 1997; Stolorow & Atwood, 2014) which seemed to speak to us in a way that further helped us with our own integration of humanistic and psychoanalytic theories and practice (see Chapter 6). This has been a great inspiration to us, and we have tried to more fully elucidate this model by showing more clearly how it applies in practice (see Chapters 7 and 10). We also felt that this work needed expanding beyond the relational strand and this led us to new areas. We explored a larger range of systemic approaches – how to take whole systems into account in the therapeutic meeting rather than just the interpersonal encounter (see Chapter 8). We also included the ecological, eco-systemic and spiritual strands of life (see Chapter 9). Some of the writers who influenced us fail to show how their theory affects their practice clearly enough – and we have engaged with this in our present explorations.

The theorists we have found helpful over the years come from a wide spectrum of schools: humanistic psychotherapists such as Rogers, Berne, Perls and Moreno; psychoanalytic psychotherapists such as Freud, Jung, Klein, Winnicott, Fairbairn, Bowlby, Balint; self psychologists such as Kohut and Stolorow; body-orientated theorists such as Lowen, Boadella; birth trauma therapists such as Grof, Lake and Emerson; eco-systemic therapists such as Abrams; and transpersonal theorists such as Assagioli, Wilber and Welwood.

In more recent years, this has also included writers and researchers in neuroscience who have contributed to our knowledge of child development, such as Schore, Seigel, Gerhardt, Van der Kolk. These are particularly important as they show how babies' brains develop along with their ability to relate and to understand their experience. Although much of this under-lines the understanding of those who researched human development using observation and phenomenology, neuroscience has confirmed these observations from a more objective material science perspective and shown them to be even more fundamentally important. We now understand that new neural pathways and patterns are forged through constant and consistent holding, soothing, smiling, playing and eye contact with caregivers (Gerhardt, 2015). This research shows how mothers who are not able to provide such contact and communication have babies emotionally and cognitively disadvantaged in later life, having difficulty in making relationships. Some psychotherapy training courses include observation of young babies and their primary carer and this can be very instructive.

In addition to theorists who have contributed to our own integration, there are integrative psychotherapists we have found useful such as Josselson (1995), Kahn (1991), Erskine (2015), Finlay (2016) and Gilbert (Gilbert & Orlans, 2011).

In teaching theory, it is important to realise that theorists are set within the cultural context of their lives and times, whether they are originators of ideas like Freud and Jung or those who developed ideas further like Winnicott and Fairbairn or more recent theorists like Robert Stolorow. This approach helps us not to introject theory as 'the truth' but, instead, investigate how and when that theory arose, seeing it in the context of the racial, class and societal culture of the time. We try to understand the intellectual culture of the school of psychotherapy in which the theorist was steeped with the other writers and approaches around at that time to which they were dialogically responding. Theory needs to be contextualised, historically and culturally, and presented alongside the psycho-biography of the theorist. We can then help students to understand these theories and use them appropriately to ensure that the theory can be useful for their work with clients, and follow them, not slavishly, as maps of the territory.

To illustrate, Melanie Klein and Donald Winnicott influenced each other but had important differences in their theories. Klein was born in 1882 to Jewish parents in Austria and later moved to England. The economic circumstances of her life, and her gender, meant that she did not train as a doctor or undertake university studies, which was very frustrating for her. Nevertheless, she had a huge influence on psychoanalysis. Her notions of child development were based on observations of her own children and so she needs to be understood in that context. It seems that she did not take her own difficulties and frustrations into account when observing her children's behaviour and analysing them. Donald Winnicott, by contrast, was born into an English, middle-class, white, Protestant home in 1896, dominated by a depressive mother, two sisters and a nanny. He was a rebellious adolescent and his subsequent teaching focusing on the need to find our 'true' self was probably connected with his avowed need to keep his mother alive through her depression. His observations of children and of mother–baby interaction took place in the context of working with children traumatised by being evacuated from cities in the Second World War as well as the context of his previous career as a paediatrician.

Teaching about cultural difference and diversity

Approaching the psycho-biography of theorists shows that theory is culturally configured, a fact that needs to be taken into account when considering psychotherapy in terms of cultural difference and diversity. Judy has written and researched elsewhere (Ryde, 2009) about how the profession of psychotherapy is very 'white' and has spent many decades trying to encourage the profession to become more diverse. We have come across a number of people who have suggested that, since psychotherapy was developed in the West and non-western countries have their own way of approaching spiritual and emotional ills, it may not be applicable to people from non-western countries. This would be more important as an argument if all differences were connected to those who come from places other than western countries. Most western nations are now very diverse themselves and many of their populations are of mixed heritage. Judy finds in working therapeutically with people who were not raised in western countries, particularly in her work with refugees, that people from other cultures and races can and do benefit from psychotherapy, provided that psychotherapists are prepared to understand and take into account difference in culture and the experience of being non-white in a predominantly white culture (Ryde, 2019). In the same way, other differences in culture such as class, gender, age and sexual orientation also need to be acknowledged and understood. Psychotherapy itself has its own culture and rules – and needs to be open enough in its response to difference to embrace a wide range of cultural ways of being.

Integrative psychotherapy that is systemic and eco-systemic is well placed to address difference and to train others to address these wider concerns. Theories about human development and the needs of those who suffer psychological dis-ease are not set in stone so that those with different understandings can be appreciated and learned from.

For instance, the western world has become extremely individualistic in its culture, as we saw in Chapter 2. This individualism has brought many psychological ills in its wake – many people have lost their sense of belonging, while other pathologies such as addictions and a narcissistic need for instant gratification are on the rise. Many non-western cultures tend to be collectivist in nature, and Judy has written elsewhere (Ryde, 2019) about the ways members of more collectivist cultures can be understood in therapy. However, from an integrative perspective, Judy has also shown how such different philosophies can be brought together and their differences resolved in theories of intersubjective and systemic integration (Ryde, 2019).

To give just one example here, the notion of the 'self' is seen very differently in individualistic and collectivist cultures. In individualistic cultures, the 'self' is seen as 'belonging' to an individual, whereas in collectivist cultures the 'self' does not exist outside the context of a group such as the family or community. For systemic intersubjectivists, the self is fluid and only exists as a set of organising principles within relationships (see Chapter 7). Learning to listen in a nuanced way, as well as being able to see and reflect on one's own culture and perceptual framing, is important in the training and development of integrative psychotherapists.

So how should this be approached in the training of psychotherapists? It is our experience that matters of culture and difference tend to be taught as something of an add on, even as an option to be chosen rather than a vital part of the training. Many people think that attention to difference should be part of every aspect of the training and therefore incorporated as part of the curriculum. Others see it more as something to be specially taught. We have come to the view that both are important. It is an aspect of the work that needs its own focus and to be a natural part of the whole.

One of the main things that student psychotherapists need to learn is not just to look through an anthropologist's binoculars to understand the culture of others intellectually, but to look in the mirror and become more aware of their own implicit culture and how it frames their thinking and being in the world; to recognise that they 'belong' to several cultures themselves, each with their own assumptions and ways of seeing. We may, for instance, belong to our family culture, our national culture, our professional culture and more. We each have our own unique mixture of cultures and cultural assumptions. In order to be open to others, we need to understand where we happen to come from so that we do not see our own assumptions as God-given truths. We must understand why we tend to respond in the way that we do.

As with other aspects of learning to be a psychotherapist, we need curiosity, openness, respect for others and their difference, insight into our own biases, and compassion for others and ourselves. Teaching students to reflect on our own reactions is a major part of the training, and part of why it takes a long time. At the heart of the work lies the vital skill of being able to reflect non-defensively on our own responses to others, which sometimes goes underground and emerges unbidden unless we are skilled at recognising it and using it for our ongoing development.

Example

A student psychotherapist had a client who was a Chinese university student. The client was very distressed because he was afraid that he would not pass his exams and would thus shame his family. The student therapist was tempted to try to help her client to see that he was under undue pressure and show him that this was counterproductive as his fear was affecting his ability to study. It was more important, however, that the therapist in supervision understood the depth of this shame within the client's cultural context, before progressing any further. For an English student, both client and therapist may have felt that the pressure to succeed was unwarranted, a view that was not shared by this Chinese student.

Conclusion

The training of psychotherapists has many facets and involves the whole person. It is wise for anyone embarking on this training to have some understanding that it is likely to disturb their normal ways of being and their understanding of the world. This is hard to fully grasp until the training is well under way, however. Because of this, the first year should be separately accredited, for example as 'basic counselling skills', so that the student can stop at this point and still have something to show for it. Another way of achieving the same end is to complete a less exacting counselling course before starting the full psychotherapy training.

Students are then in a better place to understand what is involved and to either stop, carry on or decide to take a year or two out, maybe to undertake more personal psychotherapy, and reflect on whether or not they wish to continue. Without this provision, students can feel that they have been led into an expensive training which they find more emotionally and intellectually exacting than they first expected.

Psychotherapy training is challenging but it is also very rewarding. It helps the student to more deeply understand themselves and others and to experientially and cognitively grasp the intersubjective, systemic and eco-systemic nature of the world. Through this they can find ways of responding to the multifaceted experiences of life with its traumas, losses and tragedies as well as its joys and satisfactions and understand how these show up in our own and our clients' day-to-day lives.

The training methodology of an integrative psychotherapy course helps to ensure that the learning is embodied and not just a set of introjected ideas and that the theory is wide-ranging but fully integrated into a coherent body of knowledge and experience. Students learn that they are not 'isolated minds' (Stolorow & Atwood, 1992) so their increasing self-knowledge is not just an internal matter but is held and vital within their web of relationships – personal, social and in their participation in the more-than-human world.

CHAPTER 15

Bringing it Together and Leaning into the Future

Self-transformation is precisely what life is, and human relationships, which are an extract of life, are the most changeable of all, rising and falling from minute to minute, and lovers are those in whose relationship and contact no one moment resembles another.

Rilke (1969:151)

Introduction

In his novel, *The Only Story*, Julian Barnes (2018:111) explores how everyone has a love story, whether short or long, tragic or successful. We believe that it is important in psychotherapy not just to follow the client's road of pain and distress, but also to discover their love story, their path of love, passion and purpose. Yes, there is work to do in psychotherapy – returning to areas that have been repressed or split off and need reintegrating. And, yes, we do need to complete earlier stages of maturation that have remained unfinished and which hold us back now. We do need to identify past self-narratives, limiting beliefs and assumptions and create new narratives, but we also need to work with the forward-driving internal and external life force, Henri Bergson's (1907, 2016) 'élan vital'. We need to inquire with the client about what matters most to them, what they love and are passionate about, to help them find and articulate their sense of purpose and what gives their life its deepest meaning.

Freud, we are told by Erik Erikson (1950:39), stressed the dual importance of love and work and how 'love and work are the cornerstones of our humanness'. Love can be experienced as an internal driving energy that fuels our creativity and our individual and collective evolution, that takes us forward to higher stages of development and maturity. Work can be experienced as an external call, a vocation or calling, a curriculum that life is constantly presenting to us to further our learning and development. As psychotherapists we need to help our clients look outwards, as well as look inwards; to look forwards, as well as backwards. We need to explore with our clients what they are wanting from life, but also what life is asking of them.

At the simplest level, this can mean asking the client what is necessary for them to do in their life right now. What is their world needing from them? What is life requiring from them? For some people, work is not fulfilling. They can experience it as drudgery, a means towards an end. They need our help to see beyond the immediately required tasks, to clarify what they are in service of, be that 'feeding my family', 'keeping a roof over our heads', or 'so I can travel and explore'. For some, the call of work is to clean their room, to do the cooking, to help neighbours with their shopping, volunteering to plant trees in the communal wood or campaigning for a social or political cause. Someone or something always needs you, whoever you are. Jane Goodall (2018), the great naturalist, tells us, 'You cannot get through a single day without having an impact on the world around you. What you do makes a difference, and you have to decide what kind of difference you want to make.'

At deeper levels, it can involve an exploration of the client's deeper life purpose and vocation.

There is growing evidence that purpose-focused companies are more successful than those driven by targets, goals and ambition (Renshaw, 2018; Sisodia, Wolfe & Sheth, 2007). There is also growing evidence that individuals who have a clear sense of purpose in their lives are more contented and fulfilled. Elsewhere, Peter has written about how partnerships, teams and marriages are not created by partners, but by a joint purpose which requires collaboration (Hawkins, 2017d). We suggest that, rather than thinking about how the individual creates their personal purpose, we can consider this question from the other direction: how does the purpose create the individual? This implies that the purpose is always already out there in the world, waiting for a team or individual to respond. Thus, for many years we have used the question, 'What can you uniquely do that the world of tomorrow needs?' This is a 'future-back' question, rooted in the notion of co-evolution and a belief that individual development is not just about integrating past traumas and relational ruptures, but about awakening to the developmental potential that lies just in front of us. Scharmer and Kaufer (2012) write about the importance of leaning into the future, with an open mind, open heart and open will, so we can deeply listen to what is emergent in our lives.

Psychotherapy needs to look up as well as down, looking at higher levels of maturation and development, as well as earlier levels which need completion. We must never forget that we are part of the wider endeavour to assist co-evolution in the maturation of human consciousness so, as a species, we can act appropriately and responsibly in the world we have co-created and face the challenges we have brought on ourselves.

Psychotherapy needs to look out as well as look in. To realise what that means for ourselves and the clients we relate to, we must understand that we and they are not their pathologies, or their psychometric label, or a number on the Enneagram (an ancient system model more recently used to classify personality types). They are not 'an island complete unto itself', but they embody their relationships, their family patterns, their social mores, their culture embedded in their language, verbal and non-verbal, and in their patterns of meaning-making, their biology and the current state of human evolution. There may be two bodies in the consulting room, but psychologically there are never just two people present.

Gregory Bateson, 50 years ago, was warning that we did not have 'a snowball in hell chance' of dealing with the climate crisis unless we created a radical shift in human consciousness. This has been more recently echoed by Ken Wilber (2000:137):

> Gaia's main problem – is not pollution, toxic dumping, ozone depletion, or any such. Gaia's main problem is that not enough human beings have developed to the postconventional, world centric, global levels of consciousness, wherein they will automatically be moved to care for the global commons.

Ken Wilber (Wilber, 2000:136–138, 147) is scathing about the actual capacity of system thinking and neuroscience to help us shift consciousness, and we agree that intellectual knowledge alone is not sufficient for this purpose, for it just increases what Bateson terms zero and level one learning – knowing about and solving technical, linear problems. However, we only partly agree with Ken Wilber, and have argued elsewhere that we need to move from 'system thinking' to 'systemic thinking' to 'systemic being' (Hawkins, 2017d, 2018a). Like Wilber, we argue that developing our individual and collective consciousness requires inner subjective work and intersubjective dialogue with others. This is the work of relational, systemic and ecological psychotherapy helping us to: become less reactive and more open and receptive, integrate disconnected parts of ourselves, develop an integrating self-narrative, create a stronger internal witness and core self that can integrate the many different internal and external identities, and develop a more compassionate, kind and forgiving stance to self and others, and wide-angled empathy for all human and non-human organisms, individual and collective.

This is the great work of integrative psychotherapy which we share with parents, teachers, counsellors, coaches, psychologists, spiritual guides and all members of all the helping professions. We all need to learn from each other, lower our protectionist professional walls and find language that connects across the different technical jargons we each use.

As we have shown in this book, there are many fields of academic research and study we can learn from. One of the most important in recent years has been neuroscience, but as we showed in Chapter 4, we need to work with and encourage the neuro-phenomenologists, such as Dan Siegel and Susan Gerhardt. We have liberally drawn on their work, while resisting 'neuro-reductionism' and attempts to reduce psychotherapy to reprogramming the brain and the cognitive frameworks and patterns of behaviour characterising individuals.

The dangers of being integrative as a psychotherapist

Throughout this book, we have proposed the great benefits of integrative psychotherapy, but it is also important to point out some of the dangers and limitations of this approach and how they might be addressed.

1. *The importance of clear frameworks that are transparent and understandable to the client*

   If, as we have argued throughout this book, psychotherapy is a collaborative endeavour between the client and the psychotherapist, then it is important that they develop a shared and clear framework for the work they do together. It can be difficult with such a complex integrative approach to find the simplicity at the other side of complexity which can be shared and developed in each psychotherapeutic relationship.

2. *The strength that comes by being held by a tradition and lineage*

In the Islamic Sufi tradition, there is an important prayerful practice, where you mention the name of your spiritual teacher, then their teacher, and then theirs, and so on right back to Ali and the Prophet. Roman Catholic Christian baptism has a lineage that goes back through the priest, to the bishop, to the Pope, and right through the line of Popes, back to Saint Peter and thence to Jesus. Similarly, in the early days of psychoanalysis, psychoanalysts mention that they were analysed by psychoanalyst x, who in turn was analysed by Freud. In writing a research doctorate, each academic needs to include a literature review, anchoring their thinking in those who have come before them. We all stand on the shoulders of our ancestors in our line of endeavour.

The integrative psychotherapist may draw on many traditions and many fields of study. At best, they might be what the archetypal psychotherapist James Hillman described as the 'Knight Errant', but at worse they can become the itinerant wanderer, with a rag-bag collection of unintegrated and undigested theories, approaches and models. Integration needs to be both vertical, tracing our roots back in time as we have done in Chapters 5 and 6, and integrative horizontally, interweaving approaches from many contemporary sources.

3. *The strength that comes from being part of a continuing community of practice, rooted in appropriate accountability and governance*

The complexity of the field of human consciousness is such that we are all myopic and limited in our perceptions and responses. We only know the other through the developmental level of our own epistemology and can only perceive the wider system through our own systemic position. We are all capable of being unethical and, as we have shown in this book, our ethical and moral choices are greatly enhanced when we actively practise transparently, exposing our work to others, and with their help holding ourselves accountable for what we have done. We believe that integrative psychotherapists need to have ongoing regular supervision and also be part of an ongoing community of practice, and to be re-accredited every five years (or more frequently). Fitness to practise, once achieved at initial accreditation, does not remain constant, nor do the standards we expect from professional psychotherapists. We each need to be accountable for maintaining our fitness to practise, through our continuing personal and professional development, through supervision and through keeping abreast of latest developments in the field.

The dangers in not being integrative as a psychotherapist

1. *Theory and method become more important than the client or the work*

   For the modern psychotherapist, faced with the challenges of uncertainty and the complexity of our worlds of experience, clinging to the theories and methodology of our initial training can be felt as a lifeline. Some schools of psychology argue for, and insist on, 'methodological fidelity', always applying their method in the same way. Without this, they argue, the work can never be scientifically or empirically assessed. This can lead to the psychotherapist being more in love with their methods than the client in front of them, so that the methodology and theory stand between the client and therapist. We contend that theory and method do need to be learned, but metaphorically it should stand behind us, supporting us, not blocking the co-creative space for dialogue and grace between psychotherapist and client. Jung is reported to have said, 'learn my theories until you know them inside-out, but when you enter the consulting room, let them go!' He is often quoted as saying, 'I would rather be Jung than a Jungian.' We concur with both sentiments.

2. *Ruled by the book of received wisdom*

   Studying the development of religions and other belief systems, writers like Max Weber (1947) describe how organisations start with a 'charismatic phase' organised around a revered individual teacher or prophet, such as Buddha, Moses, Jesus, Mohammed, Guru Nanak. Schools of psychotherapy also often have such a starting phase, with great charismatic innovators and founders of schools, such as Freud, Klein, Jung, Rogers, to name but a few. After the teacher or prophet is dead, some disciples will move on to find a new teacher, but many will sanctify the dead leader. Their works will be collected, interpreted and annotated. Splits will occur between different interpretations of what the teacher said or meant. The teachings will become codified and removed from their original historical and dialogical context and be passed down as 'the letter of the law' all adherents must keep to.

   In time, this 'bureaucratic phase' gives way to external challenge and internal critique, revision and reformation. New times call for new approaches. Each of these stages has its dangers and, like James Hillman before us, we have always argued for pluralism, and dialogue between faiths – be they religious faiths or psychotherapeutic schools.

3. *Control by the elders*

Being trained within one school, where the trainers, supervisors and one's own psychotherapist all come from and are approved of by that school, facilitates a process of control by the elders, ensuring newly trained psychotherapists follow the paths laid down by their lineage. Elsewhere, Peter has written about the way that supervision itself can become a way of enculturating new practitioners in the culture of those who have been trained previously, rather than being inspired by the learning lungs of the profession constantly learning from new challenges arising at the cutting edge of practice (Hawkins & Shohet, 2012: Chapter 14).

4. *Sectarianism*

Psychotherapists can be trapped in their own sectarian beliefs and become dogmatic, closed to new thinking and potentially seeing all other approaches as heretical or nonsense. Psychotherapy, from its early origins in Vienna and Freud's circle, has developed a deeply rivalrous and competitive culture, which has led to splits, factions and sectarianism. The small group of early Freudians were caught up in what has been termed the 'Freud wars', with their rivalry, mutual critique and condemnation (Gomez, 2005).

Some schools of psychotherapy ignore new developments in other fields and see new schools of psychotherapy as threats to their orthodoxy.

5. *Reinventing the wheel*

In our own journey through integrative psychotherapy over 40 years, and recently in writing this book, we have been struck by the fact that similar discoveries have been made by psychotherapists from different and separated traditions, without any obvious link or referencing between them. We notice how new theories and models are created within bounded psychotherapy schools, as if it were the first time humans ever thought of or have been shown these particular discoveries, oblivious to the fact that they have been written about and practised for some time in another school, to which they seem wilfully blind.

We have elsewhere described the powerful and widely held myth that the great innovative leaps forward in understanding and ways of working originate in gifted individual humans. Yet the reality is that the heart of human progress has always been collaborative, coming to life from collective thinking and experimentation (Harari, 2014, 2015; Sloman & Fernbach, 2017).

Integrating, developing and expanding our sense of self

One of the key threads running throughout this book has been the centrality in psychotherapy of the three tasks of integrating, developing and expanding our sense of self.

Psychotherapy helps us integrate and find coherence between our many selves. One of the most fundamental integrations is between our narrative self and our experiencing self – the story we have about our self, originating in our left hemisphere neo-cortex, and how we experience our embodied self in each and every moment. Often our narrative self is also divided many ways: there can be the story we tell ourselves and the story we relate to others; the story about ourselves we tell our family, the story we tell when we are going for a job, and the story we tell a prospective new partner. Then there are the stories that others tell about us. Often our life is restricted by living with a historic narrative we have accepted about our self. Psychotherapy helps us rework our narratives and become self-authoring in a way that does not reduce our many-sided selves to one single narrative, but provides meaningful connection and coherence between each one.

In developing our self in psychotherapy, we are increasing the capacity to reflect on the many different aspects of our self, from a place of inner witness. We learn to increasingly respond to situations with a greater sense of choice, rather than emotionally react. This comes from the ability to see not just the others in a situation, but also the context, and witness our reactions, rather than act from them. Wilber describes this as the process by which increasing amounts of the 'I' that is perceiving and reacting to the world become the 'me' which the 'I' can see. He describes all development as 'envelopment'.

In developing our self, we also recognise that our life is embedded in many layers of context that, in turn, become part of our internal text. We develop relationally, first within and then with our mother, then others. We become part of a family with its own unwritten and spoken rules, and ways of relating and being. We grow up within different tribes – people like us – and these may be extended families, or local communities, our school, sports club or other wider belonging. These in turn are contained within shared cultures, which may be regional, national, religious or ethnic, which share language, both verbal and non-verbal, ways of being and perceiving the world, beliefs and shared mindsets. Beyond the cultures that divide us, all *Homo sapiens* are part of one species, which has evolved over many millennia on this Earth and shares distinct species characteristics. This species has, in very recent history, become more globally interconnected, much more numerous and even more exploitative of and damaging to the rest of our shared ecology than ever before.

Thus, arriving in the psychotherapy consulting room is an individual self, relational self, family self, tribal self, national, religious, ethnic self, global human self and our ecological or eco-self. We are not just systemically nested within our family, culture and ecology, but they are also deeply nested within us, in every fibre of our being, the way we live, move, talk, hear, feel and see the world and think, as well as the way we construct our narratives. The work of psychotherapy is not only to separate and find our own unique identity, but also to re-own each of these widening aspects of our extended self; to own not only our personal history, but also those of our families, communities and culture. Only through this process can we each find our belonging, our rootedness, and a fullness of participation in the world, which is both out there, but also intimately within us. It is through this psychotherapeutic approach that we regain a participatory consciousness, and a life of grace and gracefulness (Bateson, 1979; Reason, 2017). Through this process we find the ever-widening path to a fuller life in our eco-self, where the ecological environment is part of us and there is a two-way flow of caring and being cared for.

For a psychotherapist to help a client on this journey, they too must have walked and be walking this path. Their training needs not just to involve understanding individual human psychology and development, but also to embrace relational, systemic and ecological perspectives. We need to learn how to participate with our clients intersubjectively, not just as two individualised subjective beings, but as two people, each deeply embedded in their family, community and culture life worlds, and two people who are each just a small part of a much, much larger evolving eco-system.

We also need to learn not just how to deepen our empathy and compassion for each individual client, but also how to develop what we have termed 'wide-angled empathy' – that is, empathy for every individual, organisation, system and being in their story and the connections between them. So often, psychotherapists are so deeply trained in empathy for the client that they begin to react against the others in the client's narrative, seeing them through the client's eyes. This can easily lead to confluence with the client or the playing out of Karpman's (1968) drama triangle of client as victim, others in their story as persecutors and therapist as rescuer, which can become a self-perpetuating cycle, kept turning by all three parties.

'Wide-angled empathy' also needs to be extended so that we can empathise as another individual, and can meet their family, tribal, national and cultural self from those levels within us. Consider this example from a recent supervision.

Example

The psychotherapist was struggling to empathise with her client, an asylum seeker who was finding it hard to adequately care for his family. He was filled with fury that was aimed at another group of refugees who he saw as using influence inside the council to get much more help than his family received. He wanted to attack and even murder them and was furious that, unlike in his own country, he could not carry out a revenge killing. The psychotherapist felt alienated by and judgemental of his murderous intent. 'Why can't he see they are struggling too?' Other supervision group members agreed that his response was 'immoral' or 'wrong', even allowing for the cultural background. The supervisor invited them to contact their own inner tribal self – times when they had desperately wanted their people to win out over another group. One group member mentioned how he was an ardent football supporter and found himself shouting at the referee to give his team a doubtful penalty. Another mentioned feeling stranded with her family at a foreign airport when two plane flights were cancelled and doing everything she could to get her family ahead of others on another airline's one remaining flight out. Another said she was aware of how her grandparents talked about the 'spirit of the Blitz' when Londoners came together and their joint murderous hatred of the German 'Hun'. From this sharing, the group found a different level of what we now term 'deep-level empathy', finding the family, tribal, community or cultural self within us that can empathise with those levels in the client and without which we remain an outsider, struggling to empathise and caught in external judgement.

Our work is to learn to go even beyond 'wide-angled' and 'deep-level empathy' to 'eco-empathy', where we find the natural responsiveness and compassion for all aspects of life, not from our separate self, but from being part of the connected web of life. It is from this place that judgemental morality drops away and we acknowledge all life as part of us.

The future challenges for integrative psychotherapy

We know so much more now about what enables healthy human development, through neuroscience, psycho-social research and many years of case work in mental health and psychotherapy.

We are blessed to have so much more of the ancient, modern and post-modern maps and methods of higher spiritual development that were unavailable to our predecessors, yet as the world becomes ever more secular and dominated by materialistic scientism, much of this is ignored, derided or hidden. If we are to manage the challenges of the next 50 years, we desperately need a great leap forward in the evolution and maturation of human consciousness.

As we learn more and more about the inner workings of the brain and the nature of intersubjective human relating, we know that the mind is a complex systemic living process operating through our bodies and brains and flowing through our external engagement with others and our environment. We must never forget that the individual and collective mind are endowed with a natural process of self-regulation and healing. Siegel writes about the 'mind's natural drive to heal – to integrate, brain, mind and relationships, in the triangle of well-being' (Siegel, 2010:76). Nature and the wider eco-systemic levels are also capable of self-healing, if we humans can only allow the more-than-human world the space and time to do so, without constant toxic interference by human greed and exploitation.

Conclusion

Ken Wilber writes, 'Each new generation has a chance to move the integral vision forward in a substantial way, simply because new information, data, and discoveries are constantly being made' (Wilber, 2000:84–85). Our hope is that this book has made a significant contribution in bringing together relational, systemic, ecological and spiritual approaches to psychotherapy and interweaving them into a new integration. We are not trying to start a new orthodoxy but to open new dialogues between practitioners from different schools, and between psychotherapy and the enormous amount of exciting new thinking in many parallel domains. We also hope that we have made some small contribution to revision psychotherapy in a way that helps to make it 'future fit' for the ever-increasing challenges facing the human species and the planet humans now dominate. Psychotherapy has to join with many other fields of endeavour in the urgent task of evolving human consciousness for our species to be fit to continue to have a place on this one Earth we share with so many other living organisms.

In providing our contribution, we are also aware, like Wilber, that, 'Whatever contributions any of us might make will only be the shoulders upon which others soon will stand' (Wilber, 2000:85).

Thank you for joining us in this exploration and may it help each one of you to make the greatest contribution that lies in your potential.

References

Abram, D. (1996). *The Spell of the Sensuous*. New York, NY: Vintage.

Adler, A. (2009, first published 1931). *What Life Could Mean to You*. Oxford: Oneworld.

Adler, A. (2013). *The Science of Living*. London: Routledge.

Alcoff, L. M. (2015). *The Future of Whiteness*. Cambridge: Polity Press.

Alexander, F. (1963). The dynamics of psychotherapy in the light of learning theory. *American Journal of Psychiatry*, 120, 440–448.

Altman, N. (2015). A Meeting of Minds: Mutuality in Psychoanalysis. In A. Harris and S. Kuchuck (eds) *The Legacy of Sándor Ferenczi: From Ghost to Ancestor*. Hove: Routledge.

American Psychiatric Association (2013). *Diagnostic and Statistical Manual of Mental Disorders*. Arlington, VA: American Psychiatric Publishing.

Amidon, E. (2014). *Non-Dual Sufism*. Available at: www.sufiway.org/teaching/notes-from-the-open-path/14-teachings/96-nondual-sufism, accessed 9 January 2018.

Appiah, K. (2005). *The Ethics of Identity*. Princeton, NJ: Princeton University Press.

Armstong, K. (2006). *The Great Transformation: The Beginning of Our Religious Traditions*. New York, NY: Knopf.

Assagioli, R. (1965). *Psychosynthesis*. London: Turnstone Books.

Atwood, G. E. & Stolorow, R. D. (1993). *Faces in the Cloud*. Northvale, NY: Jason Aronson.

Aurobindo, S. (1999). *The Human Cycle: The Psychology of Social Development*. Twin Lakes, WI: Lotus Press.

Baker Miller, J. (1987). *Toward a New Psychology of Women*. London: Penguin Random House.

Baldwin, J. M. (1902). *Social and Ethical Interpretations in Mental Development*. Oxford: Macmillan.

Barnes, J. (2018). *The Only Story*. London: Jonathan Cape.

Barr, S. (2017). The average Brit checks their phone 10,000 times a year, study finds. *The Independent*. Available at: www.independent.co.uk/life-style/gadgets-and-tech/average-briton-check-phone-10000-times-year-uk-study-iphone-samsung-smartphone-a8086631.html.

Bateson, G. (1972). *Steps to an Ecology of the Mind*. San Fransisco, CA: Chandler.

Bateson, G. (1979). *Mind and Nature: A Necessary Unity*. New York, NY: Dutton.

Bateson, G. (1992). *Sacred Unity: Further Steps to an Ecology of Mind*. New York, NY: HarperCollins.

Becvar, D. S. & Becvar, R. J. (2008). *Family Therapy: A Systemic Integration*. London: Pearsons.

Belbin, R. M. (2010). *Team Roles at Work*. Abingdon: Routledge.

Belk, R. W. (1984). Cultural and historical differences in concepts of self and their effects on attitudes toward having and giving in NA. *Advances in Consumer Research*, 11.

Bergson, H. (1907). *L'Evolution créatrice*. (Published in English as *Creative Evolution*.) Paris: Alcan.

Bergson, H. (2016). *Creative Evolution*. New York, NY: Perennial Press.

Berne, E. (1967). *Games People Play*. Harmondsworth: Penguin Books.

Bernheimer, C. & Kahane, C. (1985). *In Dora's Case*. London: Virago.

Berry, W. (1983). *Standing by Words*. San Fransisco, CA: North Point Press.

Berry, W. (2015). *Our Only World: Ten Essays*. Berkeley, CA: Counterpoint.

Bertalanffy, L. v. (1960). *Problems of Life: An Evaluation of Modern Biological Thought*. London: Harper Torch Books.

Bertalanffy, L. v. (1968). *General System Theory: Foundations, Development, Applications*. New York, NY: George Braziller.

Bertalanffy, L. v. (1972). The history and status of general systems theory. *The Academy of Management Journal*, 15(4), 407–426.

Bion, W. (1961). *Experiences in Groups*. London: Tavistock Publications.

Blanckenburg, P. B. (1951). *The Thoughts of General Smuts: Compiled by his Private Secretary*. Boston, MA: Houghton Mifflin.

Bohm, D. (1996). *On Dialogue*. London and New York, NY: Routledge.

Bohn, R. & Short, J. (2012). Measuring consumer information. *International Journal of Communication*, 6, 980–1000.

Bohr, N. (1934). *Atomic Physics and Human Knowledge*. New York, NY: Wiley.

Bollas, C. (1987). *The Shadow of the Object: Psychoanalysis of the Unthought Known*. London: Free Association Books.

Bollas, C. (1992). *Being a Character: Psychoanalysis and Self Experience*. New York, NY: Hill and Wang.

Bollas, C. (1995). *Cracking Up*. Hove: Routledge.

Bond, T. (2015a). *Confidentiality & Record Keeping in Counselling and Psychotherapy*. London: Sage.

Bond, T. (2015b). *Standards and Ethics for Counselling in Action*. London: Sage.

Bowlby, J. (1953). *Child Care and the Growth of Love*. Harmondsworth: Pelican Original.

Breakwell, G. M. (1986). *Coping with Threatened Identities*. London: Methuen.

Breakwell, G. M. (2012). Diary and Narrative Methods. In G. M. Breakwell, J. A. Smith and D. B. Wright (eds) *Research Methods in Psychology*. London: Sage.

Bronfenbrenner, U. (1979). *The Ecology of Human Development*. Cambridge, MA: Harvard University Press.

Buber, M. (2002, first published 1947). *Between Man and Man*. Abingdon: Routledge.

Buber, M. (2004). *I and Thou*. London and New York, NY: Continuum.

Buzan, T. (2009). *The Mind Map Book*. Harlow: BBC Active.

Cain, D. J. & Seeman, J. (2006). *Humanistic Psychotherapies*. Washington DC: American Psychological Association.

Camus, A. (1942). *L'Etranger*. Paris: Gallimard.

Capra, F. (1988). *Uncommon Wisdom: Conversations with Remarkable People*. New York, NY: Simon & Schuster.

Capra, F. & Luisi, P. L. (2016). *A Systems View of Life: A Unified Vision*. Cambridge, UK: Cambridge University Press.

Carlyle, T. (1841). *On Heroes and Hero Worship and the Heroic in History*. Public domain book.

Carroll, M. & Shaw, E. (2013). *Ethical Maturity in the Helping Professions: Making Difficult Life and Work Decisions*. London: Jessica Kingsley Publishers.

Casement, P. (1985). *On Learning from the Patient*. London: Tavistock.

Casement, P. (1990a). *Further Learning from the Patient*. London: Routledge.

Casement, P. (1990b). *Learning from Life*. London: Routledge.

Clarkson, P. (1995). *The Therapeutic Relationship*. London: Whurr.

Clarkson, P. & Mackewn, J. (1993). *Fritz Perls*. London, Newbury Park, New Delhi: Sage.

Commons, M. L. & Richard, F. A. (1984). A General Model of Stage Theory. In M. L. Commons, F. A. Richards and C. Armon (eds) *Beyond Formal Operations* (Vol. 1 Late Adolescent and Adult Cognitive Development). New York, NY: Praeger.

Corbridge, C., Brummer, L. & Coid, P. (2018). *Cognitive Analytic Therapy: Distinctive Features*. Abingdon: Routledge.

Corsini, R. J. & Wedding, D. (2008). *Current Psychotherapies*. Belmont, CA: Brooks/Cole.

Crick, F. (1994). *The Astonishing Hypothesis: The Scientific Search for the Soul*. New York, NY: Scribner.

Csikszentmihalyi, M. (1999). If we are so rich, why aren't we happy? *American Psychologist*, 54(10), 821–827.

Damasio, A. (1999). *The Feeling of What Hapens*. London: Heinemann.

Dartnall, E. (2012). Supervisors' Perceptions of the Impact of Supervision on Therapeutic Outcomes: A Grounded Theory Study. Doctoral dissertation, City University.

Davies, D. & Neal, C. (1996). *Pink Therapy: A Guide for Counsellors and Therapists Working with Lesbian, Gay and Bisexual Clients*. Buckingham: Open University Press.

Dennett, D. (1991). *Consciousness Explained*. Boston, MA: Little, Brown.

Diamandis, P. H. & Kotler, S. (2014). *Abundance: The Future is Better Than You Think*. New York, NY: Free Press.

Dollard, J. & Miller, N. E. (1950). *Personality and Psychotherapy*. New York, NY: McGraw-Hill.

Dunn, K. (2018). The Therapeutic Alliance. In P. Weitz (ed.) *Psychotherapy 2.0: Where Psychotherapy and Technology Meet*. London: Routledge.

Durning, A. T. (1992). *How Much is Enough?: The Consumer Society and the Future of the Earth.* New York, NY: W. W. Norton & Company.

Edinger, E. F. (1996). *Ego and Archetype: Individuation and the Religious Function of the Psyche.* Boston, MA: Shambhala.

Eliot, T. (2002). *Collected Poems.* London: Faber and Faber.

Elkington, J. & Zeitz, J. (2014). *The Breakthrough Challenge.* San Francisco, CA: Jossey-Bass.

Elton, C. (2001). *Animal Ecology.* Chicago, IL: University of Chicago Press.

Elton Wilson, J. (1996). *Time Conscious Psychological Therapy.* London: Routledge.

Emerson, W. (1996). The vulnerable prenate. *International Journal of Prenatal and Perinatal Psychology and Medicine, 7*(3), 271–284.

Endicott, L. (2001). *Ethical Sensitivity Activity Booklet 1 Nurturing Character in the Middle School Classroom.* Available at: https://cee.nd.edu/curriculum/documents/actbklt1.pdf.

Erikson, E. (1950). *Identity and the Life Cycle.* New York, NY: W. W. Norton & Company.

Erikson, E. (1982). *The Life Cycle Completed.* New York, NY: W. W. Norton & Company.

Erskine, R. (2015). *Relational Patterns, Therapeutic Presence: Concepts and Practice of Integrative Psychotherapy.* New York, NY: Routledge.

Finlay, L. (2016). *Relational Integrative Psychotherapy.* Chichester: Wiley.

Foucault, M. (2006). *Madness and Civilisation.* London: Penguin Social Sciences.

Foulkes, S. H. (1948). *Introduction to Group Analytic Psychotherapy.* London: Karnac Books.

Foulkes, S. H. (1964). *Therapeutic Group Analysis.* London: George Allen and Unwin.

Foulkes, S. H. & Anthony, E. J. (1957). *Group Psychotherapy.* Harmondsworth: Pelican.

Frankl, V. (1961). *From Death Camp to Existentialism: A Psychiatrist's Path to a New Therapy.* Boston, MA: Beacon Press.

Frankl, V. (1969) *The Will to Meaning: Foundations and Applications of Logotherapy.* New York and Cleveland: World.

Frankl, V. (2013). *Man's Search for Meaning.* London: Penguin Random House.

Fredrickson, B. and Losada, M. F. (2005). Positive affect and the complex dynamics of human flourishing. *American Psychologist, 60*(7), 678–686.

French, T. M. (1933). Interrelations between psychoanalysis and the experimental work of Pavlov. *American Journal of Psychiatry, 89,* 1165–1203.

Freud, S. (1912). *Recommendation to Physicians Practising Psychoanalysis.* London: Hogarth Press.

Freud, S. (1938). *The Psychopathology of Everyday Life* (Vol. 5). Harmondsworth: Penguin Books.

Freud, S. (1973). *The New Introductory Lectures on Psychoanalysis.* London: Pelican Books.

Freud, S. (1974). *Introductory Lectures on Psychoanalysis.* Harmondsworth: Penguin Books.

Freud, S. & Breuer, J. (2004, first published 1893). *Studies in Hysteria*. London: Penguin Books.

Fuchs, T. (2007). Psychotherapy of the lived space: A phenomenological and ecological concept. *American Journal of Psychotherapy*, 4, 423–439.

Gauch, H. G. (2003). *Scientific Method in Practice*. Cambridge: Cambridge University Press.

Gawande, A. (2015). *Being Mortal: Illness, Medicine, and What Matters in the End*. London: Profile Books.

Gazzaniga, M. S. (2011). *Who's in Charge?* London: Constable and Robinson.

Gergen, K. J. (1999). *An Invitation to Social Construction*. London: Sage.

Gergen, K. J. (2001). *Social Construction in Context*. London: Sage.

Gerhardt, S. (2015). *Why Love Matters*. Hove and New York, NY: Routledge.

Gilbert, M. & Orlans, V. (2011). *Integrative Therapy: 100 Key Points and Techniques*. Hove: Routledge.

Gold, J. R. (1996). *Key Concepts in Psychotherapy Integration*. New York, NY: Plenum.

Goleman, D. (2009). *Emotional Intelligence: Why It Can Matter More Than IQ*. London: Bloomsbury.

Gomez, L. (1997). *Object Relations*. London: Free Association Books.

Gomez, L. (2005). *The Freud Wars*. London: Routledge.

Goodall, J. (2018). *Mother Earth*. Available at: https://vimeo.com/214288898?f bclid=IwAR2DoYKICdv_1jCS1t0N-mkmZAqlVMKwzfPz1-X-613-jJ_Vb-6kFFElbm8.

Gramsci, A. (1975). *The Prison Notebooks*. Vol 1. New York, NY: Columbia University Press.

Gray, A. (2014). *An Introduction to the Therapeutic Frame*. Hove: Routledge.

Greenfield, S. (2009). *ID: The Quest for Meaning in the 21st Century*. London: Sceptre.

Greenfield, S. (2011). *You and Me*. London: Notting Hill Editions.

Grof, S. (2016, first pulished 1975). *Realms of the Human Unconscious: Observations from LSD Research*. London: Souvenir Press.

Habermas, J. (2015). *The Lure of Technocracy*. Cambridge: Polity Press.

Hanh, T. N. (1997). *Stepping into Freedom*. Berkeley, CA: Parallax Press.

Hall, K. (2014). How the outside comes inside: Ecological selves in the therapy room. *Self and Society*, 41(4), 22–27.

Hall, K. (2018). Coming home to Eden: Animal-assisted therapy and the present moment. *The British Journal of Psychotherapy Integration*, 14, 53–63.

Harari, Y. N. (2014). *Sapiens*. London: Penguin Random House.

Harari, Y. N. (2015). *Homo Deus*. London: Penguin Random House.

Harris, T. A. (1995). *I'm Okay, You're Okay*. London: Arrow Books.

Harrison, T. (2000). *Bion, Rickman, Foulkes and the Northfield Experiments*. London: Jessica Kingsley Publishers.

Hasbach, P. (2016). Prescribing Nature: Nature Connectedness, Belonging and Social Identity in a Mental Health Ecotherapy Programme. In M. Jordon and J. Hinds (eds) *Ecotherapy: Theory, Research and Practice*. London: Palgrave.

Hawkins, P. (1985). *Humanistic Psychotherapy Supervision: A Conceptual Framework*. *Self and Society: Journal of Humanistic Psychology*, 13, 2, 69–79.

Hawkins, P. (2005). *The Wise Fool's Guide to Leadership*. London: O Books.

Hawkins, P. (2011a). The heroic leader is gone: Long live the team. *Chief Executive Magazine*, 7 April 2011.

Hawkins, P. (2011b). Building Emotional, Ethical and Cognitive Capacity in Coaches: A Development Model of Supervision. In J. Passmore (ed.) *Supervision in Coaching*. London: Kogan Page.

Hawkins, P. (2014). *Leadership Team Coaching in Practice; Developing High Performing Teams*. Philadelphia, PA: Kogan Page Publishers.

Hawkins, P. (2015). Cracking the shell: Unlearning our coaching assumptions. *Coaching at Work*, 10(2), 42–46.

Hawkins, P. (2017a). *Leadership Team Coaching: Developing Collective Transformational Leadership*. London: Kogan Page.

Hawkins, P. (2017b). The Necessary Revolution in Humanistic Psychology. In R. House and D. Kalisch (eds) *The Future of Humanistic Psychology*. London: Routledge.

Hawkins, P. (2017c). *Tomorrow's Leadership and the Necessary Revolution in Today's Leadership Development*. Henley: Henley Business School.

Hawkins, P. (2017d). *Partnerships Are Not Created by Partners: From Bartering to Partnering*. Available at: www.renewalassociates.co.uk/2017/04/partnerships-are-not-created-by-partners-from-bartering-to-partnering.

Hawkins, P. (2018a). *Leadership Team Coaching in Practice*. London: Kogan Page.

Hawkins, P. (2018b). A Systemic Primer. *Renewal Associates*. Available at: www.renewalassociates.co.uk/resources, accessed 3 January 2019.

Hawkins, P. (2018c). Coaching Supervision. In E. Cox, T. Bachkirovo and D. Clutterbuck (eds) *The Complete Handbook of Coaching*. London: Sage.

Hawkins, P. (2019). Resourcing – The Neglected Third Leg of Supervision. In E. Turner and S. Palmer (eds) *The Heart of Coaching Supervision – Working with Reflection and Self-Care*. Abingdon: Routledge.

Hawkins, P. & McMahan, A. (in press). *Supervision in the Helping Professions* (fifth edition). Maidenhead: Open University Press/McGraw-Hill.

Hawkins, P. & Shohet, R. (2012). *Supervision in the Helping Professions* (third edition). Maidenhead: Open University Press/McGraw-Hill.

Hawkins, P. & Smith, N. (2006). *Coaching, Mentoring and Organiational Consultancy*. London: McGraw-Hill.

Hawkins, P. & Smith, N. (2013a). *Coaching, Mentoring and Organisational Consultancy: Supervision and Development*. Maidenhead: McGraw-Hill.

Hawkins, P. & Smith, N. (2013b). Transformational Coaching. In E. Cox, T. Bachirova and D. Clutterbuck (eds) *The Complete Handbook of Coaching* (second edition). London: Sage.

Hawkins, P. & Turner, E. (2019). *Systemic Coaching: Delivering Value Beyond the Individual*. Abingdon: Routledge.

Hawkins, P. L. & Nestoros, J. N. (1997). Beyond the Dogmas of Conventional Psychotherapy: The Integration Movement. In P. L. Hawkins and J. N. Nestoros (eds) *Psychotherapy: New Perspectives on Theory, Practice and Research*. Athens, Greece: Ellinika Grammata.

Hazan, C. & Shaver, P. R. (1994). Attachment as an organisational framework for research on close relationships. *Psychological Inquiry*, 5(1), 1–22.

Heffernan, M. (2011). *Wilful Blindness: Why We Ignore the Obvious*. London: Simon and Schuster.

Heimann, P. (1950). On countertransference. *International Journal of Psychoanalysis*, 31, 81–84.

Heisenberg, W. (1958). *Physics and Philosophy*. New York, NY: Harper Torchbooks.

Heron, J. (1981). Philosophical Basis for a New Paradigm. In P. Reason and J. Rowan (eds) *Human Inquiry: A Sourcebook of New Paradigm Research*. Chichester: John Wiley and Sons.

Hillman, J. (1975). *Re-visioning Psychology*. New York, NY: Harper and Row.

Hillman, J. (1982). *Anima Mundi: The Return of the Soul to the World*. Washington DC: Spring Publications.

Hillman, J. (1995). A Psyche the Size of the World: A Psychological Foreword. In T. Roszak, M. E. Gomes and A. D. Kammer (eds) *Ecopsychology: Restoring the Earth, Healing the Mind*. Berkley, CA: Counterpoint.

Hinchelwood, R. D. (1991). *A Dictionary of Kleinian Thought*. London: Free Association Books.

Hobson, R. E. (1985). *Forms of Feeling*. Hove: Routledge.

Holmes, J. (2014). Countertransference before Heimann: An historical exploration. *Journal of the American Psychoanalytic Association*. Available at: https://journals.sagepub.com/doi/abs/10.1177/0003065114546164.

Hycner, R. & Jacobs, L. (1995). *The Healing Relationship in Gestalt Therapy: A Dialogic/Self Psychology Approach*. Gouldsboro, ME: Gestalt Journal Press.

Ismail, S. (2014). *Exponential Organizations: Why New Organizations are Ten Times Better, Faster, and Cheaper Than Yours (And What To Do About It)*. New York, NY: Diversion Books.

James, W. (1890). *The Principles of Psychology*. New York, NY: Henry Holt & Co.

Janis, I. L. (1982). *Groupthink: Psychological Studies of Policy Decisions and Fiascoes*. Boston, MA: Houghton Mifflin.

Jaspal, R. & Cinnirella, M. (2010). Coping with potentially incompatible identities: Accounts of religious, ethnic, and sexual identities from British Pakistani men who identify as Muslim and gay. *Journal of Personality and Social Psychology*, 49, 335–343.

Jetten, J., Haslam, C. & Haslam, S. A. (2012). *The Social Cure: Identity, Health and Wellbeing*. Hove: The Psychology Press.

Josselson, R. (1995). *The Space Between Us: Exploring the Dimensions of Human Relationships*. London: Sage.

Jourard, S. M. (1971). *The Transparent Self*. New York, NY: Van Nostrand.

Jung, C. G. (1918). *Theory of Psychoanalysis*. New York, NY: Nervous and Mental Disease Publishing Company.

Jung, C. G. (1935). The Practice of Psychotherapy. *In Collected Works*. London: Routledge and Kegan Paul.

Jung, C. G. (1938). *Psychology and Religion*. New Haven, CT: Yale University Press.

Jung, C. G. (1966). Two Essays on Analytical Psychology. *In Collected Works 7. On the Psychology of the Unconscious*. Princeton, NJ: Bollingen Paperbacks.

Jung, C. G. (1969). *Synchronicity: An Acausal Connecting Principle*. Princeton, NJ: Princeton University Press.

Jung, C. G. (1977). *C.G. Jung Speaking: Interviews and Encounters*. Princeton, NJ: Bollingen Paperbacks.

Jung, C. G. (1981). The Development of the Personality. *In Collected Works*. Princeton, NJ: Bollingen Paperbacks.

Kahn, M. (1991). *Between Therapist and Client: The New Relationship*. New York, NY: W. H. Freeman and Company.

Kahneman, D. (2012). *Thinking, Fast and Slow*. London: Penguin.

Kareem, J. & Littlewood, R. (1992). *Intercultural Therapy*. London: Blackwell.

Karpf, F. B. (2015). *The Psychology and Psychotherapy of Otto Rank*. New York, NY: Philosophical Library.

Karpman, S. (1968). Fairy tales and script drama analysis. *Transactional Analysis Bulletin*, 1–9, 51–56.

Kegan, R. (1982). *The Evolving Self: Problem and Process in Human Development*. Cambridge, MA: Harvard University Press.

Kegan, R. (1994). *In Over Our Heads: The Mental Demands of Modern Life*. Cambridge, MA: Harvard University Press.

Kelly, G. (1955). *The Psychology of Personal Constructs: A Theory of Personality*. New York, NY: W. W. Norton & Company.

Klein, M. (1946). Notes on Some Schizoid Mechanisms. In J. Mitchell (ed.) *The Selected Melanie Klein* (pp.176–193). London: Penguin Books.

Klein, M. (2011). *Envy and Gratitude and Other Works 1946–1963*. London: Penguin Books.

Koestler, A. (1967). *The Ghost in the Machine*. London: Hutchinson.

Kohlberg, L. (1981). Essays on Moral Development. *In the Philosophy of Moral Development* (Vol. 1). San Francisco, CA: Harper and Rowe.

Kohut, H. (1971). *The Analysis of the Self*. New York, NY: International Universities Press.

Kolb, D. (1984). *Experiential Learning: Experience as the Source of Learning and Development*. London: Prentice Hall.

Krishnamurti, J. (1989). *Think on These Things*. San Francisco, CA: HarperOne.

Kubie, L. (1934). Relation of the conditioned reflex to psychoanalytic technique. *Archives of Neurology and Psychiatry*, 32, 1137–1142.

Kubler-Ross, E. (2005). *On Grief and Grieving*. London: Simon and Schuster.

Laing, R. D. (1967). *The Politics of Experience and The Bird of Paradise*. London: Penguin Books).

Laing, R. D. (1990). *The Politics of Experience and The Bird of Paradise*. London: Penguin Books.

Laing, R. D. & Anthony, D. S. (2010). *The Divided Self: An Existential Study in Sanity and Madness*. London: Penguin Classics.

Lake, F. (2007, first published 1966). *Clinical Theology: A Theological and Psychiatric Basis for Clinical Pastoral Care*. Lexington, KY: Emeth Press.

Lambert, M. (1992). Psychotherapy Outcome Research. In J. Norcross and M. Goldfried (eds) *Handbook of Psychotherapy Integration*. New York, NY: Basic Books.

Lambert, M. & Barley, D. E. (2001). Research summary of the therapeutic relationship and psychotherapy outcome. *Psychotherapy Theory Research & Practice*, 38(4), 357–361.

Landsberger, H. A. (1958). *Hawthorne Revisited*. Ithaca, NY: Cornell University Press.

Latour, B. (2017). *Facing Gaia*. Cambridge: Polity Press.

Laungani, P. (2004). *Asian Perspectives in Counselling and Psychotherapy*. Hove: Brunner-Routledge.

Lazarus, A. A. (1973). Multimodal behaviour therapy: Treating the 'BASIC ID'. *Journal of Nervous and Mental Disease*, 156(6), 1137–1142.

Lazarus, A. A. (1992). Multimodal Therapy: Technical Eclecticism with Minimal Integration. In C. J. Norcross and M. R. Goldfried (eds) *Handbook of Psychotherapy Integration* (pp.231–263). New York, NY: Basic Books.

Leakey, R. & Lewin, R. (1996). *The Sixth Extinction: Biodiversity and its Survival*. London: Phoenix.

Levy-Bruhl, L. (1966, first published 1927). *The 'Soul' of the Primitive* (L. Clare, trans.). New York, NY: Frederick A. Praeger.

Lewin, K. (1935). *The Dynamic Theory of Personality*. New York, NY: McGraw-Hill.

Lewin, K. (1952). *Field Theory in Social Science*. London: Tavistock.

Loevinger, J. (1976). *Ego Development: Conceptions and Theories*. San Francisco, CA: Jossey-Bass.

London, P. (1988). Metamorphosis in psychotherapy: Slouching towards integration. *Journal of Integrative and Eclectic Psychotherapy*, 7(1), 3–12.

Lovelock, J. (1979). *Gaia*. Oxford: Oxford University Press.

Lovelock, J. & Margulis, L. (1974). Biological modulation of the Earth's atmosphere. *Icarus*, 21, 471–489.

Macy, J. & Johnstone, C. (2012). *Active Hope*. Novato, CA: New World Library.

Magurran, A. & Dornelas, M. (2010). Biological diversity in a changing world. *Philosophical Transactions of the Royal Society of London*, Series B, 365, 3593–3597.

Mahon, B. J. (2002). *Forgetting Oneself on Purpose: Vocation and the Ethics of Ambition*. San Francisco, CA: Jossey-Bass.

Main, M. & Solomon, J. (1986). Discovery of a New, Insecure-Disorganized/Disoriented Attachment Pattern. In M. Yogman and T. B. Brazelton (eds) *Affective Development in Infancy* (pp.95–124). Norwood, NJ: Ablex.

Malan, D. (2007, first published 1995). *Individual Psychotherapy and the Science of Psychodynamics* (second edition). London: Hodder Education.

Marcuse, H. (2002). *One-Dimensional Man: Studies in the Ideology of Advanced Industrial Society*. London: Routledge Classics.

Maroda, K. J. (2004). *The Power of Countertransference*. Hillsdale, NJ: The Analytic Press.

Maslow, A. H. (1972). *The Farther Reaches of Human Nature*. London: Penguin Books.

Maturana, H. & Varela, F. (1980). *Autopoiesis and Cognition*. Dordrecht, Netherlands: Springer.

Maturana, H. & Varela, F. (2008). *The Tree of Knowledge*. Boston, MA: Shambhala.

May, R. (1969). *Existential Psychology*. New York, NY: McGraw-Hill.

McCleod, J. (1993). *An Introduction to Counselling*. Buckingham: Open University Press.

McGilchrist, I. (2009). *The Master and the Emissary: The Divided Brain and the Making of the Western World*. New Haven, CT: Yale University Press.

Mill, J. S. (2001). *Utilitarianism* (second edition). Indianapolis, IN: Hackett Publishing Company.

Mitchell, J. (2000, first published 1974). *Psychoanalysis and Feminism: A Radical Reassessment of Freudian Psychoanalysis*. New York, NY: Pelican Books.

Mitchell, S. A. (2000). *Relationality: From Attachment to Intersubjectivity*. Hillsdale, NJ: The Analytic Press.

Mollon, P. (1993). *The Fragile Self*. London: Whurr Publishers.

Montaigne, M. E. (1965). *The Complete Essays of Montaigne* (D. Frame, ed. and trans.). Stanford, CA: Stanford University Press.

Moreno, J. L. (1947). *The Theatre of Spontaneity*. Boston, MA: Beacon House.

Moreno, J. L. (1972). *Psychodrama*. Volume 1. New York, NY: Beacon House.

Mumford, L. (2015). *Technics and Human Development: The Myth of the Machine, Volume One*. Cambridge, MA: Harvard HBC Books.

Naess, A. (2016). Ecology of Wisdom. London: Penguin Classics.

National Health Service (2014). Adult Psychiatric Morbidity Survey. Available at: https://digital.nhs.uk/data-and-information/publications/statistical/adult-psychiatric-morbidity-survey, accessed 3 January 2019.

Norcross, J. C. & Goldfried, M. R. (1992). *Handbook of Psychotherapy Integration*. New York, NY: Basic Books.

Norcross, J. C. & Grencavage, M. R. (1989). Eclecticism and integration in counselling and psychotherapy. *British Journal of Guidance and Psychotherapy: Major Themes and Obstacles*, 17, 227–247.

O'Leary, E. (2006). The Need for Integration. In E. O'Leary (ed.) *Integration in Psychotherapy*. New York, NY: Routledge.

Orange, D. (1997). *Emotional Understanding*. London and New York, NY: The Guilford Press.

Orange, D. (2010). *Thinking for Clinicians*. New York, NY: Routledge.

Orange, D., Atwood, G. E. & Stolorow, R. D. (1997). *Working Intersubjectively: Contextualism in Psychoanalytic Practice*. London and Hillsdale, NJ: The Analytic Press.

Orbach, S. (2010, first published 1978). *Fat is a Feminist Issue*. London: Arrow Books.

Parlett, M. (1991). Reflections on field theory. *British Gestalt Journal*, 1(2), 69–81.

Parlett, M. (2015). *Future Sense*. London: Troubador Publishing.

Perls, F. (1969). *Gestalt Therapy Verbatim*. New York, NY: Bantam Books.

Perls, F. (1992, first published 1969). *Ego, Hunger and Aggression*. Gouldsboro, ME: Gestalt Journal Press.

Peterson, C. (2013). *Pursuing the Good Life*. Oxford: Oxford University Press.

Piaget, J. (1955). *The Child's Construction of Reality*. London: Routledge and Kegan Paul.

Piaget, J. (1977). *The Grasp of Consciousness: Action and Concept in the Young Child*. London: Routledge and Kegan Paul.

Polanyi, M. (1969). *Knowing and Being: Essays*. Chicago, IL: University of Chicago Press.

Quitangon, G. (2015). *Vicarious Trauma and Disaster Mental Health*. London and New York, NY: Routledge.

Rank, O. (1932). *The Myth of the Birth of the Hero and Other Writings*. New York, NY: Random House.

Rank, O. (2014, first published 1929). *The Trauma of Birth*. New York, NY: Routledge.

Reason, P. (2017). *In Search of Grace*. Arelsford, Hampshire: Earth Books.

Reason, P. & Bradbury, H. (2001). Introduction: Inquiry and Participation in Search of a World Worthy of Human Aspiration. In P. Reason and H. Bradley (eds) *Handbook of Action Research*. London: Sage.

Reason, P. & Marshal, J. (2001). On Working with Graduate Research Students. In P. Reason and H. Bradbury (eds) *Handbook of Action Research*. London: Sage.

Renshaw, B. (2018). *Purpose: The Extraordinary Benefits of Focusing on What Matters Most*. London: LID Publishing.

Resnick, R. (1995). Gestalt therapy: Principles, prisms and perspectives. *British Gestalt Journal*, 4, 3–13.

Revans, R. W. (1982). *The Origins and Growth of Action Learning*. London: Chartwell-Bratt Bromley & Lund.

Rieder, J. (2013). *Gospel of Freedom: Martin Luther King, Jr's Letter from Birmingham Jail and the Struggle that Changed a Nation*. New York, NY: Bloomsbury Press, Kindle edition.

Rilke, R. M. (1969). *Letters of Rainer Marie Rilke 1894–1910*. New York, NY: W. W. Norton & Company.

Rock, D., Siegel, D., Poelmans, S. A. Y. & Payne, J. (2012). The Healthy Mind Platter. *Neuroleadership Journal*, 4.

Rogers, C. (1958). The characteristics of the helping relationship. *Personnel and Guidance Journal*, 37, 6–16.

Rogers, C. (1959). A Theory of Therapy, Personality and Interpersonal Relationships as Developed in the Client-centred Framework. In (ed.) S. Koch, *Psychology: A Study of Science. Vol 3: Formulations of the Person and the Social Context*. New York: McGraw Hill.

Rogers, C. (1961). *On Becoming a Person*. Boston, MA: Houghton Mifflin Company.

Rogers, C. (1965). *Client Centred Therapy*. Boston, MA: Houghton Mifflin Company.

Rogers, C. (1990). The Therapeutic Relationship. In H. Kirschenbaum and V. Land Henderson (eds) *The Carl Rogers Reader*. London: Constable.

Rooke, D. & Torbert, W. (2005). Seven transformations of leadership. *Harvard Business Review*, April, 67–76.

Rosenzweig, S. (1936). Some implicit common factors in diverse methods of psychotherapy. *American Journal of Orthopsychiatry*, 6, 412–415.

Ryde, J. (2009). *Being White in the Helping Professions: Developing Effective Intercultural Awareness*. London: Jessica Kingsley Publishers.

Ryde, J. (2019). *White Privilege Unmasked*. London: Jessica Kingsley Publishers.

Ryle, A. (2002). *Introducing Cognitive Analytic Therapy*. Chichester: John Wiley and Sons.

Ryle, G. (1967). *The Concept of Mind*. Chicago, IL: University of Chicago Press.

Samuels, A. (1993). *The Political Psyche*. London: Routledge.

Sartre, J. P. (2001). *The Age of Reason*. London: Penguin Classics.

Saxe, L. (2010). Kurt Lewin 1890–1947. In J. M. Levine and M.A. Hogg *Encyclopedia of Group Processes and Intergroup Relations*, (pp.533–535). London: Sage.

Scharmer, O. (2009). *Theory U: Leading from the future as it emerges*. San Francisco: Berrett Koehler.

Scharmer, O. & Kaufer, K. (2012). *Leading into the Emergent Future*. San Francisco, CA: Berrett Koehler Publishers.

Schwab, K. (2016). *The Fourth Industrial Revolution World Economic Forum*. Cologny/Geneva: World Economic Forum.

Scott, T. (2004). *Integrative Psychotherapy in Healthcare*. Basingstoke and New York, NY: Palgrave Macmillan.

Searles, H. F. (1955). The Informational Value of the Supervisor's Emotional Experience. In *Collected Papers of Schizophrenia and Related Subjects*. London: Hogarth Press.

Sears, R. R. (1944). Experimental Analysis of Psychoanalytic Phenomenon. In J. M. Hunt (ed.) *Personality and the Behaviour Disorders*. New York, NY: Ronald Press.

Seed, J., Macey, J., Flemming, P. & Naess, A. (1988). *Thinking like a Mountain: Towards a Council of all Beings*. Philadelphia, PA: New Society Publishers.

Seligman, M. (2011). *Flourish*. Boston, MA: Nicholas Brealey Publishing.

Seligman, M. & Csikszentmihalyi, M. (2000). Positive psychology: An introduction. *American Psychologist*, 55, 5–14.

Senge, P. (2014). *Systems Thinking for a Better World*. Talk at the Systems Analysis Laboratory Aalto University Finland, 7 December 2014. Available at: https://wiki2.org/en/Peter_Senge, accessed 31 January 2019.

Shama, O. (2009). *Theory U*. Oakland, CA: Berrett-Koehler Publishers.

Shapiro, D.A. (2018). Obituary: Robert Hobson. *The Independent*. Available at: www.independent.co.uk/arts-entertainment/obituary-dr-robert-hobson-1129581.html, accessed August 2018.

Siegel, D. (2010). *Mindsight*. London: Oneworld Publications.

Siegel, D. J. (2012). *Pocket Guide to Interpersonal Neurobiology: An Integrative Handbook of the Mind*. Kindle Android version. Retrieved from Amazon.com: W. W. Norton & Company.

Sisodia, R., Wolfe, D. & Sheth, J. N. (2007). *Firms of Endearment: How World-Class Companies Profit from Passion and Purpose*. London: Financial Times/Prentice Hall.

Skinner, B. F. (1991, first published 1938). *The Behavior of Organisms*. Cambridge, MA: B. F. Skinner Foundation.

Sloman, S. & Fernbach, P. (2017). *The Knowledge Illusion: Why We Never Think Alone*. New York, NY: Penguin.

Smuts, J. C. (1926). *Holism and Evolution*. London: Macmillan.

Soloman, A. (2014). *Far from the Tree*. London: Vantage.

St Fleur, N. (2016). Signs of the 'Human Age'. *New York Times* [online]. Available at: www.nytimes.com/interactive/2016/01/11/science/anthropocene-epoch-definition.html, accessed 13 January 2016.

Stefana, A. (2017). *History of Countertransference: From Freud to the British Object Relations School*. Abingdon: Routledge.

Stern, D. N. (1985). *The Interpersonal World of the Infant: A View from Psychoanalysis and Developmental Psychology*. New York, NY: Basic Books.

Stern, D. N. (2018). *The Interpersonal World of the Infant*. London: Routledge.

Stevens, A. (1991). *On Jung*. London: Penguin Books.

Stiehm, J. H. & Townsend, N. W. (2002). *The U.S. Army War College: Military Education in a Democracy*. Philadelphia, PA: Temple University Press.

Stolorow, R. D. & Atwood, G. E. (1992). *Contexts of Being*. Hillsdale, NJ: The Analytic Press.

Stolorow, R., D. & Atwood, G. E. (1996). The intersubjective perspective. *The Psychoanalytic Review*, 83, 181–194.

Stolorow, R. D. & Atwood, G. E. (2014). *Structures of Subjectivity*. Hillsdale, NJ: The Analytic Press.

Stolorow, R. D., Atwood, G. E. & Brandchaft, B. (1994). *The Intersubjective Perspective*. London and Northvale, NJ: Jason Aronson.

Stolorow, R. D., Atwood, G. E. & Orange, D. (2002). *Worlds of Experience: Interweaving Philosophical and Clinical Dimensions in Psychoanalysis*. New York, NY: Basic Books.

Stone, J. E. (2019). *Integrating Technology into Modern Therapies: A Clinician's Guide to Developments and Interventions*. London: Routledge.

Sullivan, H. S. (1947). *Conceptions of Modern Psychiatry*. Washington DC: William A. White Psychiatric Foundation.

Szasz, T. (1961). *The Myth of Mental Illness*. New York, NY: Harper and Row.

Tajfel, H. & Turner, H. C. (1986). The Social Identity Theory of Intergroup Behaviour. In S. Worchel and W. G. Austin (eds) *Psychology of Intergroup Relations* (pp.7–24). Chicago, IL: Nelson Hall.

Taylor, C. (1964). *Multiculturalism: Examining the Politics of Recognition*. Princeton, NJ: Princeton University Press.

Taylor, C. (1991). *The Ethics of Authenticity*. Cambridge, MA: Harvard University Press.

Torbert, W. (2004). *Action Inquiry: The Secret of Timely and Transforming Leadership*. San Francisco, CA: Berrett-Koehler.

Turner, J. C., Hogg, M. A., Oaks, P., Reicher, S. D. & Weatherall, M. S. (1987). *Rediscovering the Social Group: A Self-Categorization Theory*. Oxford: Blackwell.

Van der Kolk, B. (2015). *The Body Keeps the Score: Mind, Brain and Body in the Transformation of Trauma*. London: Penguin.

Verny, T. (1995). Working with pre- and perinatal material in psychotherapy. *International Journal of Prenatal and Perinatal Psychology and Medicine*, 7(3), 271–284.

Vignoles, V. L., Regalia, C., Manzi, C., Colledge, J. & Scabini, E. (2006). Beyond self-esteem: Influence of multiple motives on identity construction. *Journal of Personality and Social Psychology*, 90, 308–333.

Wachtel, E. F. & Wachtel, P. L. (1986). *Family Dynamics in Individual Psychotherapy: A Guide to Clinical Strategies*. New York, NY: Guilford Press.

Wachtel, P. L. (1977). *Psychoanalysis and Behaviour Threrapy: Toward an Integration*. New York, NY: Basic Books.

Wachtel, P. L. & McKinney, M. K. (1992). Cyclical Psychodynamics and Integrative Psychodynamic Therapy. In J. C. Norcross and M. R. Goldfried (eds) *Handbook of Psychotherapy Integration*. New York, NY: Basic Books.

Wampold, B. (2001). *The Great Psychotherapy Debate: Models, Methods and Findings*. Mahwah, NJ: Lawrence Elbaum.

Watzlawick, P., Beavin, J. & Jackson, D. D. (1967). *Pragmatics of Human Communication: A Study of Interactional Patterns*. New York, NY: W. W. Norton & Company.

Weaver, K. (2007). Ethical sensitivity: State of knowledge and needs for further research. *Nursing Ethics*, 14, 141–155.

Weber, A. (2017). *Matter and Desire: An Erotic Ecology*. White River Junction, VT: Chelsea Green Publishing.

Weber, M. (1947). *Theory of Social and Economic Organization*. New York, NY: The Free Press.

Weintrobe, S. (2012). *Engaging with Climate Change: Psychoanalytic and Interdisciplinary Perspectives*. London: Routledge.

Weitz, P. (ed.) (2018). *Psychotherapy 2.0: Where Psychotherapy and Technology Meet*. London: Routledge.

Whitehead, A. N. (1939). *Process and Reality: An Essay in Cosmology*. New York, NY: Macmillan.

Whitehead, A. N. (2010). *Process and Reality*. New York, NY: The Free Press.

Wilber, K. (1996). *A Brief History of Everything*. Dublin: Gill and Macmillan.

Wilber, K. (2000). *Integral Psychology*. Boulder, CO: Shambhala Publications.

Willi, J. (1999). *Ecological Psychotherapy: Developing by Shaping the Personal Niche*. Cambridge, MA: Hogrefe & Huber.

Wilson, C. (1956). *The Outsider*. London: Gollancz.

Wilson Schaef, A. (2013, first published 1987). *When Society Becomes an Addict*. San Francisco, CA: Harper.

Winnicott, D. W. (1947). Hate in the Countertransference. In *D. W. Winnicott, Collected Papers: Through Paediatrics to Psycho-Analysis*. London: Tavistock Publications.

Winnicott, D. W. (1960). The theory of parent–infant relationship. In M. Kahn (ed.) *The Maturational Processes and the Facilitating Environment*. Abingdon: Karnac Books.

Winnicott, D. W. (1964). *The Child, The Family and The Outside World*. Harmondsworth: Penguin Books.

Winnicott, D. W. (1965). *The Maturational Processes and the Facilitating Environment*. London: Hogarth Press.

Winnicott, D. W. (1969). The theory of the parent–infant relationship. *International Journal of Psychoanalysis*, 41, 585–595.

Winnicott, D. W. (1971). *Playing and Reality*. London: Penguin Books.

Winnicott, D. W. (1988). *Human Nature*. London: Free Association Books.

Wolpe, J. (1969). *The Practice of Behavior Therapy*. Oxford: Pergamon Press.

World Health Organization/Global Health Observatory (2017a). www.who.int/gho/child_health/mortality/mortality_under_five_text/en.

World Health Organization/Global Health Observatory (2017b). www.who.int/news-room/fact-sheets/detail/mental-disorders.

Yalom, I. D. (1980). *Existential Psychotherapy*. New York, NY: Basic Books.

Yalom, I. D. (2011). *Staring at the Sun*. London: Piatkus.

Yontef, G. (1981). Gestalt Therapy: An Introduction. In R. J. Corsini and D. Wedding (eds) *Current Psychotherapies*. Itasca, IL: F. E. Peacock.

Yontef, G. (1993). *Awareness, Dialogue and Process*. Gouldsboro, ME: Gestalt Journal Press.

Subject Index

Author Index

CPI Antony Rowe
Eastbourne, UK
November 18, 2022